THE
COLONIAL HISTORY
SERIES
No. 82

General Editor
D. H. Simpson
Librarian of the Royal Commonwealth Society

HISTORY OF THE SPANISH AMERICA

COLONIAL HISTORY SERIES

This series of reprints aims at presenting a wide variety of books; their link is that they all deal with some aspect of the relations between European powers and other parts of the world–including such topics as exploration, trade, settlement and administration. Historical studies, and books which furnish the raw material of history, will find a place, and publications will not be restricted to works in English. Many titles reprinted will have new introductions by authorities on the subject.

A
CONCISE HISTORY
of the
SPANISH AMERICA

compiled by
John Campbell

with a new introduction
by
D. H. Simpson

BARNES & NOBLE PUBLISHERS
Founded 1873
New York
and
DAWSONS OF PALL MALL
Folkestone, England
1972

First published in London 1741
Reprinted with new introduction 1972

Dawsons of Pall Mall
Cannon House
Folkestone, Kent, England

ISBN: 389 04592 6

Introduction © Wm. Dawson & Sons Ltd., 1972

LC # 72 - 187267

Printed in Great Britain
By Unwin Brothers Limited
The Gresham Press, Old Woking, Surrey, England
A member of the Staples Printing Group

INTRODUCTION

John Campbell, the compiler of *A Concise History of the Spanish America*, was one of the most prolific writers of his age. He was born in Edinburgh on 8 March 1708, the fourth son of Captain Robert Campbell of Glenlyon. At the age of five he was brought to Windsor by his mother and in due course became a clerk in an attorney's office. He forsook the law for literature, however, his first major work, in 1736, being *Military History of the late Prince Eugene of Savoy and the late John, Duke of Marlborough*. It was based largely on French historians, and most of his literary activity was in the form of compilations from other writers. Such publications were in considerable demand in the eighteenth century, when a library was a recognised part of a gentleman's home.

In 1739 Campbell wrote *The Travels and Adventures of Edward Brown, Esq.*, allegedly the autobiography of a merchant, describing his travels in Europe and the Near East, but actually a collection of information on the countries concerned linked by a fictitious narrative. From the same year dates *Memoirs of the Duke de Ripperda* listed at the end of this volume. Soon after, he began to contribute to the *Ancient Universal History* and later wrote many sections for the *Modern Universal History*.

A Concise History of the Spanish America was published in 1741; like many of Campbell's works it did not contain his name. The "Desire which the Publick discovers being thoroughly acquainted with the past and present Situation of the Spanish West Indies" to which he refers in his preface arose from the war which began in 1739. There had been long-

standing disputes between Britain and Spain regarding contraband trade in the Spanish West Indies by
British merchants, among them Captain Robert
Jenkins, the loss of whose ear was, in popular eyes,
the reason for hostilities.   Another cause for tension
was the boundary dispute between Spanish Florida
and the English colony of Georgia, founded by
General Oglethorpe in 1733, referred to by Campbell
on pp. 100–1.

An early success of the war was the capture of
Porto Bello by Admiral Vernon in November 1739
(page 188). In April 1740 General Oglethorpe
attacked Florida, but without success (pp. 101–2);
he did, however, repel a later Spanish attack, in 1742,
on St. Simon's Island.   The high repute of Vernon
is indicated by Campbell (p. 289) but shortly after
the book's appearance a large-scale attack on Carthagena, in which he led the naval forces, was repelled.
Campbell's prophecy "how loud soever the French
may bark, they will never attempt to bite, for fear
of beating out their Teeth" (p. 306) was falsified, for
France and Britain were shortly afterwards involved
in the war of the Austrian succession.

The book itself falls into three parts; an outline of
the discovery and conquest of Spanish America, a
careful account of each colony, which is a valuable
survey of the Spanish Empire, then "the largest
Dominions of any Prince in the World" (p. 74), and
finally Campbell's reflections on the failure of the
Spanish to make the most of their possessions owing
to their short-sighted policy of exploitation, so that
eventually much of the commerce of Spanish
America was in the hands of merchants of other
nations.   He also gives an outline of the growing

influence of other European countries in the area. As in most of his works, he looked for conclusions and lessons which would advance the national interest—what Burke later called his "endeavouring every where, with so much good sense and eloquence, to rouse that spirit of generous enterprise, that can alone make any nation powerful or glorious." If his judgement in this respect was not always justified by later developments, his comments are an interesting reflection of contemporary ideas, and the language in which he presents them usually vigorous and characteristic. Several further editions appeared under various titles.

Thomas Winnington (1696–1746), to whom the work is dedicated, was M.P. successively for Droitwich and Winchester from 1726 until his death. He was "bred a Tory", but achieved high office by joining the Whigs, a matter somewhat delicately indicated by Campbell. He held several major Treasury posts and was an able politician, though his principles in public and private life hardly justified the eulogies of the dedication. He does not appear to have had any particular associations with Spanish America, but was presumably regarded as an influential man whose patronage would assist the book.

Campbell's next major work was *Lives of the Admirals*, issued in four volumes in 1742–44, a valuable survey, though containing some errors in nautical matters, which reached three editions in his lifetime and was re-issued for many years after. *Navigantium atque Itinerantium Bibliotheca or a Complete Collection of Voyages and Travels* appeared in two folio volumes in 1744–48. It was nominally

an enlarged edition of John Harris's collection of the
same name of 1702–5, but was virtually a new work,
since apart from including additional information,
Campbell had a much more systematic and disci-
plined approach to the presentation of material than
his predecessor.[1] Some historical passages from the
volume on Spanish America were embodied in it.
Apart from his factual information, Campbell urges
greater boldness in the extension of Britain's com-
mercial enterprises overseas, and attacks restrictive
trading companies. He contributed numerous memoirs to the first four volumes of *Biographica Britannica*, which began in 1745, and his *The Present
State of Europe* (1750) was widely read and went into
many editions. In 1754 he received the degree of
LL.D. from the University of Glasgow.

Campbell brought to his work great industry, a
retentive memory, and a wide knowledge of lan-
guages. Samuel Johnson said of him, "Campbell is
not always rigidly careful of the truth in his con-
versation; but I do not believe there is any thing of
this carelessness in his books" and "he has very
extensive reading; not, perhaps, what is properly
called learning, but history, politics, and in short
that popular knowledge which makes a man very
useful. In the third place, he has learnt much by
what is called the *vox viva*. He talks with a great
many people." Speaking of him personally, Johnson said, "I loved Campbell", and commented "I am
afraid he has not been in the inside of a Church for
many years; but he never passes a Church without

1. G. R. Crone and R. A. Skelton assess Campbell's editorship
   of this work on pp. 93–7 of *Richard Hakluyt & his Successors*,
   edited by E. Lynam (Hakluyt Society, 1946).

pulling off his hat. This shews that he has good principles." Boswell thought that Johnson was unfair to Campbell's religious observances in this remark.[2]

Campbell's continued interest in overseas developments was shown by his *Candid and Impartial Considerations on the Nature of the Sugar Trade* written in 1763 at Lord Bute's request to show the value of the newly acquired islands of St. Lucia and Grenada —his view of their potentialities for sugar production was over-optimistic—and in 1765 he was appointed agent for the colony of Georgia. In 1772 he wrote *A Treatise upon the Trade of Great Britain to America.* During his writing career he also wrote books and pamphlets on religion, politics, history, social and medical subjects, and was described by Johnson as "the richest author that ever grazed the common of literature."[3]

His last work, published in 1774, was *A Political Survey of Britain: being a series of reflections on the situation, lands, inhabitants, revenues, colonies, and commerce of the island. Intended to shew That we have not as yet approached near the Summit of Improvement, but that it will afford Employment to many Generations before they push to their utmost Extent the natural Advantages of Great Britian.* It is a massive work in two quarto volumes totalling 1500 pages— discursive, crammed with facts on the natural resources, geography, and history of Britain, often drawing on his wide reading to suggest, from the example of other countries, how a particular commodity might

2. J. Boswell, *The Life of Samuel Johnson* (Everyman Library, 1949), vol. I, pp. 258–9; vol. II, p. 176; *Boswell's Journal of A Tour to the Hebrides* (1936), p. 316.
3. Boswell, op. cit., vol. I, p. 259.

be better exploited.   Pages 560–694 of volume 2 deal with the colonies.

In the nature of his works and the elaborateness of his titles, Campbell was a man of his time, but the conclusions of his *Political Survey* show him ahead of it.   He advocates public purchase of "Tracts of Heath, Moor, and other Waste Lands" to be utilised for grazing and, where suitable, for cultivation.   He urges better educational facilities, and suggests a scheme for cottage homes for elderly people who have brought up three or more children—"competent Provision for such Persons in the Evening of ther Days should be made, not in the Mode of Charity, but as the just Reward and Distinction due to them from Society."   A specially bound copy of this work was sent to the Empress Catherine the Great of Russia who had sent Campbell her portrait.

The general reception of the work was indifferent, and Johnson said to Boswell that "he believed Campbell's disappointment on account of the bad success of that work, had killed him."[4]   Chalmers attributes his death to "a decline"; he died in his 68th year on 28 December 1775 in his house in Queen's Square, Ormond Street, London. He was survived by his wife, Elizabeth, daughter of Benjamin Vobe, and by one of their seven children.[5]

September, 1971.

4. Boswell, op. cit., vol. i, p. 618.
5. The main sources for Campbell's life are the *Memoir* by Andrew Kippis in *Biographia Britannica;* Alexander Chalmers's *General Biographical Dictionary*, vol. VIII, pp. 151–9, 1813; and Francis Espinasse's entry in the *Dictionary of National Biography*, vol. VII, pp. 373–5. These give an indication of the extent of his published works, only a few of which have been described here, but contains some errors.   See also Halkett and Laing *Dictionary of Anonymous and Pseudonymous Literature* (1934) *passim.*

A Concise

HISTORY

OF THE

SPANISH AMERICA;

CONTAINING

A fuccinct Relation of the Difcovery
and Settlement of its feveral Colonies:
A circumftantial Detail of their refpective
Situation, Extent, Commodities, Trade,
&c. And a full and clear Account of the
Commerce with *Old Spain* by the Galleons,
Flota, &c. As alfo of the Contraband
Trade with the *Englifh, Dutch, French,
Danes,* and *Portugueze.*

Together with

An APPENDIX,

In which is comprehended an exact Defcription of *Paraguay.*

Collected chiefly from Spanifh WRITERS.

LONDON:

Printed for JOHN STAGG in *Weftminfter-Hall,* and
DANIEL BROWNE at the *Black Swan* without
Temple-Bar. MDCCXLI.

To the Honourable

Thomas Winnington Efq;

Cofferer to His Majefty's Houfe-
hold, Recorder of *Worcefter*, and
Reprefentative in Parliament for
that City.

S I R,

IN writing this little W o r k all
imaginable Care has been taken
to avoid flattering any Party, and to
offend none. It was proper therefore to purfue the fame Plan in this
Dedication, which encouraged me to
addrefs it to You in whom all Parties
delight.

If

DEDICATION.

If Cenfure be that Tax, to which none but the Eminent are liable, Praife is a Tribute which can only be claimed by them; and as it is Sacrilege to proftitute it to the Undeferving, it is not lefs impious to refufe it to the moft worthy of Mankind.

All the Virtues which render a Man amiable in private Life joined to Eloquence, Publick Spirit and Heroick Refolution, the moft fhining Qualities which can adorn a publick Station are fo confeffedly in the Poffeffion of Mr. *Winnington*, that I look upon myfelf to be as fecure from the Sufpicion of Flattery in this Addrefs, as I am confcious it is remote from my Intention.

I am, SIR,

Your moft obedient, and

moft devoted humble Servant.

THE

PREFACE.

THAT Defire which the Publick difcovers of being thoroughly acquainted
with the paft and prefent Situation of the
Spanifh Weft Indies *firft infpired the Author with an Ambition of undertaking this
Work. His Aim was to draw within a
narrow Compafs whatever might contribute
to give a tolerable View of the Hiftory,
prefent State, and Nature of the Commerce
of the* Spanifh America. *In order to make
thefe Things the plainer, he thought it neceffary to treat of them feparately, having
obferved that moft of the Books he confulted on this Occafion, were not a little confufed, through the continual blending of thefe
Subjects, and in Confequence thereof frequent
Repetitions,*

Repetitions, which serve only to distract and disgust the Peruser.

His Design in giving the History of the Discovery and Conquests of his Catholick Majesty's American Dominions, was to shew the fatal Consequences of wrong Steps taken at the Beginning; for, whoever peruses the following Pages, will see that the Errors into which the Spaniards fell, when they first came into the new World, have never been amended, but, on the contrary, spread to such a Degree as to produce those Evils of which the Court of Spain are much more sensible than capable of affording them any Remedy. A Thing which could never have been thoroughly understood, but for this necessary Introduction, which sets it and its Causes in the clearest Light.

If ever the Spanish Ministry should be prevailed upon to take such Measures, as by degrees might contribute to put their Affairs to rights, they must be compelled to it by the Disasters of an unsuccessful War, which would not only point out the true Method of correcting whatever is amiss in the Indies, but also afford an Opportunity of entering on the necessary Regulations, effectually, and without Loss of Time. In such a Case, the Affairs of Spain would soon wear a new Face, the Credit of the Crown, and the Happiness

pineſs of the *People*, *would be reſtored toge-*
ther.

This, *inſtead of turning to our Prejudice,*
muſt neceſſarily prove our greateſt Advan-
tage, ſince, of all the Nations in Europe,
we are moſt capable of doing them either
Good or Hurt. As an Ally, we are more
concerned than any other to protect and to
promote their Intereſts, becauſe they never
can interfere with ours ; and in reſpect to
Commerce, we can ſupply their Wants cheap-
er and more effectually than any other Na-
tion, and alſo take more of their Goods in
Return. On the other hand, if at Variance,
we can at any Time defeat all their Pro-
jects in Europe, *and in a great meaſure cut*
off their Intercourſe with America.

We may *eaſily diſcern, that the Influence*
of French *Councils can never turn to the*
Advantage of Spain, *or make her at all for-*
midable to us. Whatever contributes to the
rendering Spain *uſeful to* France, *muſt alſo*
contribute to weaken and diſtreſs her. For,
as Intrigue and Negotiation ſerve the Pur-
poſes of the French, *ſo they never can ſerve*
thoſe of the Spaniards. *Oeconomy at home,*
and Peace abroad, are what they ſtand in
need of, in order to reſtore, I may ſay to pre-
ſerve, their Monarchy. In Times of Proſpe-
rity they may be, as moſt Nations are, inſo-
lent

lent and obſtinate; but, as Things ſtand now, it cannot be long before the wiſe Heads in that Nation (and ſure there are ſtill ſome ſuch) muſt diſcern the Neceſſity of acting for their own Advantage, and of no longer ſacrificing all that is dear and valuable to Mankind, to promote the Views of a deſigning Neighbour, or to flatter the Ambition of an Italian *Princeſs.*

TABLE

TABLE

OF

CONTENTS.

BOOK I.

Containing the Spanish *Discoveries and Conquests in* America.

CHAP.

TABLE of CONTENTS.

CHAP.

Table of Contents.

TABLE of CONTENTS.

A Concise

HISTORY

OF

SPANISH AMERICA.

CHAP. I.

Of the Accidents conducing to the Dif-
covery of the New World.

T is a Point in which Divines,
Philofophers, and Politicians, una-
nimoufly agree, that Sciences have
their Seafons, or in other Words,
that Arts of the greateft Confequence to Mankind, have, by a Concurrence
of happy Circumftances been quickly brought
to Perfection in one Age, though little Progrefs had been made in them in others. So
that

that the general Fund of Knowledge poffeffed.
by Mankind increafes irregularly as well in
point of Time as Place. For as Science at
firft travelled from the Eaft, fo in the Courfe
of Ages, it became a great Point of Knowledge
to find the Way thither again ; and, as we
fhall hereafter fee, a Defire of finding a new
Rout to the *Eaft Indies*, firft difcovered to us
the *Weft*.

In the fifteenth Century many ingenious
Men, and fome great Princes applied themfelves to the Improvement and Encouragement of Navigation, which had for fome A-
ges before been too little efteemed, and left,
generally fpeaking, to Men of mean Educa-
tion, and barbarous Difpofitions. The Difcovery of the *Canaries*, or rather the retriev-
ing them, for they were known to the Ancients, and fome Voyages had been made to
them in the thirteenth Century ; but they
were unaccountably loft again ; and therefore
I fay the Difcovery of them in 1417, by *John
de Bethencourt*, a Gentleman of *Normandy*,
in Virtue however of a *Spanifh* Commiffion,
was one of the firft Fruits of that laudable
Spirit of incouraging the ufeful and noble
Art of Navigation, which began now to difcover itfelf in various Parts of the World.

The *Canaries* are feven Iflands lying from
Eaft to Weft, pretty near the Coaft of *Africa*, and are the fame which were heretofore
ftyled *the Fortunate Iflands*. When I fay
feven,

feven, I mean that there are feven of principal Note; for, befides thefe, there are feveral leffer Iflands which yet have their Commodities, and would be valuable in the Hands
of any other Poffeffors than the *Spaniards.*
The Noife of *Bethencourt*'s Settlement concurring with the active Temper of the Infant
Don *Henry*, fourth Son to the then reigning
King of *Portugal*, occafioned various Expeditions under his Aufpice, in confequence of
which the Iflands of *Madeira* and *Porto Santo* were difcovered and fettled by the *Portuguefe.* The next Step was the Difcovery of
the *Azores*, or as the *Spaniards* call them,
Açores. Some *Flemings* had left a Colony
there in 1447, but *Gonçalvo Velho* failing
from *Portugal* in 1449, feized upon them,
and fecured them for that Crown, to which
they have belonged ever fince.

The vaft Advantages alfo which the *Portuguefe* derived from their Commerce with
the *Eaft Indies*, the Rout to which by the
Cape of Good Hope was likewife very lately
difcovered, occafioned much Difcourfe in the
World, and put many quick Wits, and enterprifing Seamen, on aiming at a farther Profecution of fuch profitable Adventures. The
Ufe of the Compafs, which it is faid was invented by *John Goias*, a Native of the little
City of *Malfi*, in the Kingdom of *Naples*,
was now thoroughly underftood, and Mari-
ners were no longer afraid of fteering without
                                                Sight

Sight of Land. By this Means they gave a greater Opportunity to the Winds and the Waves to facilitate their Views by carrying them at times out of their intended Courses, and thereby affording them Occasions of making Remarks, which otherwise they had never met with. Thus for Instance, a *Spanish* Pilot steering for a Port in the West of *Ireland*, was by a violent Tempest driven out to Sea fourteen Days, during which Time he saw, or fancied he saw, but at a great Distance, certain Islands, which have been since supposed part of *America*.

Two Sorts of Indications chiefly supported the Notion which then passed current among the wiser Navigators, *viz.* That there was yet a considerable Part of the Universe undiscovered. These Indications were first positive Assertions found in the Works of the Ancients; and secondly, Fables or Romantic Stories which seemed to be raised however on a Ground of Truth.

As to the first, we will speak of them briefly, because little has been said, worthy of Notice at least in our Language. *Plato*, in two of his Dialogues, mentions the Island of *Atlantis*; and there is yet extant a Description of it in *Greek* Verse, ascribed to *Solon*, on whose Credit, indeed, the whole Story depends, which runs in few Words thus: That great and good Man travelling into *Egypt* to improve his Knowledge, met there with a
Priest,

Prieſt, who entertained him with a Tradition
of this ſame Iſland, which ſeems to be either
an Allegory or a Fable. However, the Curious may read and conſider it, if they think
fit, in the Works of this celebrated Author.
The next Authority is taken from a Book generally attributed to *Ariſtotle,*, wherein it is
alledged, that the *Carthaginians* diſcovered
beyond the Streights of *Gibraltar* a certain
Iſland, large in Extent, fertile in its Soil, and
full of navigable Rivers at the Diſtance of
ſome Days Sail from the Continent ; but it
ſeems it was uninhabited. The firſt Diſco-
verers fixed there ; but the *Carthaginians*,
by an odd Stroke of Policy, forbad any of
their Subjects to ſettle there for the future,
and diſlodged thoſe who were already planted
therein. *Diodorus Siculus* gives us a far more
accurate and probable Account of this Matter,
deſcribing at large this celebrated Iſle, and then
ſhewing why it remained uninhabited. He
ſays the *Tyrians* would have planted a Colony there, but that the *Carthaginians* op-
poſed it for two Reaſons, firſt, becauſe they
were afraid too many of their Citizens would
incline to tranſport themſelves into this Iſland,
which might be prejudicial to their Affairs as
a trading People ; ſecondly, becauſe they defired to reſerve this Iſland as an Aſylum, to
which they might at any time retreat, if op-
preſſed by intolerable Misfortunes. Many
have inclined to think this Iſle the biggeſt of
the

the *Canaries*, which I confefs feems to me improbable for many Reafons; but particularly, becaufe all the *Canaries* are but indifferently provided with Water, whereas in this our Author exprefsly fays there were feveral navigable Rivers.   There is a Paffage in *Seneca* the Tragedian, which is much to our Purpofe, though it is rather a Prophecy than a Defcription.   It is very fhort, and therefore I will give it in the Author's own Words:

>——*Venient Annis*
> *Sæcula feris, quibus Oceanus*
> *Vincula Rerum laxet, & ingens*
> *Pateat tellus, Typhifque novos*
> *Detegat Orbes; nec fit terris*
> *Ultima Thule.*

Media, Act. iii. ℣ 375.

A Time fhall come, tho' it be late,
When the proud Ocean fhall abate
Of its vaft Empire; Men defcry
New Ifles, new Countries where they lie;
Nor fhall bleak *Thule* longer ftand,
To us, the laft difcovered Land.

There is yet another Paffage in an Author perhaps more ancient than any of thefe, I mean *Theopompus*, a *Greek* Writer, of whofe Works there remain now only fome Fragments, and amongft them this relating to a new World, wherein are two great Cities, one inhabited by Warriors, and another by Pietifts. The whole is vifibly an Allegory, and therefore

fore all that we can conclude from the Sum of thefe Authorities taken together is this, that fome of the wifeft of the Ancients thought there might poffibly be a large Proportion of the World undifcovered in their Time, and therefore made Choice of it, as a proper Scene wherein to lay Schemes of fuch Common-wealths as exifted only in their Fancies. In fhort, they dreamt of a new World, and have left us fome broken Account of thefe Dreams.

I come next to the Fables, or rather Romantic Stories which might be fuppofed to indicate that there was a great Part of the habitable World undifcovered ; and of thefe I fhall mention but three, though I could eafily have enlarged the Number. The firft of thefe is the Expedition of *Madoc* Prince of *Wales*, who is fuppofed to have been the firft Difcoverer of *America* ; he flourifhed in the twelfth Century, and was the Son of *Owen Guyneth*, Prince of *North Wales*. His Brothers raifing a Civil War about the Divifion of his Father's Dominions, he chofe rather to go to Sea with a few of his Friends, and feek out new Habitations, than run the Hazard of what might happen in the Iffue of this Difpute. Accordingly about the Year 1170, fteering due Weft, and leaving *Ireland* on the North, he came to an unknown Country, where he fettled a Colony, and returning thence into *Wales*, carried a fecond Supply of People, but was never heard of more.

That

That the Country he went to was really *A-merica*, is more, I think, than can be thoroughly proved; but that this Tale was invented after the Discovery of that Country, on purpose to set up a prior Title, is most certainly false. *Meredith ap Rhese*, who died in 1477, and was a famous *Welsh* Poet, composed an Ode in Honour of this *Madoc*, wherein was contained an Account of his Discoveries. Now as this was several Years before *Columbus* made his first Voyage, we may be sure that this was really a *British* Tradition, and no Tale of late Invention.

William of *Newberry* tells us a strange Story of two green Children, a Boy and a Girl, which in the Time of King *Stephen* were found in a Field, and who asserted that they came from the Land of St. *Martin*. The Story is indeed a wild one, and but indifferently told. But notwithstanding all this, it is a clear Proof that our Ancestors had some confused Notions of the Possibility of discovering some far distant Continent, which is all that from hence I attempt to prove. But the clearest and most intelligible Report of another World, which preceded the Discovery of *America*, was the Tale of the Island of the seven Churches, which in brief was this: Certain *Portuguese* Sailors having been driven in a small Bark several Days to Sea, reported on their Return, that they had been on Shore in a certain Island, the Inhabitants of which

were

were Chriftians defcended from the *Spani-ards*, who flying from their Country on the firft Invafion of the *Moors*, had difcovered this Ifle and planted it. Thefe *Portugueze* were compelled to put again to Sea, in order to recover the Land they talk'd of, from which Time they were never heard of; but the Story continued to be much talk'd of, and by the Vulgar believed.

C H A P. II.

Of the Difcovery of America *by* Columbus, *and of a prior Title thereto, which might be claimed by the* Englifh.

THOUGH the Opinion mentioned in the former Chapter, had paffed current in the Mouths of Men for many Years, yet we do not find that any Perfon undertook, by probable Arguments, to prove that there really was another Continent, and that a Paffage from this to that was practicable before the famous *Chriftopher Columbus*, who began and perfected his Difcovery in a very fhort Space of Time.

This excellent Perfon was, by Birth, a *Ge-noeze*, but of what Family we are ignorant, though feveral noble Ones in *Italy*, lay Claim to him, but with what Right, his Son Don *Ferdinando* knew not how to determine ; how then fhould we ? He addicted himfelf, from

from his Youth, to the Study of Navigation, and to the Practice of it ; for he went, while a Boy, to Sea, where he ferved under an Admiral of his own Name, who was a celebrated Corfair, and afterwards failed in a Merchant Ships to almoft all Parts of the known World. In all Probability, he took the firft Hint of his Difcovery from the common Opinion, that another World there was; but if he did, that detracts nothing from his Merit, fince the advancing Arguments in Proof of this, and ftriking out the Means of difcovering it, were entirely the Effects of his own Sagacity.

To run through all the Reafons which this great Man alledged in Support of his Judgment, would take up too much Room, it fhall therefore fuffice that we obferve, that he concluded right from falfe Premifes, and by the Happinefs of his Genius, ftruck out this important Truth from a Suppofition which was abfolutely falfe. Having long confidered the Form of this Terraqueous Globe, he became at length perfuaded that the *Indies*, which the *Portuguefe* had lately difcovered in the *Eaft*, was no other than a great Continent, balancing thofe Parts of the Univerfe already known ; and therefore he conceived that thofe who failed Eaft, muft come to their Weft Coafts; and that confequently, by failing Weft, it was as practicable to reach their Eaftern Shores. Which
Suppo-

Suppofition of his was the Caufe that he called the Iflands he difcovered the *Weft Indies*. He brought his Notions into Order about the Year 1480, when he propofed going on this Difcovery to the State of *Genoa*, which Project of his was rejected. He next offered it to the King of *Portugal*, in whofe Dominions he had refided fome Years. Commiffioners were appointed to treat with him, who, when by provoking with Objections, they had drawn out of him all they could, advifed the King to fit out a Veffel, and to fend it to try if the thing was practicable, whereby they meant to rob *Columbus*, both of the Honour and Advantage refulting from the Difcovery. The Defign mifcarried, through the Want of Courage and Conduct in the Perfons employed; but *Columbus* finding out the Trick, was exceedingly incenfed, fo that though the King of *Portugal* would have treated with him a fecond Time, being himfelf a better Judge of fuch Projects than any other Prince of his Age, yet he declin'd it, and refolved to apply elfewhere.

This was in 1487. In the fame Year, having fully inftructed his Brother, *Bartholomew*, in his intended Project, he fent him into *England*, with Directions to apply himfelf to *Henry* VII, who was reputed one of the wifeft Monarchs in Chriftendom, in Hopes that he would embrace a Propofal manifeftly tending to his Profit; and in the
mean

mean time he prepared himfelf to go into *Spain*, on the fame Account. *Bartholomew Columbus* was fo unfortunate as to fall into the Hands of Pyrates, who ftripped him of all he had. On his coming into *England* in this poor Condition, he fell ill of a Fever, and when he recovered from that, he fpent fome Time in making Maps, and felling them, before he put himfelf into fuch an Equipage as enabled him to addrefs himfelf to the King. This however he did in 1488, was well received, and actually entered into Argument with that Prince, in the Name, and on the Behalf of his Brother, feveral Years before he clofed with their Catholic Majefties, as his Son tells us in his Life. By Virtue of this Agreement, it fhould feem that our Title to the new World is prior to that of *Spain*. This is arguing in their own Way ; and if they plead the actual Difco-very of the Iflands in bar to us, I fhall here-after fhew, that we may plead the fame thing, with Refpect to the Continent, againft them. But the Bufinefs is now to profecute, in few Words, the Story of *Columbus*.

He follicited for feveral Years, and in Spight of repeated Difappointments, their Catholic Majefties *Ferdinand* and *Ifabella*. At laft being on the very Point of departing, in or-der to carry his Scheme into *France*, Queen *Ifabel*, a Princefs of great Wifdom and Cou-rage, fent for him back, and agreed with him

on

on his own Terms, which were pretty round ones, and such as discovered the Confidence he had of succeeding in his Design. He made this Agreement soon after the taking of the City of *Granada*, whereby the *Moors* were driven out of *Spain*, part of which they had possessed 770 Years, so that two of the most fortunate Events which ever happened to the *Spanish* Monarchy, fell out the same Year.

Columbus was furnished with three Carvels, and a hundred and twenty Men at *Palos de Moguere*. *Martin Pinson* was Pilot of one, *Francis Pinson* of another, and *Ditus Pinson* of the third, all three Brothers, and departed the third of *August* 1492. They came to the Island of *Gomera*, one of the *Canaries*, where they refreshed: From thence he sailed thirty-four Days West without seeing Land, insomuch that his Company murmured, and contrived his Death; but he satisfied them with good Words and Promises; at last he spied a thick Cloud, which proved Land, on the eleventh of *October*, whereat they all rejoyced, thanked GOD, and kissed *Columbus*'s Hands. The first Land they fell in with was called *Guinaya*, one of the Islands of *Lucaios*; from thence he went to *Hispaniola*, then called *Haitu*, where the Admiral's Ship was lost, but all the Men and Furniture saved.

The

The *Indians* fled from them, all but one Woman, whom they took and cloathed, and ufed courteoufly, and let her go again ; which did fo much imbolden the *Indians*, that they reforted to the *Spaniards*, and helped them to unlade their Ship that was loft, and did them other Services ; and with the Good-will of the King, they built a Caftle of Wood, and left thirty-eight *Spaniards* in it under a Captain ; and this was the firft footing the *Spaniards* had in the *Indies*. *Columbus* took ten Parrots, fome Turkeys, and other Things the Land afforded, and return'd to *Palos* in *Spain*, in fifty Days. The King and Queen were at *Barcelona* when *Columbus* arrived, whither he went with his *Indians*, and other Rarities, the third of *April*, a Year after he departed from thence.

At his coming to the King the *Indians* were baptized, the King, Queen, and Prince being prefent, who were their Godfathers and Godmother. They caufed *Columbus* to fit by them, which was never done to any Subject. They confirmed the Privilege of the Tenths, and gave him the Title of Admiral of the *Indies*; and to his Brother *Bartholomew*, that of *Adelantado*. The Queen favoured this Difcovery more than the King, and would not for a while, let any *Arrogonians* go to the *Indies* without Licence. The King rewarded many of *Columbus*'s Company ; but the Mariner who firft difcovered
the

the Land, not being recompenfed to his Content, fled into *Barbary*, where he turned *Turk*.

The *Indians* confeffed to *Columbus*, that there were many Prophecies amongft them, that they fhould be fubdued by white Men with Beards, with Apparel on their Backs, with bright Swords that fhould cleave a Man infunder, and fhould girt their Swords to their Sides.

Columbus in his fecond Voyage had feventeen Ships, and one thoufand two hundred Men, Mares, Sheep, Cows, and Corn to fow. The firft Land he fell in with was the Ifland of *Defcada*; and coming to *Hifpaniola*, he found his thirty-eight *Spaniards* flain, through their own Fault, for injuring the *Indians*. He built a Town, and in Honour of the Queen, called it *Ifabella*. And at this time began the *Spaniards* and *Columbus* to difagree.

There never was perhaps a Man better qualified for the great Defigns he undertook, than *Chriftopher Columbus*; but the Gravity of his Behaviour, and the fevere Difcipline he maintained while it was in his Power, raifed him Enemies amongft a mutinous, licentious Crew; and thefe Difputes occafion'd Appeals from both Parties to *Spain*, whereupon one *Francis Bobadilla* was fent over to enquire into thefe Matters, and to do Juftice according to the Light in which Things fhould ſhould appear to him. This Man to gratify a Biſhop who had taken ſome Pique to *Columbus*, cauſed the Admiral to be ſeized, together with his Brethren, put them in Irons, and ſent them in that Condition into *Spain*.

They arrived at *Cadiz* on the 25th of *November*, 1500; and as ſoon as their Catholic Majeſties were informed of the Treatment the Admiral had met with, they ordered him to be ſet at Liberty, expreſſing great Concern for his Sufferings, eſpecially the Queen, who was his very ſincere Friend, but it was a good while before he could procure a new Governor to be ſent to *Hiſpaniola*, which at laſt however he did. When he had carried this Point, he ſollicited Leave to make a fourth Voyage for Diſcoveries, which with much ado he obtained. It was in this his laſt going into the *Weſt Indies*, that he firſt ſaw the Continent, lying ſome time at Anchor at the *Baſtimentos :* This was in 1502. Some farther Diſcoveries he made on the ſame Coaſt ; but before he could thoroughly inform himſelf of the State of the Country he was obliged to alter his Courſe, and ſteer for *Hiſpaniola*. Some time he remained there, but at length new Diſputes and Diſorders riſing, he reſolved to return back into *Spain*, in order to give their Majeſties the beſt Account he could of thoſe Parts, that this Diſcovery might be made as advantagious to them as poſſible.

It

It was towards the latter End of the Year 1504, that he came for the laſt Time into *Spain*, where the firſt News he met with was that of the Death of Queen *Iſabella*, which ſtruck him to the Heart, inſomuch that his Health apparently declined thenceforward. He did not, however, fail to apply himſelf to the Court, where he met with very indifferent Uſage ; for though he was treated with great Reſpect, and had many fair Words given him, yet the Senſe he had of the King's Coldneſs, and of the Ingratitude of the *Spaniſh* Courtiers, made ſuch an Impreſſion upon him, as, after a few Months Illneſs, broke his Heart. This happened on the 20th of *May*, 1506, at *Valladolid*. As ſoon as the Court was informed of his Death, Orders were given for his being buried with the utmoſt Pomp and Splendor. But the Admiral himſelf had given ſome Directions concerning his Interment, which ſerved to perpetuate the Memory of his ill Treatment ; for he ordered the Irons which he had worn to be put into his Coffin with him. His Epitaph deviſed, as ſome Hiſtorians ſay, by King *Ferdinand* himſelf, ſuited the Dignity of the Perſon, and the Service he had render'd the *Spaniſh* Nation. It conſiſts only of two Lines:

Per Caſtilla, *y por* Leon,
Nuevo Mundo hallo Colon.

Caſtile and *Leon* to *Columbus* owe
That *World*, his Wiſdom only could beſtow.

To

C H A P. III.

*Of other Discoveries made in the Life-time
of* Columbus, *particularly those by* John
Cabot.

THE Report of the many and great Advantages accruing to *Spain* from the
mighty Discoveries made by *Columbus*, raised
an earnest Desire in other great Princes, to
make some Experiments in the same kind.
Among the rest, King *Henry* VII, of *England*, who, as I before observed, had first accepted the Proposal of *Columbus*, though the
Author himself knew not so much, having
still in his Dominions a Foreigner of a bold
enterprizing Genius, and withal well versed
in Navigation, resolved to employ him without Loss of Time, that, if possible, his Subjects might share in the Wealth of the new
Indies. This Foreigner was *John Cabot*, by
Birth a *Venetian*, who obtained his Letters
Patent to himself and his three Sons, for
making Discoveries in any Part of the World.
These bore date the 5th of *March*, 1496,
being the eleventh Year of that King's
Reign.

Immediately after obtaining these, he sailed
from *Bristol*; and in the Month of *June*,
1497,

1497, difcovered *Newfoundland*, failing afterwards along the Coaft of *America* to *Florida*; and may therefore be juftly reputed
the firft Finder of the Continent in thofe
Parts. If therefore there be any Ground of
Title, as the *Spaniards* pretend, from the firft
Difcovery, though Poffeffion be not taken,
then have we a better Title to the main Land
of *America* than they: But if fettling and
improving give a Right, then ours is full as
good as theirs.

In 1498 *Americus Vefputius*, a *Florentine*,
but failing with a *Spanifh* Commiffion, made
fome Difcoveries in the *Weft Indies*. From
him *America* received its Name, though, as
moft Writers agree, very unjuftly, fince it is
certain he was not the firft Difcoverer; and
many have doubted whether he difcovered
any thing at all; but he was a Man of great
Addrefs, and knew better how to glofs his
Actions than any who had gone before him.
After this he made another Voyage in the
Service of *Spain*, but on his Return he de-
ferted this, as before he did his Country's
Service, and entered into that of the King of
Portugal, for whom he went alfo twice into
the fame Part of the World. There is a
ftrong Spirit of Rancour apparent in moft
of our modern Writers againft this Man,
wherein perhaps they may be fomewhat in-
fluenced by the Reports of the *Spanifh* Writers, who very poffibly may have fome Prejudice

judice beyond what hitherto has been fuſpec-
ted, on Account of his leaving them to ſerve
the *Portugueze.*   Yet this is certain, that he
cannot, with any Propriety, be ſtyled the
Diſcoverer of *America*; though by his firſt
publiſhing his Voyages, he found Means to
give it his Name.

In 1500 *Peter Alvarez Capralis,* Admiral of a Fleet for *Emanuel* King of *Portugal,* ſteering to the *Eaſt Indies,* was by a
Storm carried on the Coaſt of *Brazil,* which
he firſt diſcover'd, and which has ſince prov'd
of ſuch infinite Benefit to his Nation.   From
hence one might be inclined to believe, that
if *Columbus* had not gone expreſly in ſearch
of the new World eight Years before, Chance,
or, to ſpeak more in the Dialect of the Chriſtian, Providence would have opened a Paſſage thither now.

The *Pinçons,* and others who had accom-
panied the Admiral *Columbus* in his Voyages,
did alſo make ſome Diſcoveries at their own
Expence, by Virtue of Commiſſions given
them by King *Ferdinand.* But two Cauſes
eſpecially hindered the Progreſs that might
otherwiſe have been expected from the Diligence of the *Spaniards* in theſe Parts.   The
firſt was the Avarice of the *Spaniſh* Government, which meaſuring the Capacity and
Worth of Adventures, barely by the Returns
of Wealth they ſent into *Spain,* they were
thereby led to act ſo rapaciouſly, as frequently
to

to hazard, for the Sake of a little Gold, the Poffeffion of whole Countries full of Commodities of great Value. Secondly, The Diftance they were at from *Spain*, and the Neceffity there was of trufting feveral Commanders with independant Commiffions, occafioned not only numberlefs Mutinies, but infpired the *Spanifh* Officers with fuch a Spirit of Cruelty againft the native *Indians*, as tended to the depopulating of thofe Countries, and thereby rendering them far lefs beneficial than otherwife they would have been.

C H A P. IV.

Of the principal Difcoveries made by the Spaniards, *after the Death of* Columbus.

THE main Caufe which retarded thofe Difcoveries which might otherwife have been made in the new World, was the Temper of King *Ferdinand*. He valued himfelf extremely on his political Knowledge, which inclined him to fhew a great deal of Refpect, but at the fame time to give very little Encouragement to *Columbus*. He was jealous of the Authority which that great Man had obtained in Virtue of the Agreement made with him, when he firft failed in fearch of the *Indies*, and this feems to be the true Reafon why he rather thwarted than encouraged the Admiral's making any farther
Difco-

Difcoveries in the latter Part of his Life. This appears more probable from the King's Conduct after his Deceafe; for he then readily granted Commiffions for new Difcoveries, and treated all fuch as made them very favourably.

The only Part of the Continent, which *Columbus* ever faw, was the *Ifthmus* of *Darien*; and he died in a full Perfwafion that this was the fame Continent with the *Eaft Indies*. The Natives helped to confirm him in his Miftake, by their Reports; for whatever Queftions he afked, they anfwered in the affirmative, from a foolifh Defire of flattering their new Mafters. But when the Admiral was once dead, nobody pretended to make Difcoveries, by Rule or Reafon, but by Chance, and as Reports led them; and this though it fometimes had happy Confequences, yet it frequently drew them into vaft Inconveniencies; for not knowing how to proportion their Forces to the Exploits upon which they went, the *Spanifh* Captains very frequently loft the greateft Part of their Men by War and Sicknefs, and inftead of inriching, brought themfelves to ruin.

Some Adventurers fettled themfelves in *Darien*; and amongft them there was one *Bafco Nunez de Balboa*, a Man only confiderable for his great Parts and high Spirit; for as to his Fortune, it was intirely wafted, by having been engaged in a former Defign

of

of difcovering, which came to nothing. Thofe with whom he was now embarked, were alfo brought to the Brink of Ruin, when by his Advice they were faved, and by repeated Acts of Courage and Conduct, brought into a profperous Condition. The Perfon who had the King's Authority was very unfit for the Employment he enjoyed. The People faw this, and that *Nunez* was much more capable of commanding. Their Wifhes concurring with his Ambition, he affumed the fupreme Authority; and from a private Man, became Commander in chief, by mere dint of Merit.

His Conduct in Power confirmed thofe who had raifed him to it in their Hopes; for by acting juftly and honourably towards the *Indian* Chiefs, he eftablifhed a folid Reputation, and procured fuch Intelligence as prov'd highly advantageous. By the Advice of one of thefe *Indian* Princes, he made a very troublefome March through the Mountains, till on the 25th of *September*, 1513, he difcovered, what no *European* had ever feen before, the *South Seas*; and had an imperfect Account of the great Empire of *Peru*. This opened a new Field for Difcoveries, and was in itfelf a much greater Exploit than any of his Countrymen hitherto had undertaken. But the *Indians* who raifed his Hopes by reporting prodigious Things of the Wealth of the great Kingdom, as they called it, at the

fame

same time embarraffed him not a little by
their pofitive Affertions, that the Inhabitants
of this Country were a numerous and warlike People; that they had great Veffels like
thofe of the *Spaniards*; and that it was in
vain for them to think of the Conqueft of
fuch a Country with the Handful of Men under his Command.

Upon this *Pafco de Nunez,* though a Man
of daring Courage, refolved to attempt nothing till fuch Time as he received a Commiffion, and a Reinforcement from *Spain,* in
order to which, he, and the People who were
with him, made choice of two Agents to be
fent home. Unluckily for them, the News
of their depofing the King's Officer had reached *Spain,* and the King always jealous of his
Authority, had immediately named one *Peter Arias,* Governor in thofe Parts, and difpatched him thither with a confiderable Force.
However, on the coming of thefe Agents
we have before-mentioned, and their bringing
with them a great Quantity of Gold on the
King's Account, *Ferdinand* feemed to forget
what was paft, and fent *Bafco de Nunez* a
Commiffion, appointing him *Adelantado,* or
Lieutenant of the *South Seas,* which however was far from anfwering the Purpofe for
which it was granted.

On the firft Arrival of *Peter Arias, Bafco
de Nunez* paid him all imaginable Refpect;
but very quickly perceiving that the Governor
exceed-

exceedingly difliked him, he no longer made his Court to him, but on the contrary, became an open Malecontent. This naturally produced bad Confequences, the rather, becaufe the new Governor, though a very brave and a very enterprifing Man, was very far from being fortunate, through his Want of Knowledge of the Country, and his not caring to afk the Advice of fuch as had been longer there.

Amongft the reft of the *Spaniards*, who came over with the new Governor, there was a Bifhop, a Man of great Parts, and of no lefs Piety. He reprefented to *Bafco de Nunez* the Folly and Wickednefs of inflaming the People againft their Governor; and, on the other hand, he took pains to fhew *Peter Arias* his Error in neglecting the *Adelantado*, whofe Succefs before his Arrival had procured the Province the Title of *Caftilla del Oro*, or *Golden Caftile*; whereas, fince his Arrival, the *Spaniards* had acquired neither Fame nor Riches. By the Perfuafions of this Prelate, a Reconciliation was brought about. Real on the Side of *Bafco de Nunez*, but feigned only by *Peter Arias*, who intended nothing more than to gain thereby an Opportunity of deftroying *Nunez*, whom he declared his Son-in-Law, contracting him to the Lady *Mary*, his only Daughter, who was as yet in *Spain*, but who, as he pretended, was to come in the next Ships.

Not

Not long after this Reconciliation, *Peter de Arias* fent *Bafco Nunez* with three hundred Men to make Difcoveries in the *South Seas*. He refolved to do nothing rafhly, and therefore fixed in that Part of the Country where *Panama* has been fince built, where he caufed great Quantities of Wood to be cut down, intending to make Veffels of feveral kinds, that he might not be diftreffed in landing, or if he was obliged to keep long at Sea. The Confidence all Men had in his Conduct made Things go on chearfully, and great Expectations were formed of the Succefs of his Voyage, when all on a fudden he was recalled to *Darien*, where upon a Charge of treafonable Expreffions, fupported by falfe Witneffes, *Peter Arias*, after a formal Trial, caufed his Head to be ftruck off, thereby ridding himfelf of a Rival, though at the fame time he blafted the Hopes, and broke the Spirits of his People.

The Ifland of St. *Juan de Puerto Rico*, fometimes though corruptly called *Borriquen*, had been difcovered by *Columbus*, but it was firft fettled by *John Ponce de Leon*, a *Spanifh* Gentleman, of fome Courage, and great Fortune. This was fo early as in the Year 1509, but it was fome Years before it was thoroughly fubdued and inhabited. Confiderable Quantities of Gold were extracted out of the Streams of two of its Rivers; and *Ponce de Leon* having by this means acquired

a very

a very large Eſtate, upon his being removed from the Government of the Iſland, reſolved to go upon new Diſcoveries. His Reputation, as a prudent Commander, and his known Generoſity, procured him many Followers; ſo that he was quickly in a Condition to execute his Deſign.

It was in the Beginning of the Year 1512, that he ſailed from *Puerto Rico*, and after a good deal of hard Weather, he at laſt approached the Continent, where he went on Shore, and took Poſſeſſion of it, calling it *Florida*; but whether, as ſome ſay, from its beautiful Appearance in the Spring Seaſon of the Year, or becauſe he landed in *Eaſter-Week*, which Feſtival the *Spaniards* call *Paſqua de Flores*, is uncertain. However, he was but a bare Diſcoverer, or at moſt he took a nominal Poſſeſſion of the Country; for the Natives being a brave, and well-armed People, forced him to reimbark his Forces, and to return to *Puerto Rico*, without being able to make any Settlement upon the Continent. Many Years afterwards *Ferdinand de Soto* undertook the Conqueſt of *Florida*, with a much greater Force, but after ſtruggling for five Years with many Difficulties, the *Spaniards* were once again obliged to abandon the Deſign.

Yucatan was diſcovered in 1517, by *Hernandez de Cordova*, a very gallant Man, who had a hundred Soldiers under his Command;
he

he attempted to have taken Poffeffion of at leaft that Part of the Country where he landed ; but the *Indians* affembling in great Numbers, vigoroufly oppofed him ; fo that at length he was conftrained to abandon his Defign, and to return again to *Cuba,* having fifty of his Men wounded in an Engagement, wherein he himfelf alfo, is reported by fome Authors, to have been hurt in thirty-three Places. *Francis de Monteyo,* with five hundred *Spaniards,* went over to the fame Country, and with fome Difficulty at firft fettled there, by degrees cultivating a Friendfhip with the Natives, they made themfelves very eafy, and intermarrying with them, began to take up their Cuftoms, and fo lived in Eafe and Plenty, without thinking any more of Conquefts, or the Toils of War. Indeed this Part of *America* has been always better peopled by the Natives than any other, in confequence of which, the *Spaniards* have been forced to behave better there than in other Places, and to ufe their Power with greater Mildnefs than is natural to that haughty Nation.

CHAP.

CHAP. V.

Of the Conquest of Mexico, *by Don* Ferdinand Cortez.

THE narrow Compaſs in which it is deſigned to bring the hiſtorical Part of this Work, will not allow us to enter minutely into the Detail of this great Conqueror's Exploits ; but for all this we cannot help entertaining the Reader with a conciſe Character of the moſt illuſtrious Perſon after the Admiral *Columbus*, who diſtinguiſhed himſelf in theſe Parts of the World. This we ſhall the rather do, becauſe many of our *Engliſh* Authors have reported various Falſehoods concerning him.

Ferdinand Cortez was born at *Medellin*, a ſmall Town of *Eſtramadura* in *Spain* in the Year 1485 ; his Father's Name was *Martin Cortez de Monroy* ; his Mother's, *Catherina Pizarro Altamarino*, both noble, though not in extraordinary Circumſtances. They found a good deal of Difficulty in bringing up this Son of theirs, who was of a very weak and tender Conſtitution, till he reached the Age of fourteen Years. He then grew ſtrong and healthy, which induced his Parents to ſend him to *Salamanca*, to purſue his Studies, intending, that when he grew up he ſhould have applied himſelf to the Law. But this

not

not fuiting at all with his Inclinations, he
quickly left the Univerfity, and returned home.
Some fhort Time after he refolved to pafs
over into *Italy*, in order to ferve under the
Command of *Gonçalvo de Cordova*, who is
better known by his Title of the *Great Captain*. But a very fevere quartan Ague obliged the young *Cortez* to lay afide this Defign,
and when he was thoroughly recovered from
this Diftemper, his Father procured him Letters of Recommendation to *Nicholas de O-
bando*, Governor of *Hifpaniola*, a very worthy Perfon, and a Native alfo of the Province
of *Eftramadura*.

In the Year 1504 he embarked at *Sevil*, on
board a Veffel commanded by *Alonzo Quintero*, who with four other Veffels failed for
the *Indies*. Through the Obftinacy and In-
difcretion of the Captain, they had but a very
indifferent Paffage, in which, however, *Cortez* gave fignal Proofs of all thofe fhining
Qualities, by which he became afterwards fo
much diftinguifhed. On his Arrival in *Hifpaniola*, he was very kindly received, and
had a Place given him, in which he continued a Year or two. He was at this Time
about twenty Years of Age, extremely handfome in his Perfon, affable in his Behaviour,
and amiable in his Manners. He had a great
Facility in fpeaking without affecting Eloquence; he was very prudent, and yet quick
in his Refolutions, and ready in the Execu-
                                            tion

tion of them; he had a wonderful Presence, and no less Steadiness of Mind; a Courage equally capable of bearing, and of undertaking all things; a generous Contempt of Money, and an earnest Desire of obliging all without expecting any Return.

A just Sense of his great Abilities engaged *James Velasquez*, on his being made Governor of *Cuba*, to make Choice of *Cortez* for his Secretary. He had not been long in *Cuba* before he fell into a very great Misfortune. It seems the Governor was a little arbitrary, which created such Discontents in the Island, that several very considerable Persons caused a Memorial to be drawn up, containing a Charge of Male Administration against him, and employed *Cortez*, in conjunction with *Andrew de Duero*, a very discreet Person, and one of the most considerable Men in the Colony, to go over with him into *Hispaniola*, where at that Time there were Judges of Appeals arrived from *Spain*. But *Velasquez* having Notice of this Design, found means to apprehend *Cortez*, with whom he was so much offended, that he was on the Point of hanging him. At last, through the Persuasion of his Friends, he contented himself with causing *Cortez* to be put in Irons, and to be sent on board a Bark ready to sail for *Hispaniola*. In the Night the Prisoner found means to get off his Irons; and though he had not learned to swim, he had the Courage

rage to throw himſelf into the Sea with a Log of Wood in his Arms; unluckily for him, it was then ebb, ſo that he was carried out to Sea a League beyond the Ship : The Flood, however, brought him back and threw him on Shore, but ſo tired and bruiſed, that he was once on the Point of quitting his Log, and ſuffering himſelf to be drowned. As ſoon as he recovered Strength enough to be able to walk, he went and hid himſelf in an adjacent Grove till it was dark, and then he crept into a Church, where he took Sanctuary.

He continued there for ſome time, till an amorous Adventure brought upon him a freſh Misfortune. Hard by the Church there lived one *John Xuarez*, who had a very handſome Siſter ; *Cortez* was extremely ſmitten with her, and as he went one Day to pay his Ad-dreſſes to her, as ſhe ſtood at a Window, an Officer of Juſtice came behind him, catched him up in his Arms, and carried him to Pri-ſon. The Magiſtrates, deſirous of pleaſing the Governor, paſſed a very ſevere Sentence on him. But *James Velaſquez*, who was natu-rally a Man of great Humanity, mitigated it firſt, and then ſet him at Liberty, refuſing however to take him again into his Service, which reduced *Cortez* to very great Wants. In this low Condition he married *Catherina Xuarez*, when he ſcarce knew how to main-tain either himſelf or her. Their Condition was very little mended when ſhe was brought

to

to Bed of a Son, to whom, at his Requeſt, the Governor *Velaſquez* ſtood God-father. By degrees he recovered that Gentleman's Favour, who gave him an Eſtate in the Country, and a certain Number of *Indians* for Servants. From this Beginning he quickly grew rich, and which is more extraordinary, gained ſuch an Aſcendant over the Governor, that when he had equipped at his own Expence a very large Fleet, in order to make Diſcoveries on the Coaſt of the Continent, he gave the Command of it to this *Ferdinand Cortez.*

An Accident happened, when he was almoſt ready to depart, which had well nigh baffled all his Hopes, and brought him once more into Diſtreſs. As *Velaſquez* and *Cortez* were one Day viewing the Fleet, a Fool which the former kept cried out, Maſter Governor, if you ſend away *Cortez* with this Fleet, you muſt ſend another to look after him. This ſtruck *Velaſquez* ſo much, that he had Thoughts of changing his Admiral ; but *Cortez* being a Man of deep Penetration, he no ſooner diſcovered this, than he reſolved to ſail without taking Leave or expecting Orders; and this bold Deſign he ſuddenly and ſucceſsfully put in Execuion, being exceedingly beloved by all the Soldiers and Sailors who were employed in this Expedition.

Arriving at *Vera Cruz,* and receiving there Information of the vaſt Wealth of the King
of

of *Mexico*, he set forward towards him on the 16th of *August* 1520, with five hundred Foot, fifteen Horse, and one thousand three hundred *Indians* to carry the Baggage. After four Days March he came to a goodly Country, called *Chinchecas*; but before he came thither he had passed high Hills, full of Snow and Ice, though it was in *August*.

Next he came to *Tlascalla*, inhabited by a People who were Enemies to the *Mexicans*. *Cortez* overthrew them in three Conflicts; the Town had twenty thousand Houses very fair, and handsome Markets and Fairs: *Cortez* took it by Night, and returned to his Camp, where he found his Men in Mutiny; but appeased them by wise and mild Exhortations, doing all he could to inspire them with Piety, and to form no Ideas of conquering but out of hope they should spread abroad the Gospel of *Christ*. From thence he went to *Chalotecan*, a Country no less fruitful; where he was entertained with their kind of Musick; but they were set on by the King of *Mexico* to betray him, which was discovered by an *Indian* Woman; and *Cortez*, to secure himself, and revenge their Treachery, suddenly set upon them, and overcame them. The King of *Mexico* sent to excuse himself of this Treason, and to lay it upon the People of the Country: He likewise sent to invite *Cortez* to *Mexico*, and as he passed the Country he was well entertained, especially in *Tlatelulco* and

Xalisco,

Xalifco, the one Friend, the other Enemy to the *Mexicans.*

When *Cortez* came within half a Mile of *Montezuma,* the King fent a thoufand Courtiers, all in one Garb, to meet him, who faluted him one after another, firft touching the Ground with their Fingers, and kiffing it. Then came *Montezuma,* with two hundred better apparalled, two and two together, without Shoes, though they ufe Shoes at other Times; he leaned upon two of his Nobility, to fhew that he was upheld by his Nobles. *Cortez* was told he muft not touch the King, for that it was the Cuftom of the Country: He prefented the King with a Chain of Bugles, and fome Diamonds in it; which the King took in good Part, and gave him in requital another of Gold wrought in Snails, Crabs, and fuch Toys. He lodged *Cortez* in his Palace with great Solemnity, and made liberal Provifion for his Army. The King erected a curious Throne of State, where he directed his Speech to the *Spaniards* as follows:

Noble Soldiers, and merciful Captains to them that yield, you are welcome into this Country of ours; I would have you know that our Forefathers have told us, and our Chronicles declare it, that we are not anciently of this Land wherein we live, but brought hither by a King, who left us here becaufe we refufed to return with him in Company. Our Forefathers married, had
Iffue,

Issue, built Houses which we enjoy ; and we have ever been of Opinion, that they will come to us again, and make us Subjects to them, as they have formerly been to our Ancestors. And therefore considering from whence you come, and that you are sent from a great King, we yield to you all Obedience and Service, and make Account you are entered into your own Houses. I am not ignorant of what hath happened to you by the Way, and that the *Cimpoalans* have spoken ill of me ; they are my Enemies, and I pray you believe them not ; I know they tell you my Houses and Walls are Gold, and that I make myself a God ; but I pray you behold my Houses that are made of Wood, Lime and Stone, and myself a fleshly Man like others. Indeed I have Plate from my Ancestors, and what I have shall be yours. I must now depart, but will so provide that neither you nor yours shall want.

Cortez answered, that what he said was true, and that the King of *Spain* was the King they looked for ; and that he was sent thither purposely to let them know so much. After they had passed six Days in great Jollity, *Cortez* had News that some of his Men were murdered by the King's Apointment ; for which he was glad, thinking to take that Occasion to subdue and conquer him and his Country. *Cortez* sent for the Malefactors, and put them to Death ; they accused *Montezuma,*

tezuma, whom likewife he impriſoned, but within a while after he ſet him at Liberty ; he confeſſed his Fault, and promiſed his Allegiance ever after.

The King choſe rather to dwell in the Palace with *Cortez*, than at Pleaſure abroad. To give him Satisfaction, he ſent to diſcover Mines for him, and procured a great Quantity of Wealth to preſent him ; he wiſhed and adviſed his Nobles to obey *Cortez*, and laboured how he might ſubdue *Cacomacſin*, his Vaſſal, who wholly refuſed to ſubmit to *Cortez*. This Act of his was affirmed by public Notaries in Writing, by the Conſent of all the Nobility, and interchangeably given to each another.

Valaſquez, the Governor of *Cuba*, envying *Cortez*, ſent *Narvaes* with eighteen Sail of Ships, and a proportionable Body of Forces and Ammunition to command, and, in caſe of Refuſal, to compel *Cortez* to go out and quit *Mexico* ; at which *Cortez* was amazed, and in a Dilemma ; for, if he made Head againſt *Narvaes*, the *Indians* would preſently have revolted ; and if he did not, *Narvaes* would in time poſſeſs himſelf of the Country ; wherefore he reſolved with one hundred and ſeventy Men to go againſt *Narvaes*, leaving a Garriſon in *Tenuſtilan*, which he commended to the Care of the King. *Narvaes* had eight hundred *Spaniards*, and nineteen great Pieces of Cannon ; neverthelefs, *Cortez*

ſet

set upon, took him, and the rest yielded themselves, being better inclined to their new than to their old Commander.

In this Interim, the Citizens of *Tenustilan* revolted against the King and *Spaniards,* and affaulted the Castle, alledging, their Diflike to the *Spaniards* was for breaking down their Idol; but in truth they laid hold of this at a proper Seafon for recovering their Liberty.

Cortez haftened thither with seventy Horse, and five hundred *Spaniards,* which gave Heart to them in the Castle; the *Indians* were desperate, and desired rather to die than live; they put *Cortez* to a Retreat, which embolden'd them much, and endangered the *Spaniards* more.

Cortez afterwards used many Engines, and other Inventions; and though he flew Multitudes of *Indians,* yet they, because of their Numbers, valued it not. *Montezuma* looking out of a Window, thinking to diffuade the People from their violent Courfes against the *Spaniards,* was ftruck with a Stone, of which Wound he died within three Days. He was a Man of a good Nature, wife and prudent. The *Spaniards* gave the *Mexicans* his Body to bury, and offered the *Indians* Conditions of Peace, which they wholly refufed, vowing to thruft the *Spaniards* out of their Country, though it were with the Lofs of a thoufand Men to one. Yet within a Day they deceitfully made a Propofition of Peace, which

which *Cortez* accepted of; and, to give them the more Content, he set a Priest of theirs at Liberty, thinking it would have wrought more heartily; but the Day following, when *Cortez* had the least Suspicion of them, and sat quietly at Dinner, they attempted one of his Houses; whereupon he suddenly rose from Table, and with his Horse charged the *Indians*, where he lost diverse Men, and was himself sorely wounded, and scarce able to retire. It was now come to that pass with the *Spaniards*, that they must either perish or quit the City; and that Night they resolved to fly with *Montezuma*'s Children, and Treasure; but the *Indians* having Notice of it, pursued them, recovered the Prisoners, slew one hundred and fifty *Spaniards*, forty one Horses, and two thousand *Indians* that took their Part. Now did *Cortez* endure great Misery and Famine, and had but one dead Horse to feed on in five Days, till he came to *Tlascalla*.

The *Tlascallans* entertained him courteously, where he staid ten Days; he built many Fortresses for his own Safety and theirs, and sent for Aid into *Hispaniola:* In the mean time he gained the Love of many *Indians*, who took part against the *Mexicans*. *Cortez* built thirteen Boats; and on the other Side, the new King of *Mexico* prepared for War, and made certain Pikes to annoy the Horse, which they feared more than the Men. *Cortez* cut a Passage into the Salt Lake, for his

Boats

Boats to have a Paſſage to the Siege of *Te-nuſtitlan:* Theſe Ships intercepted all Pro-viſions, and annoyed the *Indians* infinitely. *Cortez* aſſailed the Town in four Places, ha-ving in his Army one hundred and twenty thouſand Men; ſome came for Fear, ſome for Liberty, ſome for Friendſhip, ſome out of Gain. This Siege laſted ten Weeks, and waſted ten thouſand Men with Famine and other Misfortunes. *Cortez*, by Chance, took the new King as he was ſtealing away ſecret-ly by the Lake: He ſubdued *Tinuſtitlan*, and fourt en Towns by the Lake Side; as alſo all the *Mexicans* Realms and Provinces, to the Crown of *Spain*, giving great Spoil to the Soldiers, and reſerving the Fifths to the King.

There are ſcarce any Circumſtances which can be thought of capable of raiſing the Re-putation of a Conqueror, which are not to be found in the Story of *Cortez.* He owed his Authority entirely to his Merit, and, which is wonderful, he kept it by the ſame Means, not only in Spight of his powerful Enemies in the *Indies* and *Spain*, but alſo notwith-ſtanding many Conſpiracies againſt his Per-ſon, and ſeveral very dangerous Seditions amongſt his Troops. He performed theſe mighty Things, with a very inconſiderable Body of Men. At the taking the City of *Mexico*, which happened on the 13th of *Auguſt*, 1521, he had but nine hundred *Spa-niſh*

niſh Foot, eighty Horſe, and ſeventeen ſmall
Pieces of Cannon. Indeed the *Indians* who
ſided with him were, as we ſaid before, very
numerous. His Conduct towards this Nation was ſuch as gained the Reverence and
Affection ; ſo that it may be ſaid his Perſonal
Accompliſhments were of as great Uſe in acquiring this Country to *Spain*, as a large
Army. Notwithſtanding he was ſo great a
Stateſman, and ſo able a General, yet he never did any thing inconſiſtent with the Rules
of Honour, or unbecoming that Piety which
he ſhewed in all his Actions. He was extremely loyal to his Prince, grateful and be-
nificent to his Friends, juſt, and generous to
all. Yet he wanted not many Enemies, en-
vious alike of his Merit and his Fortune,
and who therefore took abundance of Pains
to prejudice the Emperor *Charles* V. againſt
him.

In the Year 1528 *Cortez* found it convenient to return into *Spain*, in order to juſtify
his Conduct againſt his Enemies. The Emperor *Charles* V. received him with great
Reſpect, gave him the whole Vale of *Atriſco*,
with the Towns and Villages therein, con-
ferred on him the Title of Marquis of the
Vale of *Guaxaca* ; and to complete his Fa-
vours, procured him a very honourable Mar-
riage. The next Year he returned to *Mexico*,
with his Lady, but with a very limited Commiſſion, which turned more to the Diſadvan-
tage

tage of the *Spanish* Government, than to the private Loſs of the Marquiſs, who was ſo much beloved and eſteemed in that Part of the World, as to ſtand in no Need of Authority to procure him Reſpect.

He was ſome Time afterwards Captain-General, *Mendoça* being Viceroy of the Province, at which Time there happened many private Grudges between them, but yet they joined together for the finding out of the Paſſage from thoſe Seas to ours, which we properly call the *North Weſt Paſſage* ; as alſo in the Conqueſt of *Sibola* and *Quivera*, where they were perſwaded by certain Friars, that the People worſhipped the Croſs, and had other Tokens of Chriſtianity ; but all proved falſe, and few *Spaniards* returned home, their Miſery was ſo great, and the Country ſo cold and barren, the People cruel, and five hundred Leagues from *Mexico*. *Cortez*, after his taking *Mexico*, ſent to diſcover the Northern Parts, and his People arrived in a Country where *Ticoantipe Cician Pipe* was King, who received them lovingly, and ſent an Ambaſſador to *Cortez*, thinking he was come out of the Clouds, and that their Veſſels were great Whales. They wondered at their Horſes, and accepted a Friendly Peace, offering *Cortez* fifty thouſand Men to aſſiſt in conquering *Tutepee*, who was his Enemy for uſing the Chriſtians well.

Some

Some new Troubles that he met with in relation to his Difcoveries, wherein the Viceroy interfered, inclined him in the Year 1542, to make a fecond Voyage into *Spain,* where he was received with as much Honour, and yet obtained as little Satisfaction as before. To fpeak impartially, the Emperor had conceived a kind of Jealoufy, that if *Cortez* was rewarded according to his Merit, he would become too formidable for a Subject. The Marquis was a Man of too much Senfe and Penetration, not to difcern the Judgment which was formed of him at Court, when he had refided there but a little while. He was however too wife, and too much a Man of Honour to think that any Miftakes made by his Prince could cancel any Part of the Duty he owed him: For this Reafon he applied himfelf more affiduoufly than ever to merit the Emperor's Affections. He attended him in the dangerous and difafterous Expedition againft *Algiers,* and notwithftanding all his former Services, had fo low a Commiffion as to be without a Voice in the Council of War. Being unhorfed in a Charge he made againft the Infidels, he is faid to have loft in the Field two Emeralds of immenfe Value.

After his Return to *Spain* from that Expedition, he affected to lead a quiet and retired Life, employing moft of his Time in the Inftruction of his Children, of whom he had

many,

many, both legitimate and illegitimate. His
second Wife was the Daughter of the Count
of *Aguilar*, by whom he had a Son, who
succeeded him in his Titles, and some of
whose Descendants are still living. As for
the great *Cortez* himself, he died at a Village
near *Seville*, called *Castilleja de la Cuesta*, on
the second of *December* 1554, in the 63d
Year of Age ; but his Corps, by his own
Direction, was carried into *New Spain*.

C H A P. VI.

The HISTORY *of the Conquest of* Peru, *and
the Disturbances which followed thereon.*

IT has been already shewn how *Basco de
Nunez*, gave the first Notice of this Country to the *Spaniards*, and opened a Passage
to the *South-Seas*. After his Death *Peter de
Arias*, made many Attempts to prosecute
that Discovery to very little Purpose; for his
Pride and Cruelty was so great, that he was
universally hated, which was the Occasion
of his miscarrying in almost every Thing he
undertook. It was otherwise with *Francis
Pizarro*, though his Circumstances were but
very indifferent, when he first applied himself to make Discoveries.

As to his Family there is little to be said;
for though some Writers affirm his Father
was a Nobleman, yet, even these agree, that
                                                                his

his Birth was fpurious, which is the more probable, becaufe the Time thereof is not certainly known. He came into the *Indies* at leaft as early as *Cortez*, but did not rife fo quickly into Reputation, being able to make no Figure in the World, till he raifed a Stock of Wealth and Reputation of his own, which though done with all the Expedition he could, took up for all that fome Years.

The Beginning of his great Defigns happened thus: *Pizarro* and *Diego de Almagro*, being at *Panama*, were defirous, like other Undertakers, to try their Skill, and employ their Fortunes in Difcoveries. *Almagro* being rich, drew to him one *Ferdinand Luque*, a Schoolmafter and Prieft of that Town, who was likewife wealthy; and all three undertook a Difcovery, with a Vow, by which they folemnly promifed each unto the other, equally to divide the Profit that fhould accrue. It was determined amongft them, that *Pizarro* fhould undertake the Conqueft; *Almago* go and come with all Neceffaries to relieve them, and *Luque* to make Provifion for Supplies: This happened in the Year 1525. The firft Voyage that *Pizarro* made, was with one Ship, and one hundred and fourteen Men: He failed one hundred Leagues; and went afhore feveral Times, where he found fharp Encounters, loft fome of his Men, and was himfelf hurt in feveral Places, which forced
him

him to return to *Chincama*, not far from *Pa-nama*, repenting of his Enterprize.

Almagro, who ftayed behind *Pizarro*, to fupply him as you have heard, went after him with feventy Men, and came to the Ri-ver of *St. John*; and finding no Sign of *Pi-zarro*'s being there return'd; but at his going back he landed at fome Places, where he found *Pizarro* had been, and where he was hurt. *Almagro* flew and hurt feveral Men, and returned to *Panama*, thinking *Pizarro* had done the like; but underftanding that he was at *Chincama*, he went to him, and by Confent, furnifhed two Ships, and carried, to recruit his Forces, two hundred *Spaniards* and fome *Indians*. They arrived at a marfhy and waterifh Place, where the People live in Trees. They are warlike, and their Coun-try capable of Defence, which they ftood, and killed many *Spaniards*, fhewing an im-placable Averfion towards them, defpifed their Prefents, infulted their Meffengers, and called them the *Scum of the Sea*, having no Fathers; and faid they would have none in their Country that had Beards, or that would break their Cuftoms.

Pizarro and *Almagro* had a great Defire to conquer that Country, becaufe of the Shew the Inhabitants made of Gold and pre-cious Stones; but could not do it with that fmall Force, becaufe many of them were fick and weak, and not a few were dead.

Almagro

Almagro returned to *Panama* for fourscore Men more; but before his coming back, *Pizarro* indured great Want of Victuals. Upon *Almagro's* Return, they found their Forces so small, the Country so barren and unhealthful, that they left it, and went *Chatama*, where they found Plenty of all Things, and thought to make themselves so rich, that they needed not to proceed farther; but they were deceived, for the *Indians* were their Enemies, and so many that they durst not fight them. *Almagro* was to go back for more Men to *Panama*, and *Pizarro* to stay in the Island of *Guara*.

The *Spaniards* were so weak and tired, and so discontented, that they desired to retire with *Almagro*, and to leave their Hopes of Gold; but *Pizarro* would not suffer them either to go or write, lest they should have discredited the Country; and so *Almagro* would have got no Soldiers; but notwithstanding this Prohibition, the Soldiers writ, and hid their Letters in Bottoms of Thread, by which Means their Miseries came to be known, and complained of to the Governor, who commanded that no Man should stay with *Pizarro* against his Will. At *Almagro's* coming to *Panama*, one *Pedro de la Rios* was arrived for Governor, who proclaimed, That no Man should stay with *Pizarro* against his liking, and sent a Messenger to *Pizarro* to let him know so much. Whereupon

upon moſt of his Men left him, and thoſe
that *Almagro* took up, run away from him;
ſo that *Pizarro* had but twelve Men left with
him, whereof one was a *Grecian.* He went
to an Iſland called *Gorgena,* where he lived
upon Snakes, Herbs and Crab-Fiſhes, till
Almagro's Return from *Panama*; and then
he went over to the main Land, and put the
Greek aſhore who brought him News of the
Riches of that Country, and the Plenty of
Victuals, with the State of their King *Atabaliba,*
which was Matter of great Joy to them all;
for the *South-Sea* was the Fountain of their
Wealth and Happineſs, being by far the richeſt
of all their Diſcoveries.

Pizarro hereupon returned to *Panama,*
and from thence into *Spain,* to carry the Emperor News of this rich Country, of which
he deſired the Government. He alſo left
two *Spaniards* behind him to learn the Language, Cuſtoms, and Riches of the Country,
but they were afterwards ſlain by the *Indians.*
Pizarro was above three Years upon this
Diſcovery of *Peru,* and endured as much
Hunger, and other Miſeries as Man could
do; but having much Courage and Conſtancy
ſupported all with Alacrity.

Arriving at *Panama, Pizarro* imparted
the Hope of his Diſcoveries to his Aſſociates,
who though they were grown low and poor,
yet had Credit enough to borrow a thouſand
Pieces of Gold to defray the Expences of his
Voyage

Voyage to *Spain.* On his Arrival there, the Propofals he made were readily entertained, and the Emperor gave him the Title of *Adelantado of Peru*; but as to Ships or Men, he furnifh'd them with none. To procure thefe, *Pizarro* fpoke in very ftrong Terms of the Riches of the Country he had difcovered, which drew to him a fufficient Number of Adventurers, whom he imbarked without Delay. He carried with him to the *Indies* three of his Brethren, *Ferdinand, John,* and *Gonfalo. Ferdinand* only legitimate, the others Baftards. They arriv'd in *Panama* in great Pomp and Pride; but *Almagro* was offended with *Francis Pizarro,* becaufe he had taken upon himfelf all the Honour in *Spain,* and excluded him, who was at all the Expence, and Part of the Labour and Pains. *Pizarro* excufed himfelf the beft he could, which gave however but little Satisfaction.

The Expence of the *Pizarro*'s was fo great, and their Stock fo fmall, that they could not proceed upon their Enterprize without the Help of *Almagro,* whom *Francis Pizarro* laboured to win to a Partnerfhip again. In Conclufion, by Mediation of Friends, *Almagro* furnifhed him with feven hundred Pieces of Eight, and fuch Arms and Victuals as he had; fo that *Pizarro* proceeded with two Ships, and as many Men as he could carry in them. He came to a Place called *Coaque,* where he found much Wealth; but
in

in making himfelf mafter of it, endured great Mifery. From hence he fent to King *Atabaliba* for a League and his Perfonal Friendfhip; who anfwered if he would return the Wealth he had gotten, and clear the Country of his Forces, he would be his Friend, or elfe not: A Friar was fent to perfwade him, but all in vain, fo they came to a Battle. Many of the *Indians* were flain, and their King taken Prifoner, and not a *Spaniard* killed or hurt, but only *Francis Pizarro*, in the Head, as he was fnatching at the King to take him.

Before this *Pizarro* took the Ifland of *Puna*, and gained great Wealth, which he gave to his Soldiers that came to him lately. Here his People fell fick of the Pox, a natural Difeafe of thofe Parts; and here he delivered feventy Prifoners that had been taken by the Iflanders, and fent them all to *Tumbes*, whence they were. Notwithftanding this Courtefy, they incenfed the People againft the *Spaniards*, and flew three that were fent in a civil Manner to treat with them; which fo inraged *Pizarro*, that he took their Town, and chaftifing them feverely, brought them to Obedience.

Thefe Things happened before the taking of *Atabaliba* Prifoner, who now being in their Hands, offered for his Ranfom, as much Silver and Gold, as would fill a high and fpacious Room, wherein he was, which he truly

truly performed; but the Time was so long before it could be brought two hundred Miles, that *Ferdinand Pizarro* adventured to go for it, and in that Journey he learnt much of the Secrets of the Country. *Francis Pizarrro* divided the Treasure thus gotten, and gave to every Man his due; never any Soldiers in the World were so rich. He dealt justly with *Almagro*, and gave him what was his due: All Things grew exceeding dear, or rather worth much Money; a Shirt was sold at ten Pounds, a Quart of Wine at five Pounds, and one thousand two hundred and fifty Pounds was the Price of a Horse. *Pizarro* sent his Brother *Ferdinand* to the Emperor, with his Fifths, and a Relation of what had happened. Many common Soldiers went, who carried some twenty, some thirty, some forty thousand Ducats in Plate, as the Reward of their Fatigues.

There was an *Indian* call'd *Philip*, a Christian, and Interpreter to the *Spaniards*, who fell in love with one of *Atabaliba*'s Wives, and thinking to marry her after his Death, accused him of plotting the Destruction of the *Spaniards*, for which he was condemned and executed, but whether justly or not, is a Question. Before his Death he desired to be baptized, but whether from his Heart or not, is also uncertain. *Pizarro* hearing the Fame of *Cusco*, marched thither and took it, where he found as much Wealth as he had gotten

by

by the Ranſom of *Atabaliba* ; and it is thought there was as much hid that never came to Light, though no Pains were ſpared in ſearching.

Almagro had Commiſſion from the Emperor to be Marſhal of *Peru*, and Governor of one hundred Leagues of Land further than *Pizarro*, or beyond the Bounds of his Government. Whereupon he took upon him to govern *Cuſco*, and this was the firſt Beginning of the Strife betwixt them two, but for the preſent their Jarrs were accommodated; and *Almagro* went to diſcover the Country of *Chili* in 1535, where he endured much Hunger, Cold, and other Diſaſters. *Ferdinand Pizarro* returned out of *Spain* and came to *Lima*, after *Almagro*'s Departure to *Chili*, and brought a Patent to his Brother, wherein he was made a Marquis, and to *Almagro* a Patent for the Government of *New Toledo*.

He required all the Silver and Gold that was received for the Ranſom of *Atabaliba* for the Emperor, the other being a King; but the Soldiers anſwered they had paid their Fifths, which was their Duty. This cauſed a ſudden Mutiny; but *Pizarro* appeaſed it, though with the Ill-will of the Soldiers. *Mango*, whom *Pizarro* had made King, rebelled againſt him, and had almoſt taken *Cuſco*. In the Conflict he ſlew divers *Spaniards*. *Almagro* hearing the Emperor had made him Governor, as aforeſaid, returned

out

out of *Chili*, and took *Cufco* by Force, alledging it was in his Government. He imprifoned *Ferdinand Pizarro: Mango*, the *Indian* King befieged it, and now began, or
revived the old Broils betwixt *Almagro* and
Pizarro; and now did *Francifco Pizarro* receive many Loffes by the *Indians* that rebelled
againft him. *Pizarro* fent Forces to regain
Cufco from *Almagro*, but by Mediation of
Friends they were to meet and confult before
they fought, but to little Purpofe; for that
Treaty broke off, and they fought a moft
cruel Battle, in which *Almagro* was taken,
and put into the fame Prifon into which he
had put the Brother of *Pizarro*, who, being
now at Liberty, there condemned and executed
him. If the *Indians* had taken Advantage of
this Divifion, they had defeated the whole
Power of the *Spaniards*.

Almagro was of mean Birth, and it was
never known who was his Father; he could
not read, but was valiant, fincere, merciful,
and withal fomewhat haughty and vain-glo-
rious. *Francis Pizarro*, upon this Accident
fent his Brother *Ferdinand* into *Spain* with
the Emperor's Fifths, and to excufe the
Death of *Almagro*. He came to *Valladolid* in great State, and with much Wealth;
but within a While after was committed to
Prifon. *Francis Pizarro* went on with his
Expedition, wherein he experienced Variety
of Fortune, fometimes gaining great Victories,

ries, and at others endured great Hardfhips;
yet he prevailed in the End, and got great
Wealth, and made Peace with the *Indian*
Kings. *Gonſalo Pizarro* was likewiſe a principal Man in all theſe Undertakings.

Francis Pizarro returning from *Lima*,
or, as the *Spaniſh* Authors call it, the City
of the Kings, endeavoured to be reconciled
to *Diego de Almagro*, Son to him that was
put to Death; but he would accept of no
Conditions of Friendfhip; neither would
John de Rada adviſe him to it, who was left
in Charge of him at his Father's Death, with
Command to ſeek Revenge of the *Pizarros*;
and though *Francis Pizarro* was ftill inform'd
of the Practice againſt him, yet he little
eſteemed it; but notwithſtanding his Security, on the 24th of *June* 1541, *John de
Rada*, and ten others, entered upon him
whilſt he was at Dinner, and ſlew him. He
was a Man neither liberal nor covetous, nor
would he proclaim what he gave; he was a
good Huſband for the King, and a great Game-
ſter, not regarding with whom he played:
He would never wear rich Apparel, and yet
ſometimes would put on a Garment that *Ferdinando Cortez* ſent him: He took a Pride to
wear white Shoes, and a white Hat, in Imi-
tation of *Gonſalo* the Great Captain. He
uſed his Soldiers well, and thereby as he got,
ſo he kept their Affections; he was debonair,
valiant, and honourable, which made him
                                    incapable

incapable of Sufpicion, and negligent of his
Health or Life. Upon his Death, his and
Almagro's Faction had many Bickerings;
and at laſt thoſe of *Almagro*'s Party ſeditiouſly
proclaimed there was no other Governor in
Peru, but *Diego de Almagro*. He appointed
John de Rada his General; they committed
many Infolencies, Murders, and Cruelties;
they ſeized and divided all the Goods of the
Pizarros and their Friends among their De-
ſcendents, and placed whom they liſted in
Command, meaning to make *Diego de Almagro* their King.

The Emperor hearing of thoſe Tumults
in *Peru*, ſent one *Vaca de Caſtro*, a Doctor,
with Authority to puniſh them; and he coming thither, thoſe who ſtood firm for the Emperor repaired to him; whereupon *Almagro*
prepared to maintain himſelf by Force, and
marched immediately with all his Troops to
meet him, where they fought a cruel Battle,
in which *Almagro* was overthrown; though
more Men were ſlain on the other Side; few
Captains eſcaped, and thoſe that were hurt,
died by Reaſon of the great Froſt and Snow
that was in the Country. *Vaca de Caſtro*
condemned and executed thirty of the principal Offenders, and baniſhed divers others;
Almagro fled to *Cuſco*, thinking to find Relief, but his Lieutenant he left there, hearing
the Succeſs which the Viceroy had in the Battle,

tle, apprehended him, and *Vaca de Caſtro* at his coming thither cut off his Head.

This *Diego de Almagro* was a Baſtard, whom his Father had by an *Indian* Woman in *Panama*; but he was braver than the *Meſtizos* uſed to be; he was the firſt that ever took up Arms againſt the King in the *Indies*; his Followers were ſo loving and conſtant to him, that though they had often Offers of Pardon, they would not leave him. *Vaca de Caſtro* ſettled things in good Order, gave the *Indians* Content, who now began again to cultivate their Grounds, which before they could not do for the Wars; and about this Time many Mines were diſcovered.

The Emperor being informed of the Revolts in *Peru*, and the ill Uſage of the *Indians*, he diſplaced his Commiſſioners there, and choſe others, giving them an Oath to deal juſtly, and to order things uprightly. He made forty Laws, and ſigned them at *Barcelona* the 20th of *November* 1542. But theſe Laws were ill taken in *Peru*. They were certainly well intended, and very agreeable to the Rules of natural Juſtice and Equity, but in the Situation things were in, by no means expedient to be publiſhed in *Peru*, where things grew daily worſe and worſe; beſides, *Blaſco Nunez Vela*, who was appointed Viceroy in 1544, and who had Directions to ſee theſe Laws put in Execution, was a Man no way qualified for his Employment. On his Arrival

val he caufed his Predeceffor, who was a much wifer Man than himfelf, to be imprifoned, and behaved in every Refpect fo feverely, that he gained no Friends, though he provoked many to become his Enemies. Three of the Judges, who fhould have fupported him, confpired againft him, and caufed him to be imprifoned, while in the mean time *Gonfalo Pizarro* drew together Troops, and difpofed all things for a Rebellion. The Difputes between the Judges and the Viceroy facilitated his Defign; for though the latter quickly recovered his Liberty, and drew one of the Judges to his Party, yet the reft of the Judges continued to act by their own Authority, and behaved fo cruelly and fo tyrannically, that at length perceiving they had no other Refource, they were glad to admit *Gonfalo Pizarro* for Governor of *Peru*, to feal a Commiffion to him in the King's Name, and to receive him with all Demonftrations of Refpect into the City of *Lima*.

The Viceroy returned into the Province of *Quito*, where he difcovered in his Adverfity much greater Abilities, and many more Virtues than he had fhewn in his Profperity; and though his Forces were continually inferior to thofe of the Rebels, yet his own Intrepidity joined to his Loyal Difpofition, which is natural to the *Spaniards*, enabled him to make a long Difpute. At length, however, a decifive Battle was fought between him and *Gonfalo Pizarro*

Pizarro, on the 19th of *January* 1546, in which the Viceroy being wounded, and taken Prifoner, had his Head ftruck off; for whofe Death, though done by his own Command, *Pizarro* hypocritically wore Mourning. Hence forward this Man behaved himfelf rather as a Sovereign Prince than as a Governor, bufying himfelf in amaffing Wealth, and in taking all the Precautions he could think of for fecuring himfelf and his Affociates from the Effects of the Royal Refentment, which without Queftion they had Reafon to dread.

In the mean time, the Emperor, juftly alarmed at the Confequences of thefe Seditions, which threatened the Lofs of fo confiderable a Territory as that of *Peru*, came at length to a Refolution of trufting rather to the Wifdom of one Man than to the Force of many. This Man was the Licentiate *Peter de la Gafca*, who had the Title of Prefident of the Royal Court of *Peru*, and a Commiffion fo ample, that had it not fome way been limited by his Inftructions, he would in Effect have had Royal Authority; but to balance this, he had neither Men nor Money, the Court trufting altogether, though furely not very prudently, to his great Capacity. He was in few Words a Man of unfhaken Courage, deep Prudence, mild Behaviour, unblemifhed Probity, and abfolutely difinterefted. He was not afraid to go in a Manner naked againft infolent and victorious Rebels; and all the Reward he demanded

manded for the Services he fhould perform
was, that having fettled the Province in Peace,
he might be at Liberty to depart into *Spain*.

Gafca arrived at *Nombre de Dios*, and carried himfelf mildly, faying, he came not to
make War, but, according to his Profeffion, to
make Peace, and revoked the Rigour of the
Laws that caufed the War. From *Panama* he
fent the Emperor's Letters, and writ himfelf
to *Pizarro*, telling him, he was come to pardon all Offences, to draw him to Obedience,
to give Satisfaction to his People ; and, if he
refufed this Grace, to make War. *Pizarro*
was enraged at the Receipt of thefe Letters,
and would not fuffer the Gentleman that
brought them to fit down, which the Gentleman took for a great Affront. *Pizarro* called
for his Friends, to know what Anfwer to give
the Prefident's Letter. *Carvajal*, the chief In-
cendiary, was abfent, and therefore it was hoped he would accept of Grace ; yet every
Man delivering his Opinion, fome advifed to
take and raife *Panama* and *Nombre de Dios*,
that the Emperor might have no Place to receive his Men and Shipping ; and they having all the Ships in the *South-Sea*, might
without Fear keep *Peru* to themfelves, and
then doubted not but to make *New Spain* revolt too, or at leaft, they would rob all the
Towns on the Sea-Coaft, and live by Spoil
and Rapine, which indeed they might have
done

done, having the General of the Sea true to them.

Pizarro cunningly anſwered *Gaſca*'s Letter, by Conſent of thirty of his Men under their Hands, that they underſtood of his coming by *Hinojoſa*, General of the Sea, and the fair Shew of Good he pretended; but it was too late after ſo many Murders, occaſioned by the Viceroy's perſuading him to return to inform the Emperor, that they would receive no Governor but *Pizarro*, and offered to ſend ſome Man of Quality into *Spain* to make their Caſe known to the Emperor. *Carvajal* diverted *Pizarro* from all good Intentions, and would not ſuffer him to make any Acknowledgment to *Spain*. They ſent theſe Letters to *Gaſca*, and offered to give him a great Quantity of Money to return home; and if he refuſed it, they writ to their Admiral *Hinojoſa* to apprehend him. Theſe Letters being brought to *Panama*, put *Gaſca* in fear that he ſhould be killed, for they abſolutely refuſed to receive him in *Peru*. *Gaſca* dealt ſo cunningly with *Hinojoſa*, that he brought him to ſubmit himſelf and Fleet, and became a true Servant to the Emperor. This was the Overthrow of *Pizarro*, and *Hinojoſa* was continued General, and none of his Captains diſplaced. *Gaſca* now prepared again for War, and furniſhed himſelf for his Journey to *Peru*; and, before his Arrival, ſent a Pardon to all the

common

common Sort. In his Expedition he carried himfelf courteoufly and friendly.

Gafca's Carriage, and the Submiffion of the Ships, made a great Change amongft the Rebels; for happy was he that could appear for the Emperor. *Pizarro* was much grieved to hear of thefe Alterations; but, like a couragious Captain, fent to all his Friends to come to him with their Forces; but moft part of them forfook him; and the Towns of *Lima, Cufco,* and the reft took part with the Emperor. When *John de Cafta* came to *Pizarro* to *Arequipa,* they confulted what to do, having four hundred and fifty Men in the whole Country againft them: He refolved to go to *Chili,* where never *Spaniard* had been; but he was followed by one *Centeno,* with a loyal Party for the Emperor, between whom was fought a cruel Battle, *Pizarro* gaining the Victory; he loft two hundred and twenty Men, and *Centeno* many more. *Centeno* fled, but the others having fo great a Lofs did not follow him. *Pizarro,* upon the Victory, divided his Forces into feveral Parts. *Cepeda,* a principal Man of Account on his Side, perfuaded him to make Conditions with *Gafca,* which he would not do, but was angry at the Motion, and grew fufpicious of him, who out of pure Kindnefs to him had made it.

Gafca came into *Peru* with two thoufand Men, where he heard of the Overthrow *Pizarro* had given *Centeno*; and his Men being fickly,

fickly, and finding the Corn green, and not to
be eaten, they were much difcouraged ; but
Centeno coming with the Remainder of his
Forces, put them into Heart ; whereupon he
went in the Purfuit of *Pizarro*, but had great
Trouble in paffing the River *Apurima*. But
Pizarro being apprized of it, departed from
Cufco with a thoufand Soldiers. *Donna Maria
Calderon*, fpeaking againft the Tyranny of
Pizarro, *Fran. Calderon* entered her Cham-
ber one Morning, and ftrangled her in her
Bed. Now came their Armies in view of one
another, every one taking Advantage of the
Place: *Gafca* delayed giving Battle, in hopes
that moft of *Pizarro*'s Men would leave him,
but they did not ; and he being forced by
Snow, Cold and Hunger, engaged in the Heat
of the Action. *Cepeda*, (who as I faid before)
advifed to accept of Conditions, fled to *Gafca*,
which much difheartned *Pizarro*'s Side. This
Example, and others that did the like, made
moft of them yield. *Pizarro* feeing it, chofe
rather to fubmit than fly, and yielded himfelf
to *Villa Vicentia*, Serjeant Major, who carried
him to *Gafca*. Never fuch a Battle was fought,
in which, the Heads and chief Commanders
were Doctors and Scholars.

Gafca fent Forces to cut off thofe that ef-
caped in their Way to *Cufco*, and to fecure
the Town. The Day following, being the 9th
of *April* 1548, *Gafca* committed the Caufe
of *Pizarro*, and other Offenders, to Judges,
who

who condemned him and thirteen more to Death, whereof *Francis Carvajal* was one, and indeed the chief Promoter of all the Miſchief in thoſe Parts. He was eighty four Years of Age, and had been an Enſign in the Battle of *Ravenna*; he had ſerved under the great Captain *Gonçalo Fernandez*, and was the moſt noted Soldier in the *Indies*, yet never eſteem'd valiant or ſkillful. It was a Byword, *as cruel as Carvajal*, becauſe he had been the Executioner of four hundred *Spaniards*, *Pizarro* cauſed to be put to Death after *Blaſco Nunez* came into *Peru*, carrying Blacks with him continually for that Purpoſe. *Pizarro* was never overthrown, but in this Battle, though he had fought many. *Gaſca*'s Soldiers looked for a better Reward than was given them; though indeed they were well dealt with; yet they mutinied upon it, but were ſoon quieted again.

Gaſca took a Courſe for the Eaſe of the *Indians*, and to reduce them to the Chriſtian Religion; as alſo for the peaceable Government of the Kingdom. When *Gaſca* arrived at *Nombre de Dios* out of *Spain*, he brought not an hundred Men with him, nor had he any Money, but procured Credit, and at his going away paid all Debts, and carried with him to the Emperor almoſt two Millions; but for himſelf not a Penny, being the firſt Man in Authority that ever did the like; for Covetouſneſs was the Bane of all the *Spaniſh* Affairs,

Affairs, till his Time. Indeed any Nation muſt be quickly ruined where Men aſpire to Authority with no other View than to make themſelves rich.

As for this celebrated Governor, when he had thoroughly ſettled all things in *Peru,* he prepared for his Return into *Spain,* and came to *Panama,* having much Wealth there which he could not carry; but it happened that two Sons of *Rodrigo Contreras,* Governor of *Nicaragua,* with two hundred Soldiers, entered the Town, and took the Treaſure, and as much more as they could get. One of the two Brothers got himſelf with his Wealth into two or three Ships, the other followed *Gaſca,* thinking to rob and kill him. They murdered many, and ſlew a Biſhop, becauſe he ſent to their Father into *Spain* an account of their Villainies : They drew to them all factious and diſcontented People, that favoured the Party of *Pizarro.*

Gaſca hearing of thoſe Diſorders, returned with Speed, fought with, and overcame them ; one of the Brothers was drowned in paſſing a River; he diſpatched Ships after the other, and took him and all his Wealth. This proved a fortunate Affair to *Gaſca,* and got him great Honour. He embarked at *Nombre de Dios* for *Spain* in 1550, with much Wealth for others, and Reputation to himſelf ; his going, coming, and ſtaying, was little more than four Years. The Emperor made him

him Bifhop of *Placentia*, and fent for him
to *Ausburg* in *Germany*, where he then lay,
becaufe he would be informed from his own
Mouth of all Proceedings, and the State and
Condition of the People of the *Indies*.

C H A P. VII.

Of the Difcovery of that Paffage into the
South Seas, *which is called the* Streights *of*
Magellan.

WE have now feen how after many
hundred Years Difcourfe of a new
World maintained by fome learned Men, and
exploded by others, *Columbus* firft thought the
Defign of finding it practicable, and as foon
as his Propofitions were accepted by the
Court of *Spain*, actually failed to and difcovered it. We have feen how *Bafco Nunez de
Balboa* came firft to gain the Knowledge of
the *South Seas*, that is to fay, of a Sea to the
South of the new difcovered Continent. We
have feen how the great Empire of *Mexico*,
containing the beft Part of the Northern *A-
merica*, was fubdued by *Cortez*; and how
Peru, the moft eminent Monarchy in South
America, fell into the Hands of the *Spaniards* by the Means of the *Pizarros* and their
Affociates. It remains that we give fome Account of the Paffage into the *South Seas* from

ours, and then the hiftorical part of our Work will be brought to a proper Conclufion.

From the Time of the Difcoveries made under the Catholick King's Commiffions, the *Portugueze* were exceffively jealous of their Poffeffions in the *Eaft Indies*, till at length the Pope interpofed, and by a Bull, which had a decifive Authority among Princes of his own Communion, decreed all Countries dif-covered in the Eaft to *Portugal*, and all fuch as were found in the Weft to *Spain*; yet this rather fmothered than extinguifhed the Flames of Contention, both Princes continuing to liften willingly to any fuch Propofitions as tended to aggrandize one at the other's Ex-pence; and this begat another Mifchief, which was, that fuch enterprizing Men as were not gratified at one Court, immediately thought of applying themfelves to the other; which, whether a greater Inconvenience to thefe Princes, or Advantage to *Europe* in ge-neral, is not eafy to be refolved.

We have a particular Inftance in this, in the Cafe of *Ferdinand de Magallanes*, whom we generally call *Magellan*, and *Ruy Falero*, both Natives of *Portugal*, and Men of very great Experience in the Art of Navigation. It is faid their Court differed with them about fo very a Trifle as fix Crowns *per Annum* in their Salaries; whereupon they retired to *Spain*, and made Propofitions of new Difco-veries to Cardinal *Ximenes*. The *Portugueze*

Ambaf-

Ambaſſador, who was a Man of Parts, employed all the Pains imaginable to defeat their
Deſign. He ſolicited the Court to deliver
them up as Fugitives ; he got ſome Perſons to
inform the Miniſtry that *Magellan* was a bold
talkative Man, one ready to undertake any
thing, but who wanted Capacity and Courage, when it came to Performance. Under-
hand he cauſed Application to be made to
Magellan himſelf, offering him Pardon, and
great Rewards, if deſiſting from his preſent
Purpoſe he would go back and ſerve his own
Prince. All this, however, ſignified very little, for theſe People expreſſed themſelves to
the *Spaniſh* Miniſtry, who were now very a-
ble Judges in theſe Matters, in ſuch clear
Terms, and with ſo much Probability, as to
the Diſcovery they propoſed, that they were
immediately received into Favour, made
Knights of the Order of St. *James*, and had
their own Terms granted them.

The Grounds they went upon were theſe :
That the Poſition laid down by *Columbus*, of
the Poſſibility of coming to the *Eaſt Indies*
by ſailing Weſt was certainly true, though he
had not brought it to bear ; and that ſuch as
derided that great Man's Notion, were not ſo
well ſkilled in Navigation as he. That without queſtion it was very poſſible to ſail from
the *South Seas*, which were but juſt then heard
of, to the *Molucco Iſlands* ; and that it was
very probable, a Paſſage might be found into
thoſe

thofe Seas, through the *Rio de la Plata*, or
fome other Opening upon that Coaft. That
in cafe this could be done, *Spain* might reap
the Profit of both *Indies*, fince this Difcovery
being made from the Weft would fall exprefsly under the Words of the Pope's Bull. In
confequence of thefe Propofals, it was agreed
that the Undertakers fhould have the twentieth Part of the clear Profits; that the Government of any Iflands they fhould difcover
fhould belong to them and their Heirs for ever,
with the Title of *Adelantados*; and that farther, the Crown fhould furnifh them with
five Ships, and two hundred and thirty-four
Men, with Provifions for two Years.

The Fleet failed from *Seville* on the tenth
of *Auguft* 1519, under the fole Command of
Ferdinand Magellan, *Ruy Falero* being left
behind on account of his ill Health. They
failed firft to the *Canaries*, and from thence
to the Coaft of *Guinea*; at which, the Captains under *Magellan*, were extremely offended; but he refufed to give them any Satisfaction, telling them, their Duty was to follow him, and not enquire into his Inftructions. Coming on the Coaft of *Brafil*, he
failed along Southwards, examining carefully
all the Rivers and Bays he met with. The
Weather growing extremely cold, efpecially
in the beginning of the Year 1520, and being
haraffed with continual Storms, the Sailors
growing very uneafy, in the Month of
April,

April they came to the River of St. *Julian*, where they kept their *Easter*; but this being the Depth of Winter in those Parts, and his Officers perceiving that *Magellan* intended to proceed towards the *Antartick* Pole, they remonstrated against what they took to be a romantic Proceeding. On this Occasion *Magellan* shewed himself both a wise and steddy Officer. He called all his People together, to whom he made a long Speech, insisting much on the incomparable Bravery of the *Spanish* Nation, and no less on the mighty Advantages which would accrue from their going through with this Undertaking. By this Means he made himself popular, and acquired Authority sufficient to punish with remarkable Severity some Mutineers. In short, in the beginning of the Month of *November*, after suffering incredible Hardships, he discovered in fifty-three Degrees South Latitude, those Streights which have since born his Name, and will perpetuate his Fame to the End of the World.

Through these, on the 27th of *November*, he came into the South Seas, and though Provisions became then very short, he resolved to continue his Course to the *Moluccas*; but in his Passage thither he landed on the Island *Zebu*, one of the *Philippines*, where he was well received by a *Pagan* Prince, whom he converted to Christianity, but endeavouring to reduce the whole Island to the Obedience

dience of that Monarch, he was unfortunately killed in a Battle on the 27th of *April* 1581. His Death was of bad Confequence to his People, who took upon them a Power of appointing and depofing their Commanders, which brought moft of them to Deftruction.

However, *John Sebaftian del Cano,* who commanded the Ship *Victory,* found means to bring home that Veffel with about 35 Men on board to the Port of St. *Lucar,* on the 6th of *September* 1522, having fpent three Years bating fourteen Days in this Voyage ; and having the Honour to be the firft who failed round the Globe, and thereby demonftrating the Folly of thofe who held the Opinion of *Antipodes* for a Fiction and a Herefy.

The vaft Cargo of Spices brought home by the *Victory,* and the Profpect of carrying on a moft beneficial Trade to the *Indies,* by this new Rout, engaged the *Spanifh* Government to fend in 1525, *Garcia de Lovifa,* a Knight of *Malta,* with feven Ships and four hundred and fifty Men to gain a more perfect Knowledge of thefe Streights. He paffed them indeed, but it proved a moft unfortunate Voyage, for by one Accident or other all the Ships were either ftopped in *America,* or loft in the *Moluccas.* The next Year, however, a *Genoefe* Captain came to the Mouth of the Streights, and then was forced to return. *Sebaftian Cabot,* in the Service of *Don Emanuel,*

nuel, King of *Portugal*, endeavoured to find the Streights of *Magellan*, but could not. *Americus Vespusius* was as unlucky, or rather more so, for he could not find the River of *Plate*. Many other Misfortunes happening in Profecution of the fame Defign, it remained for many Years unthought of, till Sir *Francis Drake*, in the Year 1578, paffed them happily. In 1586 Mr. *Cavendifh* paffed them. In 1593 Sir *Richard Hawkins* did the fame; as did Captain *Davis*. In 1615 *Cornelius Van Schoton* failed from *Holland* on the fame Defign. He had on board him *James la Maire*; and becaufe they paffed through a new Streight on the tenth of *January* 1616, he gave it his Name; fince which the World has heard much lefs of the Streights of *Magellan* than before; thefe new difcovered Streights being found much the fafer of the two.

The beft Defcription we have of the Streight of *Magellan*, is that of our Countryman Sir *John Narborough*, who paffed it in 1670, from which it appears to be extremely difficult and dangerous. On the one Side lies the Land of *Magellan*, which is Part of the Continent of *South America*, and on the other a very large Ifland called *Terra del Fuego*, or, *The Land of Fire*, from the Lights feen thereon in the Night, which were thought to be Fires lighted by the Inhabitants, but are fince believed to proceed from a *Vulcano*.

Cano. When *Magellan*, *Drake* and *Cavendish* paſſed theſe Streights, they took this *Terra del Fuego* to be Part of an unknown Continent, ſuppoſed to extend quite to the Pole. *La Maire* found it to be an Iſland, by ſailing round it, and called *The moſt Southern Cape*, from the Name of his Ship, *Cape Horn*, which has been ſince juſtly looked upon as the moſt Southern Point of Land on the Globe. After all theſe Diſcoveries, ſo late as in the Year 1713, a *French* Ship made a new one of the Streights of *St. Barbara*, in 57 d. 20 m. South Latitude. They ſailed through the Streights of *Magellan* till they came to that Height, and then inſtead of paſſing forward through that Part of the Channel, which Sir *John Narbrough* call'd *Crooked Reach* and *Long Reach*, they ſailed through another Channel opening to the Southward, much broader and ſafer, and which brought them with Eaſe into the *South Sea*. Hence it appears that this *Terra del Fuego*, at firſt thought a Continent, and then an Iſland, is in Fact, two Iſlands, a larger and a leſſer; and by this new Rout, a Ship may paſs from the *North* into the *South Sea* in twelve Days, at moſt, and with far leſs Inconveniency than either by the old Streights of *Magellan*, or the new ones of *La Maire*. This is a Thing of great Conſequence, eſpecially at this Time, when Expeditions to the *South Seas* are talk'd of, and therefore I have dwelt ſo long upon it; beſides the Thing in itſelf

excuſes,

excufes, and therefore I hope no farther Apology will be neceffary to the Reader.

Thus we fee in how fhort a Space of Time after the new World was difcovered, the whole of it from North to South was not only furveyed, but in a great Meafure conquered and fettled by the *Spaniards,* and very great Improvements they have made there fince, though it is highly probable much greater would have been made, had this Country fallen into any other Hands but theirs. But to give a particular Account of this Matter will be the Bufinefs of the next Book, wherein we fhall exhibit an exact Defcription of the *Spanifh America* from *Spanifh* Writers, who are generally fpeaking, very accurate, fetting down what they publifh from the authentic Accounts tranfmitted to the Government; whereas all we meet with in other Writers, which is not taken from them, is no better than hearfay, and therefore little to be depended on. If we intermingle lefs concerning the Attempts made by foreign Nations on the *Spaniards* in *America,* than many of our Readers might expect, the Reafon is plainly this, becaufe our Defign is to fpeak ftrictly of the Power of *Spain,* and therefore we can take Notice only how far that was affected, as to the Rife and Progrefs of fuch Expeditions they belong to thofe Pens which are employed in defcribing the *Englifh, French* and *Dutch* Conquefts in the new World.

End of the FIRST BOOK.

B O O K. II.

C H A P. I.

Of the Spanish America *in General*.

THE common Opinion that the King
of *Spain* hath the largest Dominions
of any Prince in the World, is so well founded, that no body hitherto has ventured to
contradict it.   His *American* Territories only
are sufficient to justify this Notion; and in
Truth, when one considers the vast Extent
and prodigious Riches of those Provinces,
one cannot but wonder that his Catholic
Majesty is not much more powerful than he
appears to be.   Without Question this is
owing to nothing but Errors in Government,
which should incline other Nations to beware
of falling into a like Condition, through
Luxury and Corruption, and should also put
them upon their Guard, with respect to a
Potentate possessed of such mighty Advantages, and who may some time or other come
to have a Ministry capable of using and improving them.

In order to be convinced of the Truth of
what I have advanced, we need only remem-
ber, that the *Spaniards* are possessed of far
the greatest and best Part of the Continent

of

of *America*. The whole Coaſt from thirty-
ſeven Degrees of North Latitude, to fifty-
three Degrees of South, is on one Side intirely theirs, and on the other, there are only
the *Portugueze* Colonies in *Brazil*, with a
few inconſiderable *French* and *Dutch* Settlements, but what belongs to them or to the
Natives. In a Word, the *Spaniards* command in the *South Seas*, the moſt extended
Coaſt in the new World; that is, from *Cape
St. Sebaſtian*, the moſt Northern Point of
California, to the Streights of *Magellan*, at
leaſt two thouſand Leagues, or between ſix
and ſeven thouſand Miles. They likewiſe
poſſeſs the largeſt and moſt valuable Iſlands,
viz. Cuba, Part of *Hiſpaniola* and *Port
Rico*.

It is an Opinion commonly received a-
mongſt us, that the *Spaniſh Weſt Indies* are
very unwholſom, but like many other general Propoſitions, this may be ſaid to be true
and falſe at the ſame time. A very confiderable Part of *Mexico* and *Peru*, are in the
Torrid Zone; and yet where they have the
Advantages of a favourable Situation, are
both healthy and pleaſant. But beſides theſe,
there are many fair Provinces in both the
temperate Zones, neither can the habitable
World boaſt of more delightful Regions than
there are in the Kingdom of *New Mexico*
in the North, and about *Buenos Ayres* in
the South, as the Reader will be told more

parti-

particularly hereafter. The Truth is, that the Country about *Porto Bello* is extremely aguifh and unwholfom, and fo is Part of the Sea Coaft of *Peru*, by Reafon of the great Rains which fall there, and the Want of Inhabitants, and from hence we form an Idea of the reft, though very unjuftly. Perhaps too the Luxury of the *Spaniards*, and the Inactivity of their Lives, may contribute to fhorten their Days, and thereby difcredit the Places they inhabit; but as it is certain, that the *Indians* before their Arrival, lived to a good old Age, and many who are temperate do fo ftill, I fay all this confidered, we may conclude, that if an active and induftrious People were fettled in thefe Countries, they would not be much incommoded by the Climate.

As to the Soil of thefe Countries in general, it is wonderfully rich and fruitful, producing Corn in abundance, and fuch Paftures as are no where elfe to be feen; Trees for Fruit, Beauty, and Ufe; Shrubs odoriferous, and of phyfical Virtues; Herbs and Roots in plenty; and in fhort, every thing that can be fought for, either grows naturally, or may with very little Pains be produced here. In the Bofom of the Earth all Sorts of Metals are found, efpecially thofe which Men value moft, Silver and Gold. Springs and Rivulets are every where to be feen; and then for the Conveniency of Navigation, there

there are the nobleſt Rivers which the World can boaſt, ſuch as the River of *Plate*, the *Amazons* River, and many others which we ſhall particularly deſcribe, in ſpeaking of the Provinces through which they run.

If the *Spaniſh* Councils were turned for the Encouragement of Trade, there are in theſe Countries ſuch a vaſt Variety of valuable Commodities as might, one would think, furniſh the People poſſeſſed of them with inexhauſtible Treaſures; for beſides Gold and Silver, of which prodigious Quantities are annually exported, both from *Mexico* and *Peru*, here are Emeralds, Pearls, and various other precious Stones, not to ſpeak of Copper, and other baſer Metals, rich Drugs of all Kinds, Logwood, Santal, Redwood, and many other Sorts of Materials for dying. Tobacco, Ginger, Sweetmeats of all kinds, with a vaſt Variety of luxurious Articles ; and then as to Things of more neceſſary Uſe, *Vigonia* Wool, the Hides from *Buenos Ayres*, Tortoiſe-ſhell, Indigo, and many more might be enumerated. Neither is the Country deficient in Sea Ports, eſpecially in the North Seas, where there are ſeveral ſafe, and ſpacious Harbours, beſides good Roads, Bays and Creeks. If theſe are in a great Meaſure wanting in the *South Seas*, the *Spaniards*, not without Reaſon, eſteem it an Advantage, becauſe it makes it the eaſier for them to defend that Coaſt againſt Strangers ; and in Reſpect

spect of one Part of the Country trading with the other, this is no great Hindrance. Besides they have a good Port for the carrying on of their *East India* Trade, which is what they chiefly value on this Side; and if ever they should so far increase their Shipping as to make new Ports requisite, Engineers would quickly put them in a Way to improve the imperfect Efforts of Nature. But while they continue to act on the Maxims which they have hitherto pursued, they are not likely to think their Havens on the *South Sea* too few.

We ought not to speak of the Number of the Inhabitants, because therein consists the true Wealth and Strength of a Government, but besides, that this will be, in some Measure, elsewhere examined, we must ingenuously confess, that with any tolerable Accuracy, it is not easy to settle it at all. The *Spanish* Writers are remarkably silent on this Head; and as to what others report on this Subject, it deserves less Credit than any other Part of their Relations, because it is impossible that what they assert, should consist with their own Knowledge. This however is certain, that the *Spanish America* is but thinly peopled, if we consider its Extent; and on the other Hand it seems to be as certain, that it is much better peopled than we commonly imagine, of which I will give two apparent Proofs. Sir *Francis Drake* made his first Expedition

pedition in 1578, and with a very flender
Force acquir'd immenfe Riches, and did prodigious Damage to the *Spaniards*. In 1587,
Cavendifh did the like in a Veffel of a 120
Tons, though he had not in her above thirty
Men, landing in feveral Places, and bringing
away as much Riches as he could carry.
Thefe Succeffes eftablifhed an Opinion that
the *Spaniards* were very weak in thofe Parts,
yet all the following Expeditions which were
undertaken with much greater Force, miferably mifcarried, which induced that wife
Princefs Queen *Elizabeth* to reftrain her Subjects from fuch Attempts. This however did
not difcourage the *Dutch*, who in 1623, fitted out a grand Fleet for the *South Seas*. It
confifted of fifteen ftout Ships, and there
were three thoufand pick'd Men on board.
They came happily into thofe Parts of the
World, and made feveral Defcents, but to no
Purpofe, being conftantly repulfed, fo that
they returned with great Lofs and Shame.
Our Country Man *Gage* perfuaded *Cromwell*,
and indeed the *Englifh* Nation, that the Conqueft of the *Weft Indies* was a very practicable Defign, but it did not prove fo in the
Event; for though we made ourfelves Mafters of *Jamaica*, yet whoever confiders the
mighty Force that *Pen* and *Venables* had, will
rather wonder that much more was not done,
than admire what they did. So that it feems
to be a thing out of Difpute, that it is not fo

much

much the Weaknefs of the *Spaniards*, as
the Weaknefs of their Councils, which have
occafioned their Loffes in thefe Parts; and
to fay the Truth, we can fcarce doubt of
this, if we reflect that they have found a
Way to make their *American* Colonies contribute to the Deftruction of their Power at
Sea, though the fame Caufe is the great Source
of ours, and is the only one that can create a
Naval Power to *France*. But to return to the
Point, *viz.* the Number of People in the
Spanish Settlements. A certain Author has
gueffed that there may be in the whole three
Millions of *Spaniards*, *Meftizos* and *Negros*,
befides which there are certainly a much larger
Number of *Indians*. For though it may be,
and without doubt it is true, that the *Spaniards* practifed intolerable Cruelties, when
they firft arrived in thefe Parts, yet we are
certain that this was done contrary to the exprefs Directions of their Catholic Majefties,
and that they have long fince altered their
Policy in this Refpect, though many *Indian*
Nations are ftill their implacable Enemies,
and fo are likely to continue.

When thefe Countries were firft reduced,
the fettling many Ecclefiafticks might be a
very proper Meafure, fince it is certain that
they were in thofe Days very zealous, not
only in converting, but in protecting the *Indians*, interpofing on all Occafions in their
Favour. But Times are altered fince then,
and

and their Meafures fhould have altered accordingly. Monafteries and Nunneries, if they are not contrary to the Spirit of Chriftianity, are at leaft incompatible with that of fettling Colonies; and fo they have been found. Priefts, generally fpeaking, proceed upon narrow and felfifh Views, and fo do all Religious Orders, particularly the Jefuits, who therefore are the leaft qualified for Miffionaries, though deficient in no other Refpect, which appears from their Conduct in *Paraguay*, where the Fathers have eftablifh'd a much more regular Government than fubfifts any where elfe in *America*, and are able to raife a greater Number of regular Troops in a Week, than could be affembled by the Viceroy of *Peru* in a Year, as appears by an authentic Memorial drawn up for the perufal of the King of *Spain*, and which the Reader will find in the *Appendix*. The Corruption and Tyranny which reigns among all the Officers, who derive their Authority from the Crown, fenfibly affects the State, fince it not only ruins the Revenue, but difcourages Induftry, and extirpates public Spirit. An unaccountable Fondnefs for Gold and Silver is another Prejudice to the *Spanifh* Settlements, has prevented the Government from encouraging new Difcoveries, and fpread fuch a fordid Spirit through all its Subjects, as is vifibly productive of the worft Effects; for though Mines may be moft bene-

ficial

ficial to the Sovereign, and to the Mother Country in the firſt Inſtance, yet taking all Things together, they are the leaſt ſo, of which the State of the *Spaniſh America* is the ſtrongeſt Proof.

Having now ſpoke of the Country in general, and taken a View of its Advantages and Diſadvantages, we will next deſcend to Particulars, and treat diſtinctly of all its ſeveral Provinces in their Order as they lye from North to South, contenting ourſelves with a bare Relation of Facts from the moſt authentic Authors, and reſerving Political Reflections, and whatever has Reſpect to Trade and Manufactures for the third Book. In the Proſecution of this Buſineſs, we ſhall, for the moſt Part, follow our old Guides the *Spaniſh* Writers, as to what regards the Inland Part of the Country, paying however a due Reſpect to what other Authors have written as to the Sea Coaſts, wherein, though they may not be better informed, yet are they certainly much clearer that the *Spaniſh* Geographers, who affect Obſcurity, and never deliver themſelves but in general Terms upon this Subject. For the ſame Reaſon perhaps which leads them to this Conduct, the Pilots never ſuffer any Stranger to have a Sight of their Charts, more eſpecially of thoſe Parts of their Empire which are leaſt known, and of which, as they are the firſt in the Order,
we

we have laid down, we fhall immediately treat, as fully and clearly as the beft Materials we could collect, will allow.

C H A P. II.

Of California, *and the adjacent Ifles.*

IT is proper to begin with this, becaufe it is the moft Northern Part of the new World, difcovered, and in any Degree pof-feffed by the *Spaniards.* The Relations we have hitherto had of it are fo confufed, and fo contradictory, that we prefume it will be doing the Public fome Service, to give a di-ftinct Account of this Country from authen-tic Memoirs, which we fhall be able to per-form, and thereby remove a Multitude of Abfurdities which have been hitherto current-ly reported of this extenfive Tract of Land.

The more Southern Part of *California* was known to the *Spaniards* very foon after the Difcovery of *Mexico*, but it remained a hun-dred and twenty Years a Matter of Difpute, whether it was an Ifland or a Peninfula. In *Sanfon*'s, and other Maps in good Credit, we fee it laid down as an Ifland with a pretty wide Sea between it and the Continent of *New Mexico.* However in the lateft Maps, particularly in one publifhed in *Holland* in 1739, it is laid down as a Peninfula, as it really is. In 1595 the *Spaniards* fent a Gal-

leon

leon called *St. Augustine* to difcover its
Coafts, but it was loft in the Port *de los Reyes*,
which prevented any farther Difcovery at that
Time.   In 1602 the Count *de Monterey*,
then Viceroy of *New Spain*, fent *Sebaftian
Bifcaino* on the fame Defign with two Ships
and a Tender : He failed as high as *Cape
Mendocina*, which lies in 41°, 20' N. L.
whence he had a Sight of *Cape Blanco*, or
the *White Cape*, which lies in 43°.   In 1684
the Marquifs *de la Laguna*, Viceroy of *New
Spain*, fent two Ships with a Tender, to difcover the Lake of *California*, that is the Sea
between it and *New Mexico*, of which however he obtained but a very indifferent Account.   Thence forward the Opinion prevailed that *California* was not an Ifland, but
Part of that vaft Continent which joins *America* to *Afia*.   F. *Martin Martinez*, reports
that while he was at *Peking* in *China*, a
Chriftian Woman of *Mexico* was brought
thither as a Slave, who reported that fhe had
been brought thither all the Way by Land,
except two Days that fhe was in pafling an
Arm of the Sea, which is fuppofed to be the
Streights of *Anian*.   Be this as it will, we
owe to Father *Caino*, a *German* Jefuit, the
Certainty that *California* joins to the Continent of *New Mexico*.   He landed in the
former from the Ifland of *Sumatra*, and paffed into the latter without crofling any other
Water than *Rio-Azul*, or the *Blue River*,
into

into which the *Rio Colorado* falls in about
35° N. L. so that this Matter is now entirely
out of Dispute, after having long exercised
the Conjectures of the Learned.

According to the best Maps we have, *California* extends from 23° 40′ to 45° N. L.
Its utmost Extent from North to South, that
is, from the Streight discovered by *Martin
Aguilar* to Cape *St. Lucas*, it must be near
eight hundred Miles. Its Breadth is very
unequal, for towards the North it is two
hundred Miles broad, but it tapers away towards the South, where it is hardly above
fifty Miles over. It is bounded on the North
by an unknown Continent, on the East, by
the Province of *New Mexico*, and the Lake
of *California*, or, as some call it, the *Vermilian Sea*, and by the great *Pacific* Ocean
on the South and West.

As it lies almost altogether in the temperate Zone, it is easy to conceive that the Climate cannot be very immoderate. In the
Summer however, they experience great Heats
on the Coast, but the Inland Part is very temperate, and in the Winter it is pretty cold.

The Country is finely diversify'd with Plains
and Mountains, well wooded and watered.
Its Soil very fruitful, abounding with Fruit
Trees, and producing, when planted, all the
Kinds of Grain which grow in *Europe :*
There are two Kinds of Deer peculiar to the
Country. All Sorts of Fowls and Birds, com-
mon

mon either in *Europe* or the *Indies*, abound
here ; there is alfo prodigious Plenty of Sea and
River Fifh ; and in a Word, a more plentiful
Country cannot be wifhed for. That there
are Mines is very probable, though not certain, but it is known that here is one of the
richeft Pearl Fifheries in the World, fo that
it is not eafy to guefs why no more Pains
has been taken to fettle fo advantageous a
Tract of Land. It has feveral fmall Rivers,
and two pretty confiderable ones, *viz. Rio
Collerado*, and *Rio du Carmel*, a great Variety of fine Ports, both on the Eaft and
Weft Side, with Bays, Creeks, and Roads
innumerable, which is the Reafon why it
was fo much frequented by our Privateers in
the *South Seas*.

The Natives of the Ifland, who are ftill
in Poffeffion of it have been differently cha-
racterized by our Writers and by the *Spaniards*; it is therefore fafeft to rely on what
Father *Caino* tells us concerning them, becaufe he converfed longer with them, and
more familiarly than any other Perfon who has
left us Memoirs. He informs us, that thefe
People, who are tolerably well made, and
very ingenious, live without Houfes, contenting themfelves with the Shade afforded
them by Trees in the Summer, and dwelling in Caves in the Winter. They are not
altogether void of Religion, fince they have
been obferved to kneel and pray on the firft
Appearance

Appearance of the New Moon, and to fhew
a great Docility in receiving the Principles
of the Chriftian Religion, which however
no great Pains has been taken to propagate
amongft them. As to Government, they
are abfolutely in a State of Nature, every
Man is both a Sovereign and a Legiflator in
his own Family, which is attended with great
Inconveniencies, there being continual Feuds
amongft them, which break out fometimes
into Broils and Bloodfhed. The Men go, for
the moft Part naked, except a Fillet of fine
Cloth about their Temples, and certain Brace-
lets of Pearl, which are very beautifully
wrought. The Women are better cloathed ;
for, befides an Ornament on their Heads, they
wear generally a Mantle of Skins over their
Shoulders, a Piece of Cloth girt round their
Bodies, and Chains of Pearls on their Necks
and Arms. Such as live on the Eaftern Side,
on the Shore of the *Vermilian Sea*, are Enemies to the *Spaniards*, who very probably
have given them Caufe. But in other Parts
of the Ifland, they feem extremely well difpofed to entertain any Strangers, and might,
without much Difficulty, be converted and
civilized ; but as they are very numerous,
and their Country of great Extent, one may
reafonably fuppofe, that the *Spaniards* have
declined fending Miffionaries, through Fear
that the People, when civilized, might either
prove dangerous Neighbours, or by cultivating

ting their Lands, invite Strangers to settle amongst them.

There are in *California* two Curiosities, which as they are well supported in Point of Authority, deserve to be taken Notice of. After the Rainy Season is over, there falls in the Morning a great Quantity of Dew, which settling upon Rose Leaves, candies and becomes hard like Manna, having all the Sweetness of Sugar, though it is not so white, and consequently not so pleasant to the Eye. In the Heart of the Country, there are Plains of Salt quite firm and clear as Crystal, which, considering the vast Plenty of Fish of all Sorts, which are also found there, might prove of great Advantage to any civilized People who were possessed of this Country. But it does not appear that the Natives make any Use of this Salt for curing their Fish, which they generally eat raw, as they also do Flesh and Roots.

The *Spaniards* for a long Tract of Time, wholly neglected this valuable Peninsula, and it is but very lately that they had any Settlement there. At present they have only a Village in its Southern Extremity, near Cape *St. Lucas*, which is called by the Name of the Place itself, *California*. The *Manila* Ships touch here sometimes in their Course to *Acapulco*, and no doubt, in Time, this will become a very considerable Place by their trading with the *Indians* for Pearl.

There

There are many fmall Iflands on the Coafts
of *California*, both in the *Pacific* Ocean, and
in the *Vermilian Sea*, fuch as the Ifland of
St. Catherine, of *St. Clement*, of *Paxaros*,
of *St. Anne*, of *Cedars*, fo called from the
great Number of thofe Trees which grow
thereon, and which are of an uncommon
Size. But the Ifles which are moft known,
are three which lie off Cape *St. Lucas*, toward the *Mexican* Coaft, thefe are called *las
tres Marias*, i. e. *The three Marys*; they are
but fmall, have good Wood and Water,
abundance of Game, Salt Pits, as in *California*, and therefore the *Englifh* and *French*
Pyrates have fometimes winter'd here, when
cruizing in the *South Seas*. We will conclude this Article with obferving that Captain *Dampier*, propofed, with great Judgment, feeking a North Weft Paffage, by
doubling Cape *Blanco*, the moft Northern
Point in *California*; a Propofition which deferves to be maturely confidered.

C H A P. III.

Of the Kingdom, or Province of New Mexico.

THIS Region, which the *Spaniards*
fometimes call the Kingdom, and fometimes the Province of *New Mexico*, lies to
the Eaft of *California*, and was formerly fup-
posed

poſed to be divided from it, by that called the *Purple*, or *Vermilian Sea*, which is no other than an Arm of the *Pacific* Ocean, running up between it and *California*, and is now generally called the *Lake*.

This Country, which is of very great Extent, is bounded on the North by very high Mountains, beyond which lies a Country altogether unknown. On the Eaſt, it has the new diſcovered Country of *Louiſiana*; on the South, ſome of the Provinces of the Kingdom of *Mexico*; on the Weſt, the *Vermilian* Sea, and the *Rio Colorado*, which ſeparate it from *California*. According to the beſt Maps, it lies between 32° and 45° of N. L. and between 260° and 273° of Longitude. In Length, from North to South, it is upwards of nine hundred *Engliſh* Miles, and in ſome Places is near ſix hundred broad, though in others it is much narrower. Some Geographers divide it into fifteen, many of the *Spaniſh* Writers into eighteen Provinces, of which they give us barely the Names. The lateſt Maps ſeem to divide it only into five.

Its Climate is extraordinary pleaſant, as lying in the midſt of the temperate Zone, the Summers very warm, and the Winters pretty ſharp; but then the former are neither ſtifling nor unwholeſome, the latter clear, and by no means intemperate. The Rains do not fall here ſo heavily as in *California*; but the Weather is generally
ſpeaking

fpeaking agreeable to the Seafon, and refrefh-
ing to a *European* Conftitution.

As to the Soil, it is wonderfully good, a-
bounding with Fruit and Timber Trees, and
beautifully interfperfed with rifing Grounds
and Rivers. All Sorts of wild and tame Cattle, efpecially Cows are found here in abundance. Fowl is very plenty, the Rivers well
ftored with Fifh ; and, in one Word, this is
as pleafant, plentiful, and rich a Country as
America, or indeed any other Part of the
World affords.

There is great Plenty of Water, though
few great Rivers in *New Mexico*, fuch as the
Rio Salado, the *Rio del Norte*, or the *North
River*, which runs the whole Length of the
Country, and then turning to the Eaft, paffes
thro' the Province of *New Leon*, where it
falls into the Gulph of *Mexico:* There are
alfo feveral little Rivers which run into the
Sea of *Mexico*, and feveral Bays and Creeks
on that Coaft, which, if the *Spaniards* defired, might eafily be converted into Ports ;
but, as we fhall prefently fee, this is not like
to happen.

The greateft Part of this extenfive Territory is ftill in the Hands of the Natives, who
though they are an eafy, peaceable, and generous People, yet were not only more numerous, but better provided for their Defence
than any other Inhabitants of the New World
which the *Spaniards* had met with. Thefe
People

People were well cloathed, cultivated their Lands, had large Stocks of Cattle, tolerable Huts in their Villages, and good Stone Houfes in their Towns when the *Spaniards* firft arrived here, which was about the Year 1539. They were Idolaters, worfhipping the Sun and Moon ; and as to Government, they had their petty Princes or Caciques, whom they chofe for their Wifdom and Valour. Thefe People fhewed a greater Readinefs to embrace the Chriftian Religion than any other of the *American* Nations, but withal did not difcover any kind of Willingnefs to part with their Liberty, which in a great Meafure they ftill preferve. The *Spanifh* Authors fpeak of various Nations in this large Country, but the principal are the *Apaches*, who are diftinguifhed by the Places of their Settlement. About the latter End of the laft Century, conceiving themfelves aggrieved by the *Spanifh* Governor, they made a general Infurrection, and did a prodigious deal of Mifchief, but were at laft appeafed, and better Garrifons have been kept there fince.

The Capital of all this Country is the City of *Santa Fé*, feated on the *Rio del Norte*, in 36° of N. L and in the Longitude of 272°. It is faid to be a well built rich City ; but ftanding at the Diftance of one hundred and thirty Leagues from the Sea, it cannot be expected that we fhould have a good Account of it ; befides this, the *Spaniards* have many
other

other Towns of Note which are unneceffary for us to mention. The whole is under a particular Governor, who refides at *Santa Fé,* and who ought to have always a ftanding Force of fix hundred Horfe, for which he receives from the Crown conftant Pay. There are Mines both of Gold and Silver in this Province, which are held to be extraordinary rich ; but the *Spaniards* carry the Plate, and Horfes and Mules over Land, and affect a great deal of Caution whenever they write of this Country, whether it be that they are apprehenfive of the Natives, or afraid that Strangers fhould attempt any thing by making Defcents on the Side next *California* is uncertain. Thus much however we know, that Turkoifes, Emeralds, and other precious Stones are brought from thence to *Mexico,* where they are much efteemed and looked upon as much better than thofe which are found in other Parts of the *Spanifh America.* The Governor enjoys his Poft for five Years, and then has a Succeffor fent him, which is probably the Reafon he is fo much devoted to his own Intereft, and fo carelefs of that of the Public. Since the Acceffion of *Philip* V. Orders have been tranfmitted to the Viceroy of *Mexico* to fend a certain Number of poor Families into thefe Northern Provinces, which was certainly a very wife Step, fince the beft way of providing for the Safety of any Country is to people it.

The

The *Spaniards* are naturally cautious, and sometimes more so than they need ; but in this Case they are certainly in the right. *Dampier* more than once mentions the Possibility of penetrating to the Gold Mines by making a Descent on the Shore opposite to *California*. On the other Side, if ever the *French* should become numerous in their Settlements on the River *Miſſiſſippi*, the *Spaniards* will run no small Hazard from their Neighbourhood, as muſt readily appear to any Man who conſiders with what Addreſs the *French* have fixed themſelves in *St. Domingo*. But if there were annual Draughts of People ſent into *New Mexico*, and there ſettled in convenient Farms, they would quickly grow populous, it being natural for Mankind to increaſe more in cold than in hot Countries, eſpecially where the Conveniencies of Life are to be had with Eaſe.

C H A P. IV.

Of Florida, *and the Iſlands belonging thereto.*

WE have already obſerved that this Country was firſt ſeen by *Cabot*, and afterwards more thoroughly diſcovered by *John Ponce de Leon*, to whom it owes its Name. It coſt a great deal of Trouble before any Settlement could be made therein, and
even

even now it is but a narrow and inconfiderable Province, at leaft in refpect to the *Spaniards*; though it might be of infinite Advantage either to us or to the *French*, of which
its prefent Mafters are not a little apprehenfive. Heretofore, when they were ftronger,
they pretended to queftion the Right, both
of the *Englifh* and the *French* to their Settlements on the Main ; but now the Tables are
turned, and inftead of plundering others, they
are in pain for their own Poffeffions.

The *Spanifh* Province of *Florida* is bounded on the North by Mountains, and by the
French Settlements behind them. On the
Eaft, by *Carolina*, and the Channel of *Bahama*; on the South, by the Gulph of *Mexico*; and on the Weft, by the *French* Settlements. Thus it is in a manner cut off from
the reft of the *Spanifh* Settlements, and will
be more effectually divided from them in
proportion as the *French* increafe.

The Air is pure and temperate, and the
Country, generally fpeaking, healthy ; the
Heats are indeed fometimes very great, but
they are allayed by the Sea Breezes, and towards the *Apalatchi* Mountains the Air is
generally cool. Hence it is fuppofed the Natives derived that Firmnefs of Conftitution
which diftinguifhes them from other *Indians*,
as well as their extraordinary Size, being
larger, and more robuft than the *Mexicans*, as
alfo longer lived.

The

The Soil is rich and fruitful, abounding with all Sorts of Timber and Fruit Trees, efpecially Pines, Laurels, Palms, Cedars, Cyprefs and Chefnut Trees, but above all, Saffafras is here in the greateft Plenty; and great Quantities are exported annually from hence. The Land produces alfo Corn, Roots, and Herbs in great Abundance with little Labour. Flefh, Fowl, and Fifh, are alfo plenty, or at leaft they might be fo, if thofe who are fettled in the Country were at all induftrious; and where People are not fo, it is impoffible they fhould have Plenty.

The Country is well watered, but it muft be owned there are no convenient Ports on the *Spanifh* Coafts, the Shore being full of Shoals and Sands, which, however, the Weaknefs of their Colonies confidered, may poffibly pafs for an Advantage, at leaft it has actually proved fo, as often as they have been attacked; but perhaps no Government but their own would truft fo much to fo precarious a Defence, efpecially when Experience muft have put their Enemies upon providing againft it for the future.

The Natives of this Country are of an Olive Colour, robuft, agile, and extremely well proportioned; they go naked, both Men and Women, except only a Deer-fkin round the Middle; but, to preferve themfelves from the Injuries of the Weather, they are painted with certain Juices which leave indelible Marks.

Marks. They have long black Hair, which falls down upon their Shoulders, but they have a Method of combing, curling and twifting it about their Heads, fo as to make it look very agreeable and becoming. The Weapons they ufe are Bows and Arrows, which they manage with great Dexterity. The Women are alfo remarkably graceful and well fhaped. They are not only capable of performing all domeftic Offices, but alfo of bearing their Hufbands Company when they go either to hunt or to War. On thefe Occafions they will fwim over broad Rivers with their Children on their Backs. The *Spaniards* charge thefe People with abundance of Vices, and though fome have fufpected a little Partiality in what they fay concerning them, yet I find all who have had any thing to do with them agree that they are a bold, fubtle, and deceitful Nation. As an Inftance of this, I cannot but take Notice of a Fraud practifed by them, which one would fcarce expect from fuch unpolifhed People. There are frequently Pieces of Ambergreafe found upon their Coafts, and the *Europeans* being ready to purchafe them at a round Rate, the *Indians* have found a way to counterfeit Ambergreafe, and that fo well, as to cheat all who are not very good Judges.

As to Religion, they are bigotted Idolaters, worfhipping the Sun and Moon as fupreme Deities, and bearing an irreconcileable Hatred

to

to all Chriftians. In refpect to Government, they have their Chiefs or Heads of Clans, to whom they are very fubmiffive. Such a little Prince is ftyled by them, *Paraoufti*; he commands in chief, in time of War, and prefides in their Councils in time of Peace. Though Polygamy is not in ufe with the reft of the Nation, yet their Princes are indulged in having three or four Wives; but the Children of the firft only are efteemed legitimate, and capable of Succeffion. Their Priefts, whom they ftyle *Jaoünas*, have alfo a great Influence over them, and well they may, for they act in no lefs than three Capacities, *viz.* as Priefts, Prophets, or rather Conjurers, and Phyficians. Thefe Men are clad in long Robes made of Skins, preferve always a very grave Appearance, fpeak little, live very abftemioufly, and in fhort take all the neceffary Precautions to maintain that Empire they have gained over the Minds of their Countrymen. As Priefts, they pray and facrifice to the Sun; as Magicians, they pretend to foretel the Succefs of all Expeditions, *&c.* and as Phyficians, they bleed, bathe, vomit, and fweat the Sick till they either cure or kill them; and in either Cafe expect a Reward.

The *Spaniards*, as they have always lived in a State of War with thefe *Indians*, fo they have conftantlyreprefented them in the blackeft Colours, though fuch of our Countrymen as have had any thing to do with them, affirm

they

they are not fo bad, except as to their Subtilty and Propenfity to Fraud, of which they have more than any other Natives of *America*.

The only Towns or Places of Strength, which the *Spaniards* are poffeffed of, or have been poffeffed of for a long Time in *Florida*, are St. *Auguftine* and St. *Mattheo*. As to the former, it is feated in the Latitude of about 30°, and lies along the Shore at the Bottom of a Hill, in the Form of a Parallelogram, the Streets cutting each other at right Angles. About a Mile North from the Town ftands the Caftle, defended by four Baftions. The Fortifications heretofore were bad, but have been lately repaired, and the Place furnifhed with fifty Pieces of Cannon, fixteen of which are Brafs, befides thofe which are in the Town, fortified alfo of late by fome Intrenchments. In 1586, when this Place was fcarce fettled, Sir *Francis Drake* took and pillaged it. In 1665 it was taken again by Capt. *Davis* at the Head of a confiderable Body of Bucchaneers. As for St. *Mattheo*, which was a lefs confiderable Place than St. *Auguftine*, it lies fifteen Leagues North from thence, and was befieged by us, when we were laft at War with the *Spaniards*, but with little Advantage, not to fay any worfe of that Attempt.

In the Year 1702, the People of *Carolina* formed a Defign of conquering what the *Spaniards* ftill hold in *Florida*, and actually undertook it under the Command of Colonel

Moor

Moor their Governor. It cannot be suppofed that he could raife a very great Body of Troops, confidering the Limitations our Governors in the *Weft Indies* are under, and that he was to march no lefs than three hundred Miles by Land. However, his Forces confifted of at leaft five hundred *Englifh*, and feven hundred *Indians*. He ruined the Farms and Villages in the open Country, and befieged St. *Auguftine* three Months, at the end of which Time the *Spaniards*, who were flow enough in all their Motions, fent fome Ships to its Relief, and on their firft Appearance Colonel *Moor* raifed his Siege, and retired precipitately, though in all Probability, if he had continued in his Camp, the *Spaniards* might not have thought themfelves ftrong enough to attack him. This fo effectually difcouraged the People of *Carolina*, that tho' the War between us and the two Crowns of *France* and *Spain* continued ten Years after, yet they attempted nothing farther; and indeed their Diftance, and the Difficulties they were under, and which have been fince removed, leave us no great Caufe to wonder at the Conduct they purfued.

The fettling a Colony in *Georgia* in 1733, put Things in this Part of the World into quite a new Situation. The *Spaniards* were uneafy, and apprehenfive of our growing Power in *Carolina*, and muft confequently be much more alarmed when the Danger

drew

drew nearer. The *Spanish* General of *Florida* therefore began to make Difpofitions for a Rupture, and to talk very high, and yet on farther Confideration in 1736, he thought proper to conclude and fign a Treaty with an *Englifh* Officer fent to treat with him ; for which, as I have been well informed, he was actually fent for over into *Old Spain*, and there executed. Since the breaking out of the War, in which we are at prefent engaged, *viz.* in *April* 1740, General *Oglethorpe* undertook the Reduction of this Place, in order to which, he marched with a confiderable Body of *Englifh* Troops, and a much larger of *Indians*. The Particulars of this Expedition have as yet never been publifhed by Authority, and therefore I fhall not infift upon it long. The *Spanifh* Governor, it feems, was a Man of great Experience, and having long had Intelligence of the Vifit defigned him, had increafed his Forces to near a thoufand Men. The *Englifh* feemed to have taken Poffeffion of too many Places, fome of which were probably abandoned to them with that View. This afforded the *Spanifh* Officer an Opportunity of cutting off about one hundred and thirty Men, who were pofted in the Negro Fort, under the Command of Colonel *Palmer.* This Difafter, together with the apparent Impoffibility of doing any great Execution by the Batteries which had been raifed on the Ifland of *Euftatia*, occafioned

the

the raising of the Siege toward the latter End
of *June*, and thereby put an End to the high
Expectations which had been raised, from
this Undertaking, which if it had succeeded,
must have been attended with very extraordinary Circumstances ; of which, as my Subject is the *Spanish* Settlements only, I chuse
to say no more at present.

There is nothing more certain than that
the *Spanish Florida* is as good and fruitful a
Country as any in *America* without Exception ; and yet it is altogether as certain, that
the Inhabitants are poor and miserable to the
last degree, which must be owing to the
wretched Conduct of their Government in
these Parts, and must prove fatal to them
sooner or later, since if ever this Province
falls either into our Hands or into those of
the *French*, their Navigation will be very
precarious, and the Wealth of the Isle of
Cuba be no longer transported to *Spain*. For,
as heretofore the Inhabitants of that Isle received great Supplies of Corn and other Provisions from *Florida*, which they now have
from *La Vera Cruz*, so, were it again settled
by an industrious People, they would undoubtedly cultivate their Lands, and trans-
port the Product of them into the adjacent
Isle of *Cuba*, where the People are frequently afflicted with Dearths, in spite of all the
Precautions can be taken to prevent it. It
must be own'd, that all the Coast is so shallow,
that

that no Port, capable of receiving great Ships could be made. But as leſſer Veſſels may anchor ſafely under the Guns of Fort St. *Auguſtine*, it is not to be doubted that even with theſe the *Spaniards* might be kept exceedingly in Awe, were they once to loſe the ſmall Poſſeſſions they had here; and this it is that makes them ſo exceſſively uneaſy about their new Colony of *Georgia*.

C H A P. V.

Of the Audience of Guadalajara, *or* New Gallicia.

THE vaſt Country of *North America*, in the Poſſeſſion of the *Spaniards*, antiently ſtyled the Empire of *Mexico*, is now called *New Spain*; and though the whole be under the Obedience of one Viceroy, yet for the Sake of its being more eaſily governed, it is divided into three Audiences, *viz. Guadalajara*, *Mexico*, and *Guatimala*. Of theſe, that which we are now to ſpeak of, lies fartheſt to the North, though on the Coaſt of the *South Seas*.

It lies between 20° and 30° N. L. and between 268° and 273° of Longitude. On the North it is bounded by the Kingdom of *New Mexico*, on the Weſt by ſeveral Provinces of the Audience of *Mexico*, on the South by other Provinces of the ſame Audience, and on the

the Eaſt its Shore is waſhed by the *South Sea*. As it lies part in the temperate, part in the torrid Zone, its Climate differs pretty much; however, generally ſpeaking, it is eſteemed wholeſome, and is certainly far more temperate than any Part of *New Spain* be-ſides. The Soil is generally mountainous and woody, ſo that the Coaſt looks like a Deſart, yet it is indifferently fruitful, produces *European* and *Indian* Grain in Plenty; many valuable Drugs, and very rich Silver Mines. On the Coaſt alſo there is a good Pearl Fiſhery.

This Country was diſcovered, or at leaſt ſettled by *Nuno de Guzman* 1531. He found it inhabited by a brave and bold People, well armed, well cloathed, and who defended themſelves obſtinately againſt the *Spaniards*. Their Towns were tolerably well built and furniſhed, neither were the People at all barbarous, but managed both civil and military Affairs with great Addreſs and Regularity; however, the *Spaniſh* Writers charge them with ſome horrid and unnatural Vices, which is the more extraordinary, conſidering it is alſo affirmed that their Women were very beautiful, and of very engaging Behaviour. As it is well known theſe Conquerors treated them but roughly, ſeized their Lands, and deſtroyed their Perſons, it is no great Wonder, that in order to colour this, they have dealt pretty freely with their Characters, which they might the more readily be tempted

ed to, becaufe they had a moral Certainty
that thefe poor Creatures never could have
Juftice done them by any impartial Pen.

This Audience is fubdivided into feven
Provinces; the firft of thefe is *Cinaloa*, which
lies next to the Kingdom of *New Mexico*, on
the Shore of that called the *Vermilian Sea*.
The Capital of this Province is the City of
St. *John*, at a fmall Diftance from the Coaft;
behind this Province lies that of *New Bifcay*,
which has no Communication with the Sea;
however, the Inhabitants of it are very rich,
not only in Corn, Cattle, and other fuch like
Commodities, but in Silver alfo, of which
there are very rich Mines, in the Neighbourhood of the City of St. *John* of *Bifcay*, its
Capital; befides which, there is another confiderable Town called St. *Barbara*. Adjoining to this Province is that of the *Zacatecas*,
fo called from its ancient Inhabitants; it is
alfo an inland Province, well inhabited, and
abounding with large Boroughs, of which
the principal are *San Luis de los Zacatecas*,
almoft under the Tropic of Cancer, *Du-
rango*, a Bifhop's See, and a great Town called *Nombre de Dios*. The next Maritime
Province to *Cinaloa* is called *Culiacan*, and
lies to the South; its capital City hath the
fame Name. Next to it, immediately under the
Tropic of *Cancer*, ftretched along the *South
Seas*, lies the Province of *Chiametlan*, the
Capital of which is *Aquacara*. The moft
                                    fouthern

southern Province on the Coast is that of *Xalifco*, in which, besides the Capital of the same Name, is a very considerable Town called *Campof-tella*. Behind this Province, yet so as that a Corner of it touches the Sea, lies that of *Gua-dalajara*, properly so called, having for its Capital a City of the same Name, which is also the Head of the whole Audience, and the Seat of the Royal Courts of Justice; besides this, it is a Bishop's See of a considerable Revenue, and very pleasantly seated on the Banks of the River *Baranja*, and to the North of the Lake of *Chapala*, which is said to be forty Leagues in Compass.

It must be owned, that this is but a very short and dry Description of so large a Country, yet this may be the more easily excused, when it is considered that very few of our Writers say any thing of it at all; and even the *Spanish* Writers treat very superficially, because, as they report, it is a Part of their Dominions which has but very little Trade; but I have Reason to believe that their Silence proceeds from wiser Motives. In short, some of our Bucaneers who had been taken in these Parts about forty Years ago, have left with their Friends in *Jamaica*, Accounts of another Nature, which in few Words amount to this. The Sea Coasts are purposely deserted by the *Spaniards*, that Strangers may not be able to find any thing that may tempt them to land, or if they do land out of Curiosity, may not

know

know what to do next. The Ground of thefe
Precautions is, not only feveral Silver Mines,
which we have mentioned before, but alfo
fome of Gold, lately found in the Neighbourhood of *Campoftella*, of very great Value. The
Ore they chufe to tranfport by Mules to *Mexico*, rather than expofe fo valuable a Commerce to be intercepted by Foreigners, which
might very well happen if they ventured to
fend it in fmall Veffels by Sea.

The *Spaniards* are not very numerous
throughout this whole Audience, except in
the two great Cities of *Guadalajara* and *Campoftella*. The *Meftizo's*, however, make a
confiderable Figure in point of Number and
Eftate, but the Bulk of the People are the
Natives, who are, generally fpeaking, well
treated here, becaufe they are not of a Temper to be treated otherwife; and the Effects are
anfwerable to fo good a Caufe, fince they are
vifibly braver and politer than any of their
Countrymen, and for all that appears, are well
affected to the *Spaniards*, chiefly through the
Inftigation of their Priefts, for whom they
have a great Efteem; though they are far
from being fuch Slaves to them as in other
Parts of *New Spain*. Not only the Natives,
but the *Spaniards* live here to great Ages; and
as they drain the Marfhes, and thin the Woods,
it is obferved that the Climate grows daily
better and better, infomuch that many remove
hither

hither from other Parts of the Empire of *Mexico.*

C H A P. VI.

Of *the Audience of* Mexico.

THIS which is by far the noblest Part of the *Spanish* Dominions, hath on the North, the Country of *Florida*, on the East the North Sea, or Bay of *Mexico*, on the South, the Audience of *Guatimala*, the Gulph of *Honduras*, and on the other Side the *South Sea*, on the West, the Audience of *Guadalajara*. Its Extent is very great, its Soil fruitful, and though under the *Torrid Zone*, its Climate indifferently cool, rich in all Sorts of desirable Commodities, Gold, Silver and Precious Stones not excepted. In order however to have a just Notion of this noble Country, it will be requisite to consider it as at present divided into seven Provinces, of each of which I will speak as clearly, and at the same time, as concisely as possible.

The first of these is the Province of *Mechoacan*, of very considerable Extent. It is bounded on the North by the Province of *Panuco*, and that of *Guadalajura*, on the East by *Panuco*, and *Mexico Proper*, on the South by the last mentioned Province, and the *South Soa*, which also bounds it on the West. The Climate is extrordinary good,

and

and the Soil wonderfully fertile, which makes it so wholesome that sick People go from other Parts of *Mexico* to recover their Health there. It abounds with Lakes, Rivers and Rills of clear brackish Water, which are of admirable Use; for though the Meadows through which they run abound with a rank Kind of Grass, yet it is never found to prejudice their Cattle, but like other Salt Marshes, makes them extraordinary fat and fine. They have also a numerous Breed of good Horses, fit both for the Saddle and Draught. All Sorts of Fish are there in the utmost Plenty, as the Name of this Province imports; for though we call a certain Drug which grows there *Mechoacan*, yet in the *Indian* Language that Word signifies a Place abounding with Fish. Corn of all Sorts grows here in Plenty; and no Country in the World is better furnished either with Fruit or Timber Trees. The Commodities for which it is chiefly famous are Sarsaparilla, Sulphur, Indigo, Sassfras, Cocoa, Ambergrease, Vanillas, Hides, Wool, Cotton, Silk, Sugar, &c. but the two principal Commodities are Silver, of which there are several rich Mines; and the Root called *Mechoacan*, sometimes White Rhubarb, from its Colour and Effects; formerly it was in high Repute, and sold in *Europe* at a great Rate, but of late it is much sunk both in its Reputation and its Price, the Resin of Jalap being found to answer all Intentions better.

At

At the Time *Cortez* fubdued the Kingdom
of *Mexico*, *Mechoacan* was an independent
Monarchy, and its Sovereign of fuch Power
as to be formidable to the *Mexicans*, to whom
he was an inveterate Enemy. He was however fo much intimidated when he heard of
the Deftruction of that Empire by the *Spaniards*, that he fubmitted of his own Ac-
cord; fo that *Cortez* gained this confiderable
Country by his Reputation only. It was
then, and fome Time after very populous;
but the *Indians* are now grown thin, not fo
much through any Severity of the *Spaniards*,
as by their introducing Luxury amongft them,
which was unknown in earlier Times; for
thefe People being of a weaker Conftitution
than *Europeans*, are lefs able to fupport Exceffes, to which however they are naturally
but too much inclined.

At prefent the Cities in this Province are
numerous, but the principal of them is that
diftinguifhed by the fame Name of *Mechoacan*; it ftands very pleafantly on a large River, and not far from a confiderable Lake of
the fame Name; the *Spaniards* call it *Vale-
dolid*; it lies in the Latitude of 19° 10′ and
forty-feven Leagues from *Mexico*, large and
beautiful, adorned with a fine Cathedral, and
full of handfom Houfes belonging to rich
Spaniards, Owners of the Mines of *Gua-
naxoato*, which lie about twenty-eight Leagues
to the North, and fifteen Leagues farther
there

there are others which are ftill richer. A-
mongft the moft confiderable Places in this
Province, may be reckoned the Town of
St. Philip, that of *St. Michael*, the Conception, and the Port of *Sacatula*, at the Mouth
of a River of the fame Name: It may not
be amifs to obferve, that for Reafons before
affigned, the *Spaniards* carry on the greateft
Part of the Trade of this Province by Land,
in which they are the more excufable, confidering there are but very bad Ports here, indeed fcarce any that can be properly called
fo.

The next Province is that of *Mexico Proper*, which hath to the North that of *Panuco*, to the Eaft that of *Tlafcala*, to the
South the Pacifick Ocean, and to the Weft
the Province of *Mechoacan:* As it is the moft
confidered, fo it is alfo one of the fineft Provinces in this great Empire. The Climate is
indeed variable, fo that Strangers fometimes
complain of its exceffive Heat, and the Natives again are apt to fhrink under its Cold ;
however *Europeans*, of found Conftitutions,
agree that it is both pleafant and temperate.
The Soil is remarkably fruitful, and though
the *Mexicans* are as luxurious in their Tempers, and have as much Money wherewith
to indulge their Luxury as any other People
in the World, yet all the Neceffaries of Life
are extremely cheap, which is a pregnant Proof
of the Plenty that reigns here. As to the
Com-

Commodities of this Province, they are much
the same with those of *Mechoacan* before-
mentioned, except that the Mines afford a
much greater Quantity of Silver, and that
this Silver holds sometimes a very considerable Portion of Gold, of which we shall hereafter have occasion to speak. As to the History and Conquest of this Country, it has
been already sufficiently explained in the
former Book, and therefore we shall not med-
dle with it again here.

The Royal City of *Mexico* is the Capital
of this Province, of the Audience, and of all
New Spain, This famous City is seated at
the Foot of a Chain of Mountains, in the
Midst of a great Lake called from thence *The
Lake of Mexico*. In Point of Regularity, it
is the best built City perhaps in the Universe,
the Streets being so strait, and so exactly dis-
posed, that from any Part thereof the whole
is visible. The *Spanish* Writers place it in
the Latitude of 19° 40'. There are five En-
trances into it, over as many Causeways, and
the Want of three Things render it very remarkable, these are Gates, Walls and Artillery.
All the Buildings are convenient, some of
them very magnificent, especially the Cathedral, Churches, Monasteries and Nunneries;
of the former there are twenty-nine, and of
the latter twenty-two: You may guess at the
Riches of these from the Revenue of the
Cathedral, which amounts to at least seventy
thousand

thousand Pounds a Year, out of which the Archbishop receives annually fifteen thousand Pounds, besides prodigious Sums that accrue to him by Way of Perquisites. To say the Truth, the Church is unreasonably rich, for it enjoys the Whole of what we in *England*, would call Property, that is to say, the Clergy are the sole Ground-Landlords in this Place, which is the Reason that few *Spaniards* care to settle there. Many Writers have reported improbable, not a few incredible Things of *Mexico*. In order to avoid therefore following their Steps, I shall stick close to a *Spanish* Author who resided there long enough to be perfectly acquainted with it, and who in other Respects writes freely, and with great Sincerity; he assures us that it is above six Miles in Compass, and that it contains about a hundred thousand Inhabitants, that they are rich to an immense Degree, and that the most valuable Commodities of the *East* and *West Indies*, together with those of *Europe*, are daily exposed to Sale in their Markets; but as to what our Countryman *Gage* tells us of his seeing two thousand Coaches there driving for Diversion in an Evening, we must either believe that it happened in the Night, and that he dreamt it, or if he really look'd upon the Coaches, that at least he saw double. The far greater Part of these Inhabitants are Blacks or Mulattos, the rest *Spaniards*, who reside there as long as they continue in Office, or

till

till they have acquired fuch a Fortune as fa-
tisfies them. Befides all the King's Courts,
this City is honoured with an Univerfity, is the
Seat of an Archbifhop, and hath a Tribunal
of the Inquifition. We may form fome Idea
of the Riches of the People by the Tenths
collected from the eleven Prelates fubject to
this Archbifhop, which amounts to upwards
of half a Million of Pieces of Eight, thofe
Prelates receiving at leaft twelve hundred thoufand Pounds Sterling *per Annum.*

But there is another Method of calculating
the Wealth of *Mexico*, which I will prefent
to the Reader, becaufe I am pretty confident
he will find it no where elfe. There was
brought into the King's Exchequer at *Mexico* in the Year 1730, fomewhat better than a
Million of Marks of Silver; this was the
King's Duty from the Mines, which ought
to be one Fifth of the Metal taken out of
them. It is true moft People think the King
is pretty roundly cheated ; but becaufe this
does not appear to us, we will fuppofe he is
honeftly paid, and that this is the fifth Part of
what is dug out of the Mines. The whole
therefore muft amount to five Millions of
Marks. A Mark is a Weight equivalent to
eight of our Ounces, fo that if we compute
this Silver at 5 *s. per Oz.* then the Inhabitants
of *Mexico* receive annually from their Mines
ten Millions of Money.

We

We have neither Room nor Inclination to enter here into an Account of the Manners of the People, or if we had, faying that they are lazy and profufe, would ferve as well as if we wrote Pages about them. The immenfe Wealth which fome of them poffefs intoxicates them to fuch a Degree, that thro' meer Mifmanagement they run it out. As for the *Spaniards*, they are very unjuft and oppreffive, and their Clergy miferably ignorant, and withal Bigots to the laft degree, and of very fcandalous Morals, if their own Writers may be believed. With all this Grandeur and Wealth, the military Strength of this Place is incredibly low; the Viceroy has not about his Perfon above four or five hundred Men, which is perhaps owing to the Jealoufy of the Government at home, for otherwife he might, for an inconfiderable Expence, be much better provided. To fay the Truth, the Place is in very little Danger from Foreigners, at the fame time that it muft be owned there would be a great Rifque run in putting Arms into the Hands of fuch an unruly People as the Bulk of the Inhabitants in this City really are, who on the flighteft Grievances threaten their Viceroys to burn them in their Palaces, or to tear them in pieces if they ftir out, and who have more than once fhewn a ftrong Inclination to be as good as their Words.

One

One would imagine that this great City would hinder there being any other confiderable Places in this Province ; but it is far from being fo, for there are many, even in the very Lake, and befides thefe, not a few fcattered up and down the Country, fuch as *Petalan*, *Catalutla*, which are maritime Places, *Ostuma*, *Tasco*, *Cuernabaca*, *Atlisco*, fcattered up and down the Province, and extremely well peopled by *Indians*.

But after *Mexico*, the moft confiderable town, or that at leaft which deferves moft Notice from us, is *Acapulco*, the Haven of *Mexico* for the *South Seas*. The Town is pretty large, but not well built, whence fome have made very falfe Conclufions as to its Wealth and Importance. That the Town is but mean is indifputable, and two extraordinary Caufes there are for it. The firft of thefe is the Frequency of Earthquakes, and every body knows that it would not be only ridiculous, but very dangerous to build ftrong, fubftantial Houfes, in a Place liable to fuch Accidents, where the flighter the Houfe, the fafer thofe who inhabit it. The fecond Reafon is, the Unhealthinefs of the Place, which is fuch that, except when their Bufinefs calls them hither, few *Spaniards* are to be feen in the Town, and then they ftay no longer than needs muft, leaving their Dwelling and Warehoufes to the Care of Servants. I fufpect there may be added to this, a third Caufe, at leaft as
ftrong

ſtrong as any of the reſt, and that is the ſmall
Inclination theſe People have to dwell on the
Coaſt at any Rate. Now the Reaſon of their
repairing frequently to *Acapulco,* is its being
the grand Port of *New Spain* for the Trade of
Peru and the *Eaſt Indies,* as the Harbour of
La Vera Cruz is for the *North Seas* and the
European Trade ; but in order to form a juſt
Notion of theſe Matters, we muſt enter into
a more particular Detail.

The Port of *Acapulco* is allowed by all proper Judges to be an excellent one, far ſuperior
to any in theſe Seas. It lies 17° N. L. and its
Haven is not only ſafe and commodious, but
withal ſo very large, that ſeveral hundred
Ships may anchor therein without running any
Hazard of one injuring another. There is
a ſmall low Iſland croſſing the Mouth of the
Harbour ; it is about a Mile and a half long,
and half a Mile broad, ſtretching Eaſt and
Weſt. It leaves a good, wide, and deep Channel
at each End, where Ships may ſafely go in
or come out, taking the Advantage of the
Winds ; They muſt enter with the Sea Wind,
and go out with the Land Wind ; for theſe
Winds ſeldom or never fail to ſucceed each
other alternately in their proper Seaſon of the
Day or Night. The weſtermoſt Channel is
the narroweſt, but ſo deep, there is no anchor-
ing ; and the *Manila* Ships paſs in that Way,
but the Ships from *Lima* enter thro' the South
Weſt Channel. This Harbour runs in North
about

about three Miles, then growing very narrow, it turns fhort about to the Weft, and runs a- bout a Mile farther, where it ends. The Town ftands on the North Weft Side ; at the Mouth of this narrow Paffage, clofe by the Sea, and at the End of the Town, there is a Platform with a great many Guns. Oppofite to the Town, on the Eaft Side, ftands a high ftrong Caftle, faid to have forty Guns of a very great Bore. Ships commonly ride near the Bottom of the Harbour, under the Com- mand both of the Caftle and the Platform.

Moft of our Writers who have mention'd this Place and its Trade, have run into an Error as to its Commerce with *Peru*, which they confine to the annual Ship from *Lima*. This has no Foundation, in Truth ; for at all other Seafons of the Year, fave that where- in the *Acapulco* Ship arrives, which is about *Chriftmas*, the Trade is open, and Ships of *Peru* come thither frequently, fell their own Commodities, and carry back thofe of *Mexico* ; but inafmuch as the great Importance of this Place fprings from the annual Ships of *Lima* and *Manila* ; thefe are all the Veffels faid to come hither by our Voyage-Writers, who collect only from general Reports, and there- fore we need not wonder at their falling into Miftakes of this Nature, in contradicting which, we make ufe of the beft Authority, that of *Spanifh* Authors, who have refided long on the Spot, and have been interefted in the Commerce there.

In

In the former Book we have given an Account of the Difcovery of the *Philippine Iflands*, and their being conquered by the *Spaniards*. As they are much richer, and of far greater Importance to that Crown than we commonly imagine, fo undoubtedly the *Spaniards* are ftronger and better provided in thofe Parts than we have any Accounts of, as may be infallibly concluded from the vaft Riches which their Governors and even their under Officers acquire there. Yet the only Commerce they have with the reft of the World is this, by the Port of *Acapulco*. Our accomplifhed Admiral, Sir *John Narborough*, reported that there were feven or eight Ships concerned in this Trade ; but nothing is more certain than that he was mifinformed, for till within thefe thirty Years, there never was any more than one annual Ship which paffed between *Manila* and *Anapulco*. Now indeed there are two, one the *Galleon* or trading Ship and the other a kind of Convoy. The Convoy is a Frigate of between twenty and thirty Guns, the Galleon a prodigious, unweildy Veffel of a thoufand, fometimes twelve hundred Ton Burthen. This is the Effect of that ftrict Regulation whereby the Inhabitants are tied down to fend no more than this Ship every Year. It is laden with all the rich Products of the Eaft, fuch as Ambergreafe, Civet, Bezoar, very large oriental Pearl, vaft Quantities of Piece Goods, and the Value of about

a hun-

a hundred thoufand Pound Sterling in Gold
Duft.   This Voyage to *Acapulco* is extremely
dangerous, as it is by far the longeft from
Land to Land that can be made.   They touch
indeed at *Guam*, one of the *Ladrones*, and,
except a Day or two's Stay there, pafs three
thoufand Leagues without feeing any thing
but Sea and Sky.   Nothing certainly but the
vaft Wealth that is acquired could tempt Men
to run fuch a Hazard; but when it is confidered that the Captain of the Galleon makes
forty thoufand Pieces of Eight, the Pilot
twenty thoufand, each of his two Mates nine
thoufand, and every common Seaman a thoufand if he manages prudently, we cannot be
amazed.   They fail generally from *Manila*
towards the latter End of the Month of *June*,
and arrive at *Acapulco* within ten Days before,
or ten Days after *Chriftmas* always.

About the fame time comes the annual
Ship from *Lima*, laden with the richeft Commodities of *Peru*, and at leaft two Millions
of Pieces of Eight; thefe are to be laid out
in the Purchafe of *Indian* Commodities that
the Fair of *Acapulco*, which lafts fometimes
thirty Days, and at which fuch as come from
the *Eaft Indies* furnifh themfelves with all
Sorts of *European* Goods, brought hither
over Land from the Port of *Vera Cruz*.   It
is eafily conceived what a mighty Alteration
happens at *Acapulco* on the Commencement
of this Fair, which from a dirty dreary Village,

lage, or at leaft very inconfiderable Town, exalts it into a populous City, crowded with the richeft Commodities of both the *Indies*. When the Fair is over, the Goods belonging to the *Mexican* Merchants are tranfported over Land by Mules; thofe which are fent into *Peru* are laden not only on the annual Ship, but on many others; and the Galleon, as foon as it is poffible, prepares for her Return to *Manila*. By the Way we muft remark, that heretofore the *Lima* Ship was of very inconfiderable Force, but of late, fince our Privateers have found the Way into the *South Seas*, they never employ any Veffel carrying lefs than forty Guns, and fhe alfo is allowed a Tender, fometimes two.

The *Galleon*, in her Return from *Acapulco* to *Manila*, makes a much fafer and fpeedier Voyage than in coming, for falling down from 17° to 19° of Latitude, fhe runs away before the Wind, and performs a Courfe of about two thoufand Leagues in ten, twelve, or thirteen Weeks at the moft. Her Return is expected with great Impatience by reafon of the great Want the Inhabitants of thofe Parts have of the Goods fhe brings. Befides, in her comes Money for the Pay of all the Garrifons which are faid to coft the King of *Spain* two hundred and fifty thoufand Pieces of Eight *per Annum*, which is true; but then they reckon without any Notice taken of the immenfe Quantity of Spices and other rich

Com-

Commodities brought from thence, or even of the large Quantity of Gold mentioned before, which will much more than balance that Account.

The next Province in the Audience of *Mexico* is that of *Tlafcala*, which has the Happinefs of lying both on the *North* and *South Seas*. Its Boundaries are thus : On the North it has part of the Province of *Panuco*, on the Eaft the Gulph of *Mexico*; on the South the *Pacifick Ocean*; and on the Weft the Province of *Mexico* proper.

As to the Climate and Soil of this Province, they are much the fame with thofe of *Mexico*, only fome think the former lefs variable, and the latter more fruitful. As it is perhaps, the beft feated, fo it is beyond Queftion, the moft populous Country in all *America*, which is owing to many Caufes; fome of which it may not be improper to mention. In the firft Place we muft obferve that the *Tlafcalans* were never conquered, but as they were originally the Allies of *Cortez*, fo by his Recommendation, they have ever fince been confidered in that Light by the *Spanifh* Government, which is perhaps the only true Point of Policy they purfue. By this Means the Villages and Towns fwarm with *Indians* who are quite different People from their Neighbours; for whereas the latter are grown fenfelefs and ftupid, through the long Continuance of Slavery and Oppreffion; thefe
                                        have

have all the Fire and Spirit that is natural to a free People. They fpeak the *Spanifh* Tongue, and fcarce any other ; they are per- fectly reconciled to the *Spanifh* Cuftoms, and are fo grateful for the Countenance and Re- fpect fhewed them, that it is conceived the Government may more fafely depend upon them than upon the *Meftizos*, though the lat- ter are actually defcended from *Spaniards*. One may very well wonder that having fuch an Inftance before their Eyes, the Viceroy and his Council do not treat the *Indians* in general better; perhaps they may have their Reafons, though, to us, they feem paft find- ing out.

There are in this Province many great and rich Towns, amongft which, not to detain the Reader too long, we will fpeak but of three. *Tlafcala*, anciently the Capital of the Pro- vince, now no more than an *Indian* Town, ftands very pleafantly on the Bank of a Ri- ver which runs into the *South Sea*. It is well inhabited, and its Inhabitants are, for *Indians*, very rich. Few *Spaniards* refide here, yet fome there are. At a fmall Di- ftance from thence ftands *Puebla de los Ange- los*, i. e. The City of the Angels, which is now the Capital of the Province, and much the fineft Place in it. It vies for Beauty and Magnificence with *Mexico* itfelf, and one may guefs at the Richnefs of the Place by the Re- venue of the Cathedral and its Chapter, whch, which amounts to three hundred thousand Pieces of Eight *per Annum.*

The City of *La Vera Cruz*, which is the great Port of *New Spain*, on the North Seas, stands also in this Province, and very well deserves a particular Description. When *Cortez* landed on this Coast, in order to undertake the Conquest of *Mexico*, he founded the City of *Old Vera Cruz*, which he so named, because he landed there on *Good-Friday*; this was in 1518, but since then great Alterations have happened, and this City is partly decayed, partly destroyed, the Causes of which have been many. In the first Place the Port was found to be very bad, next the City was shewn, by Experience, to be extremely unwholesome, and lastly it proved to be very weak and defenceless. At about fifteen or sixteen Miles distance, a very strong and safe, though not capacious Port was discovered, capable of being effectually protected by a Fort built upon a triangular Rock, which Fort, when erected, was call'd *Saint John de Ulua.* By Degrees, the *Spaniards* erected a Town in the Neighbourhood of this Fort, which, in Process of Time, drained the old Town, and was thence called *New Vera Cruz.* It stands in the Latitude of 19° 16′ and is not very considerable, either for its Bulk, or for the Magnificence of its Buildings; for on the one Side being exposed to vast Clouds of dry Sand, and on the other

to

to the Exhalations of very rank Bogs, it is so very unwholefom, that fcarce any *Spaniards* of Note refide there conftantly; and to this we properly may afcribe its being at prefent, and having always been a Place of no great Strength, as appears by its having been taken by fome *French* and *Dutch* Buchaneers in 1683, and the Apprehenfions its Inhabitants are in on the Appearance of any ftrange Ships ever fince.

In Point of Trade however it is one of the moft confiderable Places, not only in the new, but perhaps in the whole World· It receives from *Acapulca* over Land, a vaft Quantity of *Eaft India* Commodities: The Ware-houfes here are generally full of *European* Goods; and the Merchants of *Vera Cruz*, carry on a Trade as great as it is poffible for *Spaniards* to carry on throughout all *America*. In its Port the Flota is obliged to winter; and on its Arrival, there is a prodigious Fair held here which quite changes the Afpect of the City for the Time it lafts, which is fometimes for many Weeks, for it is opened as foon as the Ships arrive in the Port, and does not end till they are ready to fail. Some Writers, without diftinguifhing between the City and Citizens, would have us believe that this Place is immenfely rich, which is ftrictly and literally true in the Fair Time, but can fcarce be allowed fo at any other, at leaft of late Years, fince the richeſt Merchants

chants

chants not only refide at the City of *Angels*, the far greater Part of the Year, but alfo keep their Plate there till fuch Time as the Flota is on the very Point of failing, a neceffary Precaution, fince Experience has fhewn how eafy *La Vera Cruz* may be furprized, though perhaps it might be difficult enough to keep it. Its conftant Inhabitants are only *Mulottos* and *Meftizos*, with a few *Spanifh* Factors, who ftay to make Fortunes; and long, to be fure, they need not ftay in a Place, where a Man who hath half a Million of Pieces of Eight, is not thought rich, or any thing more than what we call well to pafs. The whole of the Inhabitants of *Vera Cruz*, including Slaves, may be about three thoufand, and the Compafs of the City is about half a *Spanifh* League.

Behind the Province of *Tlafcala* lies that of *Panuco*, which is very large and finely fituated. On the North it is bounded by *Florida*, and part of the Audience of *Guadalajara*, on the Eaft by the Gulph of *Mexico*, on the South by the Provinces of *Tlafcala* and *Mexico* Proper, and on the Weft by that of *Mechoacan*. It was one of the firft Difcoveries of the famous *Cortez*, who took a great deal of Pains to conquer and plant it, though the Country be rather fruitful and pleafant than rich. Its Inhabitants made a very vigorous Refiftance, and were not fubdued without confiderable Lofs; however,

by

by the building feveral Cities, they have fince
been thoroughly bridled, which is perhaps
one Reafon why many of them chofe to retire
into *Florida*, rather than remain Slaves in
their native Country. On this Account we
find this Province but indifferently peopled,
and little Notice taken of it in feveral Authors, notwithftanding its having a very extended Sea Coaft, along the Gulph of *Mexico*, with feveral Roads and Creeks, though
no great Ports. Its Capital hath the fame
Name with the Province, as hath alfo the
River upon which it ftands, which is large
and navigable. The City of *Panuco*, which
is a Bifhop's See, lies in the Latitude of 21°
50' at the Diftance of about twenty Leagues
from the Sea ; it contains about five hundred
Families, and the Houfes therein are built of
Stone, which renders them ftrong and clean,
and are neatly thatched with *Palmetto* Leaves.
There are other confiderable Places in the
Province, fuch as that of *St. Jago de los Val-
les*, which lies higher than that of *Panuco*,
on the fame River, and fome others, which,
to avoid fwelling this Article, I fhall not
mention.

On the other Side of the Province of *Tlafcala*, lies that of *Guaxaca*, as well fituated
as any in *America*. On the North it has the
Gulph of *Mexico*; on the Eaft the Province
of *Tabafco*, and the Audience of *Guatimala* ;
on the South the *Pacific* Ocean ; and on the
Weft

Weſt the Province of *Tlaſcala*. The Climate is tolerable, and the Soil rich, producing two very valuable Drugs, Cochineal and Vinelloes, the former a rich Dye, and the latter a valuable Perfume; it grows in various Parts of the Kingdom of *Mexico*, but no where in ſuch Plenty as here, we will therefore take this Opportunity of deſcribing it. The Vinello is a little Cod full of ſmall black Seeds; it is four or five Inches long, about the Bigneſs of the Stem of a Tobacco Leaf, and when dried much reſembling it; ſo that our Privateers at firſt have often thrown them away, when they took any, wondering why the *Spaniards* ſhould lay up Tobacco Stems. This Cod grows on a ſmall Vine, which climbs about and ſupports itſelf by the neighbouring Trees; it firſt bears a yellow Flower, from whence the Cod afterwards proceeds. It is firſt green, but when ripe, it turns yellow; then the *Indians* (whoſe Manufacture it is, and who ſell it cheap to the *Spaniards*) gather it and lay it in the Sun, which makes it ſoft; when it changes to a Cheſnut Colour. Then they frequently preſs it between their Fingers, which makes it flat. The principal Uſe of this Perfume is to give a Flavour to Chocolate, and ſometimes Tobacco; in both which it is extremely agreeable. This Province of *Guaxaca* is but very thinly inhabited, for which no ſufficient Reaſon appears, ſince it wants not good Ports both on the
North

North and in the *South Seas*, such as *Aquatulco*, formerly taken by Sir *Francis Drake*, which though a small, is yet a very safe and commodious Harbour, though there is now scarce so much as a Village in its Neighbourhood. On the other Side, in the Gulph of *Mexico*, Ships ride safely at the Mouth of the River *Alvarado*. The Capital of the Province is an inland City of a middling Size, and indifferently built, seated in a fair and fruitful Plain ; its proper Name is *Antequera* ; but it is commonly called *Guaxaca* ; it is a Bishop's See of considerable Revenue, and some rich Families, descended from the old *Spanish* Conquerors, have their Habitations there. Other Places of Note in this Province are *St. Jago*, *Spiritu Santo*, and *St. Ildefonso*. I shall conclude what I have to say of this Country, by observing that a great Part of the Estates of the Family of *Cortez* lie here.

East from this Province lies that of *Tabasco*, stretched along the Gulph of *Mexico*, and of a very inconsiderable Extent. North it is bounded by that Gulph, East by the Province of *Yucatan*, South by part of the Audience of *Guatimala*, and West by the Province of *Guaxaca*. As it is a narrow Slip by the Sea Shore, neither its Soil nor its Climate are much to be boasted of, the one being far from wholesome, and the other not over fruitful. Our Logwood-Cutters were wont to frequent this Coast much, and procured

cured great Advantages to themfelves by trading with the *Spaniards*, who are very glad
of any Supplies of *European* Commodities,
having no Ports of their own, and lying at a
confiderable Diftance from *La Vera Cruz*.
There are no Mines here, which is one Reafon perhaps why it is fomewhat neglected;
yet the People have good Farms, well ftocked with Cattle, which yield them confiderable Profit ; and befides they have great Plenty
of Cocoa, which they fend laden on Mules to
Vera Cruz. The only Town of Note is in
the eaftern Corner of the Province, and is
called by the *Spaniards*, *Nueftra Sennora de
la Vittoria*, i. e. Our Lady of Victory.

The laft Province in the Audience of
Mexico is that of *Yucatan*, or, as the *Spaniards* fpell it, *Jucatan*. It is a Peninfula, furrounded on the North and on the Weft by
the Gulph of *Mexico*, on the Eaft by the
Gulph of *Honduras*, on the South by part of
the Audience of *Guatimala*, and the little
Province of *Tabafco*. It is in all Refpects a
moft noble Country, and as fuch defervedly
commended by *Herrera*, and all the *Spanifh*
Writers. The Climate is pretty warm in the
Summer, which begins in the Month of *A-
pril*, and ends in that of *September*. The
Winter Seafon is indifferently cool, excepting
the Months of *January* and *February*, which
are almoft as hot as in the Midft of Summer;
yet, on the whole, the Country is very wholefome,

fome, efpecially a fort of mountainous Tract which runs acrofs it, where when the *Spaniards* entered *America*, there were fome *Indians* three hundred Years old, and the Natives ftill live to a vaft Age. The Days and Nights are pretty near equal all the Year round ; and this, with the Sea Breezes, makes the Heat tolerable enough. The Soil is indifferently good, produces Plenty of Corn, when fufficiently cultivated, and abounds with Cattle of all Sorts ; but the principal Commodity is Logwood, for which the Bay of *Campeachy* is defervedly famous. But in as much as no Mines have been difcovered in this Country, whatever Plenty there may be of other ufeful things, the *Spaniards* are not fond of making Settlements here, which without doubt is one great Caufe of its abounding fo much with *Indians*. Thefe however live, generally fpeaking, in fubmiffive Obedience to the *Spaniards*. In the Bay of *Campeachy*, they are made ufe of in making Salt, which is a very laborious Employment, the poor Creatures being forced to endure all Extremities of Weather, without either Houfe or Hut to protect them ; they likewife keep their Cattle, and do every other fervile Office, though but unwillingly ; for when an Opportunity offers, they are fure to embrace it, and fairly run away into the Woods, or elfe take Shelter in fome uninhabited Iflands, where they live

in

in a State of Nature, though not much at their Eafe.

Some of the *Spanifh* Writers would have us believe that the Natives were extremely barbarous, till civilized by them, and particularly that they devoured human Flefh. This however feems to deferve no great Credit, fince after the ftricteft Enquiry that can be made, we have no Certainty that any of the *Indians*, how barbarous foever, either now do, or ever did eat human Flefh, except it may be in Time of War, the Flefh of their Enemies, not becaufe it was grateful to them, but becaufe it was a Mark of Victory, and a Gratification of their Revenge. Befides, thefe *Indians* live quietly enough in their Villages, and are extremely fubmiffive to their *Padres* or Priefts ; fo that the *Spaniards* have no need to invent any fuch Stories, except it be to excufe their own Cruelty, which is not fo great now as it has been, and which was always contrary to their Laws, and repeated Edicts from the Court of *Spain*, which in this, as in moft other cafes, were received with all outward Demonftrations of Refpect, and perhaps publifhed with much Solemnity, but within a few Months, when the King's Officers had made the moft of Difpenfations, as little minded as if they had never been heard of.

There are in this Province feveral little Towns, but four only of any confiderable Bignefs, and of which it is neceffary we fhould give

give the Reader fome Account. The firft of
thefe is *Campeachy*, or, as it is called by the
Spaniards, *San Francifco de Campeche*. It is
a fair Town ftanding on the Shore in a fmall
bending of the Land, and is the only Town
on all this Coaft, even from *Cape Catoche* to
La Vera Cruz, that ftands open to the Sea.
It makes a fine Shew, being built all with
good Stone. The Houfes are not high, but
the Walls very ftrong; the Roofs flattifh, after the *Spanifh* Fafhion, and covered with
Pantile. There is a ftrong Citadel, or Fort
at one End, mounted with many Guns, where
the Governor refides with a fmall Garrifon to
defend it. Though this Fort commands the
Town and Harbour, yet it has been twice taken. Firft, by Sir *Chriftopher Mims*, who a-
bout the Year 1659 having fummoned the
Governor, and afterwards ftaid three Days
for an Anfwer before he landed his Men, yet
then took it by Storm, and that only with
fmall Arms. This Man was fo bold, that
when the old *Jamaica* Privateers would have
perfuaded him to make ufe of Fraud, in taking the Place, he rejected their Counfel with
the utmoft Indignation, adding, " I come
" hither to get, and not to fteal Victories ; "
whereupon he marched to the Attack with
Drums beating and Colours flying. It was
taken a fecond Time by *Englifh* and *French*
Buchaneers by Surprize; this was in 1678 ;
and fince then, it has remained pretty quiet.
The

The chief Manufacture of the Country round about it is Cotton Cloth, which is the Clothing of all the Natives, and even some of the *Spaniards* of the poorer Sort. In the northern Part of the Province, and at a pretty considerable Distance from the Sea, stands the City of *Mereda*, which is the Capital, and the Seat of a Bishop. South East from it lies *Valadolid*, at no great Distance from the Bay of *Honduras*; it is a fair Town, and pleasantly situated, but withal very little known to Strangers. In the Isthmus, or Neck of Land, which joins this Peninsula to the Continent of *Mexico*, stands the Town of *Salamanca*, small indeed, but tolerably well built, and at present in a very thriving Condition.

C H A P. V.

Of the Audience of Guatimala.

THIS is the last Audience in the Kingdom of *Mexico*, and a noble Country it is, very little inferior to that of which we have been speaking, except in great Cities, and as capable of Improvement as any part of the *Spanish America*. It is bounded on the North by the Audience of *Mexico* and the Bay of *Honduras*; on the East by the *North Sea*, and some of the Provinces of South *America*; and on the South and West by the

Pacific

Pacific Ocean, or, as we commonly call them, the *South Seas* ; so that it enjoys as advantageous a Situation in respect to Commerce as could be wished. Its Provinces are eight in Number, of which we shall speak as succinctly as possible.

The first Province in this Audience is that of *Chiapa*, of a triangular Form, and so seated, that though it come very near the Sea, yet no part of it reaches it. It is bounded on the North by *Tlascala* and *Tabasco*, on the East by *Jucatan*, on the South by the Provinces of *Vera Paz*, and *Soconusco*, and on the West by the last mentioned Province, and that of *Tlascala*. The Middle of this Province lies sixty Leagues from either of the Seas, which renders the Air cold and dry, but withal very sharp, and very healthy. The Soil is diversified, and very fruitful, especially in Corn and Timber. Pears, Apples, and Quinces, are here in Plenty ; Cochineal grows wild ; and there is likewise both Cocoa and Cotton ; but that which is the peculiar Glory of this Province is its Breed of Horses, which are thought the very best in all *New Spain.* Heretofore there was a great deal of Gold found in this Province, but for want of *Indians*, and from the Discovery of richer Mines in other Places, this is now come to nothing. In the hilly Part near the Middle of *Chiapa*, there is such a Variety of vast and venomous Serpents, that no body will venture

to

to travel in thofe Parts. *Herrera* tells us, that thirty *Indians* going a fifhing in a Moonlight Night, as they were talking heard a loud Noife of hiffing, and turning, faw a Creature looking at them with Eyes like Fire, whereupon they ran up the Trees for Fear, whence they could fee it was a fort of Snake, having Feet about a Span long, and a kind of Wings above, the Creature about as long as a Horfe, and moved very flowly, for fear of which they never returned thither any more. Three of the *Quelene Indians* affirmed, that as they paffed over that River, they had feen the fame Creature hiffing; they defcribed it, and thought it came down to the River to drink, and one of the three, who was behind the others, died of the Fright.

There are two remarkable Cities in this Province, both of its own Name, the firft is, for Diftinction fake, called *Chiapa de los Indos*, that is, *Chiapa of the Indians*, becaufe it is inhabited by the Natives of the Country, who are beyond Exception the wittieft, wifeft, and moft civilized People in all the *Spanifh* Dominions, of which, if we had no other Proof, this might feem fufficient; that by a fpecial Grant from the King of *Spain*, the Citizens have the Privilege of chufing their own Magiftrates: The other City is called *Cividad Real*, that is, *the Royal City*, inhabited by *Spaniards*; it is a Bifhop's See, and reputed both rich and a pleafant Place. There
are

are a great many Curiofities in this little Province, which the narrow Compafs we are
bound to keep will not allow us to defcribe.

The Province of *Soconufco* lies next to that
of *Chiapa*, extending itfelf along the Coaft of
the *South Seas*, for the Space of thirty-five
Leagues. On the North it has the Province
of *Chiapa*; on the Eaft thofe of *Vera Paz*,
and *Guatimala*; on the South the *Pacific*
Ocean; the fame on the Weft, with part of
the Province of *Tlafcala*. The Air of the
Province is very far from being either healthy
or agreeable; Storms are frequent, and the
rainy Seafon continues long and troublefome;
the Soil too is none of the beft, fo that there
grows very little Corn; but this is in fome
meafure compenfated by the vaft Abundance
of Cocoa. There are however but very few
Spaniards in this Part of the Country, and
even fuch as are there, are not very rich; the
Reafon affigned for which is, the Temper of
the Natives, who are exceffively proud, more
numerous than elfewhere, and withal quar-
relfome and malicious, which renders them
cruel to each other, and much more fo to
Strangers. The fole Place of Confequence
ftands on the Shore of the *South Sea*, and in
the Language of the Natives is ftyled *Guevit-
lan*. A few *Spaniards* are fettled here, tho'
they will fcarce venture themfelves in any
other Part of the Province, which perhaps is
one

one Reason why they are desirous of having it made a Garrison.

Guatimala, properly so called, is the next Province; it also extends itself along the Coast of the *South Sea*, for upwards of one hundred Leagues; on the North it has the two Provinces of *Vera Paz* and *Honduras*; *Nicaragua* on the East, the Sea on the South, and on the West *Soconusco* : It does not rain frequently in this Province, but when it does, it falls for many Days together. Some Places are accounted as pleasant, and withal as healthy as any in *New Spain*, but generally speaking the Climate is not good. The Soil is however excellent, and fruitful beyond Comparison, especially in Corn and some valuable Fruits. Cotton is a Staple Commodity, as also Wax, for they have abundance of Bees, who make a Honey as white as the Comb itself. The Pastures also are so large and so fine, that it is impossible to form an Idea of the vast Number of Cattle which are fed in them. The Natives are naturally of a quiet, peaceable Disposition, but the *Spanish* Writers charge them with being extremely bigotted to their old Superstitions; in all Probability the Luxury of the *Spanish* Clergy, the Haughtiness and oppressive Behaviour of their Governors, and that rank Hypocrisy which is visible amongst all Degrees of Men, have prejudiced these unhappy Men against the Lights of the Gospel.

The

The ancient City of *Guatimala*, which was one of the fineft in *New Spain*, was entirely deftroyed in the Year 1541 by a Hurricane, whereby an hundred and twenty thoufand *Spaniards* loft their Lives. The Day before this dreadful Accident, fome *Indians* acquainted the Bifhop, that they heard a prodigious Noife under the burning Mountain feated 'above the City ; he treated this Information with Contempt. At Midnight however, a prodigious Noife was heard, as if in the Bowels of the Earth, and immediately a mighty Torrent of Water iffued out of the Mountain, which carried all before it, while a dreadful Earthquake heighten'd the Horror of the Scene, and hindered any of the miferable Inhabitants from making their Efcape. The *New Guatimala*, which is not only the Capital of this Province, but alfo of the Audience, a Place where the Prefident, and the Royal Courts refide, the Seat of a rich Bifhop, and the Center of Commerce in thefe Parts, ftands in a fine Plain, at a good Diftance from the *Vulcano*, which was fatal to the whole City ; however, it is far from being altogether out of Danger from Earthquakes, which are ftill frequent in thefe Parts. It is notwithftanding this, well built, and well inhabited, the Citizens carrying on a great Trade not only through all the Provinces of *Mexico*, but even into *Peru*, whereby fome become extraordinary rich, who then, generally

rally fpeaking, leave this Place, and go to refide at *Mexico*. The chief Commodities in
which they deal, are, Hides, Indigo, Anatta,
Silvefter, Cochineal, Cocoa, *&c.* and indeed
no City can be feated more conveniently for
an extenfive Trade than this is, and at the
fame time enjoy fo great a Security from the
Inroads of Pyrates and Privateers, for it ftands
eight Leagues from the *South Sea*, which, is
too far for the Buccaneers to march without
halting; and about forty Leagues from the
Gulph of *Mexico*, by which it alfo drives a
great Trade. The other confiderable Places
in this Province are *La Trenidad*, the Port
of *Acaxutla*, the Port of St. *Michael*, and
feveral other leffer Creeks and Bays. The
Vulcano near *St. Jago de Guatimala* is feen
at a great Diftance at Sea.

The Province of *Vera Cruz* lies between
Guatimala and the Gulph of *Honduras*. On
the North it has that Gulph, and the Province
of *Chiapa*; on the Eaft it has the Province
of *Honduras*, on the South that of *Guatimala*,
and on the Weft *Soconufco* and *Chiapa*. It is
but of fmall Extent, and in Figure a kind of
Oval, in Length forty-eight Leagues, and in
Breadth twenty-eight. As to the Climate,
the *Spanifh* Writers affirm that one half of
the Province is very pleafant, and withal very
healthy, whereas the other half is hot to the
laft degree, the Air participating of all the ill
Qualities which can be expected from fuch a
Tem-

Temperament. As to the Soil, the Country is very rough, and mountainous, yields little Corn, but abounds with Cedar Trees, and other useful Timber. The chief Commodities are Drugs, especially physical Gums, of which they have Plenty, as also Sarsaparilla, China Root, and Mechoacan. Formerly also there was some Gold in the *Gulfo dulce*, but of late we do not hear much of it ; and therefore it is reasonable to believe that either it is not sought for, or sought in vain.

This Province received its Name from an odd Accident ; it was brought under the Obedience of the *Spaniards* by the preaching of certain Monks. The Soldiers, on their first entering the Province, finding they had nothing to do, called it ironically *Terra de Guerra*, or the Land of War; but the graver Sort of People, with much more Propriety, *Vera Paz*, as much as to say, *the Land of true Peace.* I have a *Spanish* Writer before me, *Francisco de Coreal*, who relates a strange Thing of which he was Eye-witness in this Province. It cannot but entertain the Reader, and therefore I transcribe it precisely in his own Words. " It has been, says he, a Cus-
" tom time out of Mind, with the Clergy in
" the *Indies*, to oblige the poor Natives to
" carry Pictures to the Church ; these Pic-
" tures are always of some Saint, and they
" persuade them that this Devotion will prove
" a means of making them both rich and
                              " happy.

" happy. And the Reason assigned for it is,
" that as soon as it is set or hung up in the
" Church, the Soul of the Saint descends to
" inhabit it, and remains there so long as the
" *Indian* who brought it behaves as he ought
" to do. Thus far there is nothing amiss,
" for according to the Christianity settled in
" the *Indies*, this is no more than a pious
" Fraud of a laudable kind. But the Priests
" make it their Business to turn this Trick to
" their own Advantage, by rendering it a
" means of extorting Money from the poor
" ignorant People. In the first place he must
" be well paid for making the Soul of the
" Saint descend, then there must be an-
" nual Offerings to keep the Saint in good
" Humour with his *Indian* Patron, and his
" Family. But to my Story. It happen'd
" at *Coban*, in the Province of *Vera Paz*,
" as I passed through it, that a certain *In-*
" *dian* had paid his Priest for placing a Pic-
" ture of St. *Dominic* in a particular Place
" in the Church. It so happen'd that ano-
" ther *Indian*, who was jealous of this Man,
" and thought he would succeed too well, if
" his Saint had so advantageous a Place, came
" to the Priest, and offered him double as
" much, if he would place his Favourite
" there, who was St. *Ignatius*. Whether
" the latter Saint was more in the Priest's
" good Graces, or whether it was purely out
" of Respect to the Money, is uncertain ; but
" so

" fo it was, that St. *Dominic* was forced to
" let St. *Ignatius* take his Place.   Upon this
" a Quarrel commenced between the *Indi-*
" *ans,* which quickly fpread itfelf into two
" Parties, who after a fharp Battle of Words,
" fell to Blows, and feveral were left dead on
" the Spot, though the Saints did neither of
" them appear in the Field, but remained as
" quiet in the Church as if nothing had hap-
" pened."   The Reader will eafily perceive,
that even the Inquifition itfelf cannot hinder
fenfible *Spaniards* from treating the Frauds of
Churchmen with a juft Contempt.

The Capital of this Province is the little
City of *Vera Paz,* a Bifhop's See, rather
neatly than elegantly built; and the Inhabitants of which, if they are not extravagantly
rich, are however at their Eafe, and live free
from any Apprehenfions of being vifited by
Enemies.   All the Rivers of the Province run
into the *Gulfo Dulce,* which at length forms
a Lake, and then runs into the Bay of *Hon-*
duras, having a little Port at its Mouth,
where there are many fifhing Veffels, otherwife of fmall Trade, and very little frequented.

The Province of *Honduras* is the largeft in
all this Audience, lying from Weft to Eaft
above a hundred Leagues in Length, and
near fourfcore in Breadth.   It is bounded on
the North by the Bay of *Honduras,* on the
Eaft by the *North Sea,* on the South by the
Provinces

Provinces of *Nicaragua* and *Guatimala*, on
the Weſt by *Vera Paz*. The Air is very
wholeſome, and the Soil extremely fruitful.
It abounds with Corn, both *European* and
Indian; its Paſtures are rich and fine, and
maintain conſequently vaſt Quantities of Cattle. The Rivers of this Province, moſt of
them overflow like the *Nile*, and contribute
thereby to the Richneſs of the Soil. Its principal Commodities are Cotton, Wax, *Vigonia*
Wooll, Logwood, *&c.* beſides Gold and Silver, of which anciently there were more than
there is now, the *Indians* in this Province
being wore out, and with them the Mines.

The principal City in this Province is that
of *Valadolid*, called by the *Indians Comaya-
gua*. It ſtands at a great Diſtance from the
Sea, pretty near the Frontiers of the Province
of *Guatimala*; it is now the Biſhop's See,
which was removed in 1558 from *Truxillo*;
it is pleaſantly ſeated in a Valley, and for a
Spaniſh inland City well inhabited. Beſides
this, there is the aforeſaid Port of *Truxillo*,
and towards the weſtern Extremity another
called *Porto Cavallo*, a ſmall Town, but famous for being the Port of the City of *Guatimala*, to and from which all Commodities
are carried by a Road cut immediately through
the Rocks on Horſeback; whence the Name
of the Place, which is but thinly inhabited,
except occaſionally, when a Regiſter-Ship
arrives from *Europe*, when there is a Sort of
Fair

Fair held here ; but of late this rarely happens; and therefore this Port is on the Decay, though formerly very famous.

Nicaragua is the next Province, and lies
both on the *North* and on the *South Seas.* It
is bounded northwards by the Province of
Honduras, on the Eaſt by the Sea, on the
South by the Province of *Coſta Rica*, and the
Pacific Ocean ; on the Weſt by *Guatimala*.
The Air of this Province is the beſt and clear-
eſt in the whole Kingdom of *Mexico*, and
the Soil moſt excellent ; it abounds with Corn
and with Fruits, as alſo with very fine Timber ; Wax, Cordage, Tar, and Sugar, are the
principal Commodities it affords. One may
gueſs how pleaſant, and plentiful a Country
this is, by its being called the *Paradiſe of
Mahomet.* What adds much to its Beauty,
is the noble Lake of the ſame Name, which
is near a hundred and thirty Leagues in Circuit ; it comes within twenty Miles of the
South Sea, and iſſues into the *North Sea* by a
Canal, at the Mouth of which is the Port of
St. John. This Lake abounds with Fiſh,
which are ſo much the better on account of
its having a Flux and Reflux, like the Sea.

The *Indians* in this Province are better
treated than elſewhere, and their Towns are
neater and larger than in other Places, which
may very poſſibly be owing to their having
no Mines, for otherwiſe, no doubt, they
would have been deſtroyed in digging and
labour-

labouring to fatiate the Avarice of their Mafters.   The Spaniards employ themfelves generally fpeaking, either in Commerce or in
Farming, for both which no Country can be
more happily feated.   Its native Commodities are of great Value, particularly Cacao;
of which, though they have not the greateft
Plenty, yet the Cacao of *Nicaragua* is the
largeft and the fineft in the World.   They
have likewife Manufactures of feveral Kinds,
efpecially of Cotton, which are rare in this
Part of the World; and as Trade and Induftry make the People active and wealthy, fo
the *Spanifh* Writers obferve, that they are
very high fpirited, that is, they will not
truckle to oppreffive Governors, or fubmit
tamely to that ill Ufage which they fee plainly proves the Ruin of their Neighbours.

The City of *Leon* is the Capital of this
Province; it ftands on the Edge of the Lake,
and at twenty Miles Diftance from the *South
Sea*.   The Plain in which it is feated is fandy,
furrounded on every Side with fine Meadows,
the Houfes are not high built, but ftrong, and
large, with Gardens about them; their Walls
Stone, and the Covering Pantile.   Befides
the Cathedral, for it is a rich Bifhoprick, there
are three Parifh Churches.   In the Year 1685
it was taken and plundered by our Buccaneers under the Command of the Captains
Swan and *Townly*, who burnt it to the Ground;
but it has been fince rebuilt and fortified.   Its

Port

Port on the *South Sea* is called *Rialexa,* and is a very good one ; it ſtands in a Plain by a ſmall River ; it has three Churches and an Hoſpital, and ſerves not only for the carrying on the Trade of *Leon,* but of *Guatimala.* There are noble Warehouſes near the Sea, and many Factors reſide therein ; but the Air is bad, and therefore the Place is, generally ſpeaking, but thinly inhabited. It was taken at the ſame time with the City of *Leon,* by the Buccaneers I before mentioned. From this Port, and even at Sea, may be ſeen a burning Mountain juſt above the City laſt mentioned, and thence called by the Seamen, *the Vulcano of* Leon. It was formerly very terrible, but it has not burnt ſo much of late. On the Eaſt Side of the Lake, at the Diſtance of twenty-five Miles from *Leon,* ſtands the City of *Granada,* which is much the better built of the two, and is withal a Place of far greater Trade, as having the Conveniency of ſending Goods by the Lake to *Carthagena,* and other Places. The Navigation of the Lake is tedious, though not dangerous, chief-ly on account of the Idleneſs and Want of Application in the *Spaniards,* who from be-ing very active and vigorous as they were when they firſt ſettled in this Country, are now become ſlow, cautious, and ſo wedded to their own Opinions, that Cuſtom is always a ſtronger Argument with them than Reaſon. It is ſaid confidently, perhaps not without
Truth,

Truth, that there is a great deal of Smuggling carried on by the Help of this Navigation, which certainly might be ufed to much better purpofe than it is, if the Poffeffors of this Country were of the fame Difpofition with other Nations.

But becaufe the River which iffues from the Lake, and falls by three Mouths or Channels into the *North Sea*, is interrupted with Cataracts, they trouble not themfelves about it ; and perhaps they are afraid, if they fhoud take pains to remove thefe Difficulties, and to open, as they might, a commodious Port on this Side, it might invite Enemies to think not only of plundering, but taking Poffeffion of it, which would be a fatal Thing indeed.

The next Province is called by the *Spaniards Cofta Rica*, or the *Rich Coaft*. It lies upon both Seas, and yet the Communication between them is much obftructed by the Roughnefs of the Country, and by a long Chain of Mountains which runs acrofs it from Eaft to Weft. On the North it is bounded by the Province of *Nicaragua*, and the Sea ; on the Weft by the Province of *Veragua*, on the South by the *Pacific* Ocean, and on the Eaft by the Province of *Nicaragua*. Its Climate is far from being good, and its Soil is yet worfe, being mountainous, barren, and woody ; yet there are in it fome very confiderable Places, fuch as *Carthage*, which as it is the Capital, fo it is feated in the Heart of
the

the Province, in the Midway between *Ni-coya*, which ftands on the South, and the Port of *St. John* in the *North Seas.* The Reader will naturally wonder at feeing this Account of the Province fuit fo ill with its Name; but this Difficulty may be eafily cleared up, if we confider that thefe Places received their Appellations when they were firft difcovered, and of courfe received fuch Denominations as fuited beft with the Notions of thofe who impofed them. The Reafon they call this *Cofta Rica*, was becaufe its Inhabitants were poffeffed of a great deal of Gold, and parted with it freely ; whence the *Spaniards* concluded they came by it eafily, and that there was abundance of it in this Country. In this, however, they were in fome meafure miftaken, for as the Gold was chiefly taken out of their Rivers, fo the Quantity decreafed in proportion as the People were diminifhed, who were wont to fearch for it, a thing to which none of the *Indians* are much inclined now. Mines however there are in this Country both of Gold and Silver, though not fo rich as formerly.

The laft Province in the Audience of *Gua-timala* is that of *Veragua*, of no great Extent, but excellent in its Situation. It lies on both Seas, which bound it North and South; on the Eaft it has part of the *Terra Firma*, on the Weft the Province of *Cofta Rica*. It is in Length about fifty, and in Breadth about twenty-

twenty-five Leagues. The Climate is not to
be boasted of, its Soil very indifferent, the
Country being mountainous, and overgrown
with Woods, affording very little either of
arable or pasture Lands ; but then it abounds
in what the *Spaniards* esteem much more
than even the Necessaries of Life, that is,
Gold, of which there is more in this little
Province than in all *New Spain* besides, which
is chiefly got out of their Rivers, especially
after hard Rains or Storms. The Capital of
the Province is the *City of the Conception*, so
called in honour of the Conception of *Christ.*
It is both large and rich, standing not far
from the Coast of the *North Sea.* In the
Heart of the Country is the Town of *Santa
Fé*, near which there are Gold Mines : On
the South Coast lies the Town of *Parita*,
whence the Gulph so called takes its Name.
Some understanding Persons have thought it
very practicable to make a Descent on this
Coast, and even to take the *City of the Conception* during a War with *Spain*; which I
mention as a Matter that may deserve Enquiry.

CHAP.

C H A P. VIII.

Of the Islands in North America.

IN speaking generally of the Islands, yet in Possession of the *Spaniards* in this Part of the World, we shall divide them only into the *Lucaios,* and *Antilles.* Of the former we shall give some Account in this Chapter, and of the latter in the next.

Thefe Islands, according to the *Spanish* Orthography, are called *Lucayo. Herrera* tells us they may be divided (for indeed they are numerous enough to need a Division) into three Parts or Parcels; and of these he gives us a better Account than any other Author I have met with. The first, says he, are the *Bahama Islands,* which gave Name to the Channel where the Currents are most impetuous. The second are called *de los Organos,* and the third those of *the Martyrs,* which are next to the *Cayos* of the *Tortoises* to the Westward, which last being all Sand, cannot be seen at a Distance, and therefore many Ships have perished on them, and all along that Coast of the Channel of *Bahama,* and the Islands *Tortugas. Havana,* in the Island of *Cuba,* is to the Southward, and *Florida* to the Northward; and between them are the aforesaid Islands of *Organos, Bahama, Martyrs,* and *Tortugas,* having a Channel with a

vio-

violent Current, twenty Leagues over in the
narroweſt Place, between *Havana* and *Los
Matyres*; and fourteen Leagues from *Los
Matyres* to *Florida*, between Iſlands to the
Weſtward; and the wideſt Part of this Paſſage to the Weſtward is forty Leagues, with
many Shoals, and deep Channels; but there
is no Way for Ships or Brigantines, only for
Canoes; but the Paſſage from *Havana* to
come to *Spain*, is along the Channel of *Bahama*, between the ſaid *Havana*, the *Mar-
tyres*, the *Lucayos*, and *Cape Canaveral*.

I think it unneceſſary to trouble the Reader
with the Names of theſe Iſlands, ſince they
are generally uninhabited, though in many of
them the Air is temperate, the Soil fruitful;
and there is great Plenty both of Wood and
Water. We have already obſerved, in the
firſt Book, that one of theſe Iſlands was the
firſt Land made by *Columbus*; but they were
in another Condition then than now, being
well inhabited, and thoroughly cultivated,
whereas at preſent they are ſo many Deſerts.
The ancient Inhabitants were a fairer People
than thoſe on the Continent, were ſtronger,
and had better Health. The *Spaniards* obſerving this, tranſported them from their own
Iſlands in order to make them work in the
Mines, where they died by Thouſands, which
made their Maſters think of nothing but fetch-
ing more, till at laſt the Natives entirely a-
bandoned theſe Iſlands, and returned to the
Main,

Main, carrying with them an Antipathy to the *Spaniards*, which Time hath not been able to abate. It is undoubtedly Want of good Policy which has made the *Spaniard* quit Places of such mighty Importance, as these Islands are to him, and no doubt whenever the Administration at *Madrid* come to think seriously of providing for the Safety of their *American* Dominions, they will not fail to direct the planting or fortifying at least one or two of these Islands, which will not only secure the Passage of their Fleets, but prove in many other Respects of infinite Service.

It is pretty remarkable, that this Error in the *Spanish* Government was pointed out so long ago as in the Time of our Queen *Elizabeth*, and thence was inferred the Advantage of our settling here, which seems to have been as little minded, though perhaps it was better understood. After the Settlement of *Carolina*, some Attempts were made from thence upon these Islands, but hitherto they have been of little use, though we still keep some of them, and, if I mistake not, there was among other Bubbles in the Year 1720, one that went under the Name of the *Bahama Islands*, and, as I take it, proposed a Settlement there. Since then these Isles have been pretty much frequented by Pyrates, till they were by degrees rooted out and destroyed. At present I doubt our Colonies there are but in a very indifferent Condition, though of the highest Consequence

fequence to us in fecuring the Freedom of our
Navigation, and curbing the Infolence of the
Spaniards, which might be eafily done by
fortifying any one of thefe Iflands.

C H A P. IX.

Of the Iflands of Cuba, Hifpaniola, *and*
Porto Rica.

IN that Part of the *North Sea*, which lies
between 8, and 28 Degrees of Latitude,
and between 293° and 316° of Longitude,
there are fcattered a Multitude of Iflands, to
which the *Spaniards* have given the general
Name of *Antilles.* There have been many
Reafons affigned for their being fo called, but
I think none of them very probable, much
lefs fatisfactory, and fhall not therefore repeat them. Let it fuffice that the *Spaniards*
ufually divide them into larger and leffer.
Among the former are *Cuba, Hifpaniola*, and
Porto Rico, which are to make the Subject
of this Chapter. As for the other two Iflands,
which are ufually reckoned among the larger
Antilles, viz. *Trinidad*, and *Jamaica*, the
former is not very confiderable, and the latter
not being now in the Hands of the *Spaniards*, we have not thought it neceffary to enter into a particular Account of either.

The Ifland of *Cuba* is the moft confiderable of the three, and, to fay the Truth, is one
of

of the fineft Iflands in the Univerfe. It lies
ftretched out from Weft to Eaft, having *Florida* and the *Lucayos* on the North, *Hifpaniola* on the Weft, *Jamaica* and the fouthern
Continent on the South, and the Gulph of
Mexico on the Eaft. It lies between 19° 30′
and 23° of North Latitude, and from 293°
to 304° of Longitude. *Herrera* fays that it
is two hundred and thirty Leagues in Length,
and in the broadeft Part, which is toward the
Ifland of *Hifpaniola*, forty Leagues, in the
narroweft about twelve.

It lies within the Tropick of *Cancer*, and
is by far the moft temperate and pleafant of
all the *Antilles*. The *Europeans*, who are
generally troubled with the Heat of thefe
Parts, confefs themfelves agreeably refrefhed
by the cooling Winds, which are felt Morning and Evening throughout the Ifland. As
to the Soil, it differs pretty much in the feveral Parts of the Ifland. All the weftern
Part of the Country is plain, and if it were
properly cultivated might be fruitful, though
as it is it muft be owned that much cannot be
faid of it on that Head. The eaftern Part is
exceedingly mountainous; and from thence
there runs a Chain of Hills almoft throughout the Ifland ; but the farther Weft you go
they are the lefs rough and barren. From
thefe Hills there run down to the North and
South many Rivers, and amongft them two
pretty confiderable, which befides their be-
ftowing

flowing Verdure and Coolness as they pass,
are full of Fish, and those very large and
good. The greatest Inconveniency in *Cuba*,
is its being overgrown with Woods, which
whatever the *Spaniards* may pretend, must
be owing to their own Laziness, and nothing
else; for, as they admit, the Country was
well peopled when first discovered; it must
necessarily have been less thick set with Trees.
Amongst these, however, there are some very
valuable, particularly Cedars of an enormous
Size, and other Sorts of odoriferous Wood.
Birds there are of all kinds, more than in
any other of the Islands; and the *Spaniards*
at their first Landing having suffered some
black Cattle to stray into the Woods, they by
degrees turned wild, and have furnished the
Island with such a Breed as make now the
principal Part of its Riches. We have before observed that its Rivers abound with Fish,
to which we must now add, that they abound
also with a Creature terrible alike to Fish,
Beasts and Men, *viz.* the Aligator. It is
thought there are more of this Species here
than in any other Part of the known World.
Most Writers confound this Creature with
the Crocodile, and indeed the *Spaniards* have
but one Name, *viz. Caymanes*, to express
both; yet it is certain that there is a Difference, and amongst other Particulars, in these.
The Legs of the Crocodile are longer than
those of the Aligator; his Flesh is not musky,

as

as the other's is; the Knots on the Back are thicker, higher and firmer; but the plaineft and moft difcernible Difference, and which indeed difcovers itfelf at firft Sight is this, that the Crocodile carries his Tail cock'd and crooked, with the Tip turning back, like a Bow, whereas the Aligator drags his on the Ground.

This Ifland was difcovered by the famous *Chriftopher Columbus,* who had but a very flight View of it, which yet was fatal to the Natives, for they having prefented him with Gold, fome Pieces of which he carried into *Spain,* it occafioned an immediate Refolution to fettle in it. This was performed in 1511 by *John Velafquez,* who tranfported hither about 500 Foot and 80 Horfe. He was a haughty, cruel, inexorable Man, and the Treatment the poor People met with from him, was fuch as we want both Room and Will to relate. The worthy Bifhop of *Chiapa,* who was an Eye-Witnefs of his Barbarity, hath publifhed it to the World, and computed, that by thefe horrid Severities, near five Millions of People were deftroyed. Later Writers, inftead of fpeaking tenderly of this Matter, and making fome Amends to their Memory, do all that is in their Power to give this horrid Proceeding the Air of Juftice by reprefenting the *Indians* as the moft bafe and wicked Nation that ever lived. *Herrera* tells us, that they were a very good fort of of People, and well temper'd. They had, says he, Caciques and Towns of two or three hundred Houses, with several Families in each of them, as was usual in *Hispaniola.* They had no Religion, as having no Temples, or Idols, or Sacrifices; but they had the Physicians, or conjuring Priests, as in *Hispaniola*, who, it was thought, had Communication with the Devil, and their Questions answered by him. They fasted three or four Months to obtain that Favour, eating nothing but the Juice of Herbs, and when reduced to extreme Weakness, they were worthy of that hellish Apparition; and to be informed whether the Seasons of the Year would be favourable or otherwise; what Children would be born; whether those born would live, and such like Questions. These were their Oracles; and these Conjurers they called *Behiques*, who led the People into many Superstitions and Fopperies, curing the Sick by blowing on them, and such other exterior Actions, mumbling some Words between their Teeth. These People of *Cuba* knew that Heaven, the Earth, and other Things, had been created, and said, they had much Information concerning the Flood, and that the World had been destroyed by Water from three Persons that came three several Ways. Men of above seventy Years of Age said, that an old Man, knowing the Deluge was to come, built a great Ship, and went into it with

with his Family, and abundance of Animals ; that he fent out a Crow, which did not return, ftaying to feed on the dead Bodies, and afterwards returned with a green Branch, with other Particulars, as far as *Noah*'s Son's covering him when drunk, and the other fcoffing at it ; adding, that the *Indians* defcended from the latter, and therefore had no Coats nor Cloaks ; but that the *Spaniards*, defcending from the other that covered him, were therefore cloathed, and had Horfes.

The true Reafon, in all Probability, why the *Spaniards* deftroyed with fo little Pity fo vaft a Number of innocent People, was a covetous Defire of poffeffing the whole Ifland, and all its real and fuppofed Riches ; for at this time they fancied that the Parts of the Ifland poffeffed by the Natives were exceffively rich in Gold, of which, while they fuffered them to live, the *Spaniards* did really receive a very large Share. But fince the Extirpation of the *Indians*, there has been very little, and at prefent there is fcarce any Gold at all found ; which fome would make a Judgment on the *Spaniards* for their Cruelty. For my part, I think the Matter eafily unriddled. The Gold, I fuppofe, was taken out of the Rivers, which required not only a great deal of Time and Patience, but many Hands, and a perfect Knowledge of the Places where it was to be found. This accounts for the lofing that precious Metal with the

People,

People, and shews how weak a Point of Policy this Doctrine of Extirpation really is.

The City of *St. Jago de Cuba* is the most
ancient in the Island, and is, generally speaking, esteemed its Capital, though now the
Governor resides at the *Havana*, and only
such of the *Spaniards* as have Estates on the
Island, and are contented with their Possessions, without meddling much in Trade, inhabit this Place, which has a declining Aspect, and preserves only the Ruins of its former Greatness. Yet even this City has a noble, safe and commodious Port, inferior to
the *Havana* only in its Situation, that being
on the North West Side of the Island, towards the Channel of *Bahama*, whereas *St.
Jago de Cuba* lies on the North East, and
commands the windward Passage.

As for the City and Port of *Havana*, it
stands almost directly south of *Cape Florida*,
and consequently commands the Gulph of
that Name. It was built by *James Velasquez*, who, as we have before observed, conquered the Island of *Cuba*, and settled a little
Town, which was the Mother of this, in
1511. It was originally called *the Port of
Carennas*; afterwards, when the City by its
Alteration of Site and Encrease of Wealth
grew considerable, it was called *St. Christo-
pher of the Havana*. These Alterations
happened but by slow Degrees, as we may
conceive from the following Account of the
Accidents

Accidents which have befallen it. In 1536 it was taken by a *French* Pirate, and was of fo inconfiderable a Value, that it was ranfomed for feven hundred Pieces of Eight. It was taken fometime after by the *Englifh*, a fecond Time by the *French*; nor was it, till the Reign of *Philip* II. of *Spain*, that the Importance of it was thoroughly underftood, and any Care taken in fortifying it. What was then done, proved not fufficient, and moft of the Fortifications were in a very bad Condition, when *Francis Coreal* was there in 1666, and very little better when he vifited it again, twenty Years afterwards. Since the Acceffion of the Houfe of *Bourbon* to the Throne of *Spain*, more Pains have been taken about it, and therefore we fhall defcribe firft the City, and then the Port, in the Condition they now are.

The City of *Havanna*, according to the laft and moft exact Map of thefe Parts, lies under 23° 12′ of Latitude, and confequently within 20′ of the Tropick of *Cancer*; and its Longitude Weft from *London* is 82° 13′. It ftands on the Weft Side of the Harbour, in a very beautiful and pleafant Plain, having the Sea before it, and being furrounded on all Sides by two Branches of the River *Lagida*. The Buildings are fair, but not high, built of Stone, and make a very good Appearance, though it is faid they are but meanly furnifhed. Here are eleven Churches and

Mona-

Monafteries, and two handfome Hofpitals.
The Churches are rich and magnificent ; that
dedicated to St. *Clara* having feven Altars, all
adorned with Plate to a great Value ; and
the Monaftery adjoining contains a hundred
Nuns with their Servants, all habited in Blue.
It is not, as fome have reported, a Bifhop's
See, though the Bifhop generally refides there,
but the Cathedral is at St. *Jago*, and the Revenue of this Prelate not lefs than fifty thoufand Pieces of Eight *per Annum*. Authors
differ exceedingly as to the Number of Inhabitants in this City. A *Spanifh* Writer, who
was there in 1700, and who had Reafon to
be well acquainted with the Place, computed
them at twenty-fix thoufand; and we may
very well fuppofe that they are increafed fince.
They are a more polite and fociable People
than the Inhabitants of any of the Ports on
the Continent, and of late imitate the *French*
both in their Drefs and in their Manners.
One Part of the Ifland is under the Jurifdiction of this City, as the other is under that
of St. *Jago*; but the Diftrict belonging to
the *Havana* is by far the beft cultivated,
and has the moft Towns and Villages in it;
and thefe are not above fix in Number, which
fhews how ftrangely Things are managed in
this Part of the World.

The Port is not only the beft in the *Weft
Indies*, but perhaps one of the fineft in the
Univerfe : It is fo capacious, that a thoufand
Sail

Sail of Ships may ride there commodiously without either Cable or Anchor; and there is, generally speaking, six Fathom Water in the Bay. The Entrance is by a Channel a-bout ¼ of a Mile in Length, which is pretty narrow, and through it you come into the Bay, which lies like a Bason at the Bottom of it, with a small Island seated in the East Corner thereof. At the Entrance of the Channel there are two strong Castles, which are supposed to be capable of defending the Place against any Number of Ships. The first of these is styled *El Morro*, on the East Side of the Channel. It is a kind of a Tri-angle fortified with Bastions, on which are mounted about forty Pieces of Cannon, car-rying a Ball of twenty-four Pound Weight. From this Castle there runs a Line, mount-ed with twelve heavy Cannon, styled *the twelve Apostles*, almost level with the Water, and carrying each a Ball of six and thirty Pounds. On the other Side of the Channel stands a strong Fort, called *the Puntal* by some Authors, and indeed by the *Spanish* Writer I mostly use, styled *Mesa de Maria:* it is a regular Square, with good Bastions, well mounted with Cannon. Between this City and the Sea there is a Watch-Tower, where a Man sits in a round Lanthorn at the Top, and on the Appearance of Ships at Sea, puts out as many Flags from thence as there are Sail. Some Writers place this Tower on the

the other Side the Channel : perhaps a new
one may be built there.   The third is ftyled
the Fort : it is a fmall, but ftrong Work on
the Weft Side, towards the End of the narrow Channel, with four large Baftions and a
Platform, mounted with fixty Pieces of heavy Cannon.   Befides thefe there are two
Forts, one on the Eaft Side, called *Cojemar*,
the other on the Weft, called *the Fort of*
Chorrera, of twelve Guns each.   The Governor is, generally fpeaking, a Perfon of
known Courage and Capacity, and has a very
numerous Garrifon, as indeed he ought to have,
confidering that it is very properly ftyled *the*
Key of the Weft Indies ; and if they loft it,
the whole of the *Spanifh* Negotiation muft
lie at the Mercy of the Power poffeffed thereof.   If ever this Place fhould be attacked by
us, it muft be by a Land Force, for it is impoffible to make any Impreffion here by a
Fleet only.   The Caftles, which defend the
Channel, muft be taken before we can pretend to enter the Port ; and indeed were they
once taken, the reft of the Defign would eafily fucceed.

   We are now to fpeak of the Commerce in
this Port, which is the moft confiderable of
any in *America*.   We will, for the Sake of
Perfpicuity, divide it into the particular Commerce of the *Ifle of Cuba*, and into the general by the *Galleons*.   The former confifts
in Hides, ufually ftyled, *of the Havana,*
                                                which

which are excellent and of great Value; Sugar, which is alfo a good Commodity; Tobacco, admirable in its kind ; Ginger, Maftic, Alloes, Sarfaparilla, other Drugs, and great Quantities of Tortoifefhell. It muft be obferved, that the Commerce of the Ifland of *Cuba* is not entirely confined to the *Havana*, but extends itfelf to other Ports, particularly St. *Jago*, where there are frequently many little Veffels from the *Canaries*, and other Parts, which trade entirely for the Commodities of the Country. As to the general Commerce, this Port is the Place of Rendezvous for all the Ships which return into *Spain* from the *Indies* ; fo that here are frequently fifty or fixty Sail in the Port at once. While they ride here, there is a Fair kept on Shore, where they trade for immenfe Sums, and with fo great Honour, that it is faid they never open the Bales, but take the Goods according to the Bills of Parcels, without any Infpection. While the Fleet is in the Bay, Provifions are exceffively dear on Shore, and Money is fo plenty, that a *Spaniard* expects half a Piece of Eight a Day from a Male Slave, and half as much from a Female, out of what they earn by their Labour. The Fleet generally fails from thence through the Channel of *Bahama*, in the Month of *September*, and is the richeft in the World, fince in Silver and Merchandize there is feldom lefs than thirty Millions of Pieces of Eight on board, or fix

Millions

Millions feven hundred and fifty thoufand
Pounds of our Money.   Dr. *Gemelli Careri*,
who was here in 1698, tells us of an extraordinary Pearl that he faw here ; it was in
Shape a perfect Pear, in Weight fixty Grains,
and was abfolutely clear and ripe.   This
Pearl was taken at *Panama* by a Black belonging to a Prieft, who refufed to fell it to
the Viceroy of *Peru* for feventy thoufand
Pieces of Eight, faying, He would carry it
to his Majefty himfelf ; but he died at the
Havana ; and the Pearl was fent to the
King by another Prieft to whom he confi-
ded it.

There are in the Ifland of *Cuba* fome other
good Ports, particularly that of *Honda*, which
lies to the Weftward of the *Havana*, and is
very little inferior to it in any Refpect, though
it is not much frequented. Some other Creeks
alfo might be improved into better Ports than
moft on the Continent, but for Want of Inhabitants they are neglected.   For the fame
Reafon the Copper Mines are not wrought
to any very confiderable Profit, and perhaps
they would not be wrought at all, but that
out of them is taken the Metal requifite for
making the Brafs Cannon, not only for the
Fortifications here, but throughout the *Weft
Indies.*   The *French* have more than once
difcovered an Inclination to fettle on *Cuba*,
as well as they have done on *Hifpaniola* ; but
the Treaty of *Utrecht* has put an End to this
                                    Project,

Project, fince it gives us an unqueftionable Right to hinder them if ever they fhould attempt it.

The Ifland of *Hifpaniola*, which is alfo called *St. Domingo*, was by the Natives ftyled *Hayti*. It lies in the midft, between *Cuba*, *Jamaica*, and *Porto Rico*, and is feparated from the laft only by a narrow Channel. It is generally ftyled the fecond of thefe Iflands, *Cuba* being held the firft; but upon a more exact Computation, it is found at leaft as large, extending in Length from Eaft to Weft four hundred and eighty Miles, and in Breadth from North to South, about ninety. It is furrounded by little Iflands which are very convenient, and of great Advantage to the Inhabitants. The Climate is according to its Situation, extremely hot, yet not without fome Qualification from the Winds, which blow here at certain Seafons: It alfo rains here at certain times exceffively, yet not in all Places alike; but on the Whole it cannot be faid that the Air is by any means comparable to that of *Cuba*. The Soil alfo differs very confiderably, being in fome Places extremely rich and fertile, in others miferably poor and barren.

Chriftopher Columbus difcovered this Country in 1492, as we have fhewn in the former Book. He built here the Cities of *St. Domingo* and *Ifabella*. By degrees the *Spaniards* conquered and deftroyed the Inhabitants,

tants, though not without a great deal of Refiftance, as will be eafily conceived when the Reader is told, that in the Extirpation of thefe People there were not lefs than three Millions of Souls deftroyed. While the Natives enjoyed their Poffeffions, the *Spanifh* Inhabitants lived much more happily, and enjoyed much greater Affluence than they have done fince; for thefe People cultivated their Lands, fupplied them with Fifh, and brought them fome fmall Quantities of Gold, wherever they had it; whereas now the far greater Part of what the *Spaniards* claim rather than poffefs, is Defert, and produces them little or nothing.

The *Spaniards* were for many Years the fole Poffeffors of this Ifland, and for fome part of that Time it was a very flourifhing Colony; for as it was the firft of their Difcoveries, fo it was the Center of their Commerce in thefe Parts; but when *Peru* fell into their Hands, and they began to make great Additions to their Territories on the Continent of *North America*, this Ifland began to be flighted, which encouraged the *French* about the Middle of the laft Century to fix themfelves on the North Side of the Ifland, whence at firft they might have eafily been driven; but they are now grown fo ftrong, and have improved their Settlements fo much, that it would be not only impracticable to attempt the removing them, but
they

they might, if they pleafed, without any confiderable Difficulty, make themfelves Mafters of the whole Ifland, which in all Probability they would have done, if the Benefits which they draw from the Neighbourhood of the *Spaniards* were not greater than any which could be derived from their Expulfion.

The Commodities of this Country are Hides, Sugar, Ginger, Cocoa, Wax, Honey, Ambergreafe, various kinds of Woods for the Ufe of Dyers. There were formerly Mines of Gold, the richeft that ever were heard of, and Mines of Silver of very confiderable Value, but they are now abandoned as not worth the working ; yet for all this, fome of the old *Spanifh* Planters live here in great State and Plenty, and which is more extraordinary, confidering how ill this Climate agrees with new Comers, they live in good Health, and to great Ages, fome of them having reached to a hundred and twenty, and many of them exceeding fourfcore.

The Capital of the whole Ifland is the City of *St. Domingo.* It is feated on the South Side of the Ifland, at the Mouth of the River of *Ozama*, in a fine Plain, which renders it extremely pleafant, and fhews it to great Advantage from the Sea. It is à large well-built City, and contains feveral Edifices more magnificent than is ufual in the *Indies*. It has a fine Cathedral, feven large Monafteries,

ries, and two Nunneries; the Governor-General of the *Spanish* Islands resides here, as also the Judges of the Royal Courts, which makes it the supreme Seat of Justice, and thereby secures it from falling into Ruin, as otherwise it certainly would do through the Loss of Trade. Besides, it is also the Seat of an Archbishop, to whom the Bishops of the *Conception* in this Island, of *St. John de Porto Rico*, of *St. Jago de Cuba*, of *Venezuela* in *New Castile*, and of *Honduras*, are Suffragans: Whence it is easy to conceive that its principal Inhabitants are Lawyers and Clergy. It has also a good Port, and the greatest Part of the Trade that is carried on by the *Spaniards* is here. In 1586 it was taken by Sir *Francis Drake*, who held it a whole Month, and then burnt a Part of it, but spared the rest on the Inhabitants agreeing to give him sixty thousand Pieces of Eight by way of Ransom. It quickly recovered its Lustre, and would have maintained it if Trade had not decayed; as it is, it makes a good Appearance, and the Number of its Inhabitants, including People of all Complexions, Negroes as well as *Spaniards*, is thought to exceed twenty-five thousand, and some say there are many more.

Other Cities there were in this Island, which formerly made a considerable Figure, such as that of the *Conception*, which is a Bishop's See, *St. Jago Cavalleros*, inhabited by

by Buccaneers or Hunters; and then as to
Ports, they had *Puerta de la Plata*, and
many others, which were deftroyed fo often
by Pirates, that at length they funk into
Fifhing Villages, no longer worth the taking.
Of late Years it is faid the *Spanifh* Affairs in
this Ifland are on the mending hand.

The Streight between the Iflands of *Cuba*
and *Hifpaniola*, which is about 18 Leagues
over, is that which is fo well known to us by
the Name of *the Windward Paffage*, by
which our Ships fometimes return from *Jamaica*; but as this Paffage is both difficult
and dangerous, it is feldom that Ships make
Choice of it, but on the contrary, fail quite
round the Ifland of *Cuba*, and fo through the
Gulph of *Florida*. Hence in few Words,
the Importance of keeping thefe Paffages free
and open is made apparent, for otherwife
not only our Navigation fuffers, but by degrees the Inhabitants of the Ifland of *Jamaica*
muft be undone, and that Ifland return into
the Hands of its old Poffeffors the *Spaniards*,
even without the Trouble of an Invafion.

St. John de Porto Rico, though it be lefs
than either *Cuba* or *Hifpaniola*, is however a
very fine Ifland. It is in Length from Eaft
to Weft about 150 Miles, in Breadth between
50 and 60; the Midft of the Ifland is in the
Latitude of 18°. As to the Climate, it is exceffively hot in Summer, which lafts from
May to *September*; and very moift and rainy
in

in the Winter; the Soil however is extremely rich and fertile, abounding in fine Meadows, well ſtocked with wild Cattle, which however were originally of *Spaniſh* Breed.

This Iſland, as we have obſerved elſewhere, was by its ancient Inhabitants ſtyled *Boriquen*; it was diſcovered by Admiral *Columbus* in 1493, who called it by the Name of *Saint John the Baptiſt*. It coſt the *Spaniards* however a good deal of Trouble to reduce it, the Inhabitants being a brave gallant People, and extremely fond of Liberty. By degrees, notwithſtanding, and by dint of the mighty Advantages they had over them in the Art of War, the new Comers not only conquered, but extirpated the Natives, though at their firſt Arrival they were not leſs than ſix hundred thouſand. The Conſequence was the ſame here as elſewhere, the Deſtruction of the People has been the Ruin of the Iſland; and there is no longer any conſiderable Quantity of Gold to be met with here, which formerly was found in vaſt Quantities, and for the Sake of which theſe poor innocent People were ſlaughtered; and ſuch Effects muſt in the Nature of things always attend on ſuch baſe and bloody Expedients.

The Capital of the Iſland is the City of *Porto Rico*, which ſome ſuppoſe to have been ſo called from the Excellence of its Port, which is indeed as good as can be, and where the largeſt Ships may lie in the utmoſt Safety.

Safety. *Porto Rico* stands on the North Side of the Island, in another joined to the Continent by a Causeway, which runs directly cross the Harbour. It is the Place of Residence of the King of *Spain*'s Governor, and is likewise a Bishop's See, large and well built, and better inhabited than most *Spanish* Cities, the true Reason of which is its being the Center of the contraband Trade carried on by the *English* and *French*, with the King of *Spain*'s Subjects, notwithstanding the Severity of the Laws, and the extraordinary Precautions taken to prevent it. There is a very strong Citadel built on the South West Side of the Place, which commands and defends it; and besides this there is a very strong Castle, which protects the Port. In 1595 Sir *Francis Drake* was here, and burnt all the Ships; but foreseeing that he should not be able to keep the Place without abandoning all his other Designs, he left it. Three Years afterwards the Earl of *Cumberland* reduced it, and had some Thoughts of keeping it, but losing 400 Men in the Space of a Month by a contagious Disease, he was glad to depart, carrying with him seventy Pieces of Cannon, and an immense Booty in Plate. In 1615 the *Dutch* sent a strong Fleet hither, but with no great Success, for they only took and plundered the City, not being able to reduce the Castle, which with the other Forts are now in a better Condition than ever, this

Harbour

Harbour having been found of vaft Ufe, fince the *Spaniards* have thought it their Intereft to difturb our Commerce.

The principal Commodities, in which the Traders of *Porto Rico* deal, are Sugar, Ginger, Hides, Cotton-thread, or Raw Cotton, Caffia, Maftick, &c. They have alfo great Quantities of Salt, and make a confiderable Profit of the Sale of their Oranges and Lemons, as Fruit, and in Sweetmeats. They have a great many good Veffels, in which they fail to various Parts of *America*; and this it is that affords them an Opportunity of carrying on the illicit Trade before-mentioned. Befides *Porto Rico*, there are feveral confiderable Towns, fuch as *Arezibo*, *Guadiamila*, *St. Germain*, &c. The Genius of the People, and the convenient Situation of this Ifland, would render it the moft flourifhing of all the *Spanifh* Colonies, if fome great Inconveniencies did not keep the People under. Thefe are principally three; great Droughts which are but too frequent, and which bring the Inhabitants to the very Point of ftarving; Hurricanes, which happen alfo very often, and do incredible Mifchiefs at Sea and on Shore; and laftly, the Defcents of Privateers, which have been fo frequent and fo fatal, that all the Sea-Ports have been ruined over and over; and perhaps this is one Reafon why the *Guarda Coftas*, fitted out from *Porto Rico*, are remarkably cruel. It is not eafy to

fix

fix the Number of People upon this Ifland; but fome who pretend to be extremely well acquainted therewith, affure us that they do not exceed ten thoufand.

The Ifland of *Mona*, which is very fmall, according to fome Writers not above three Leagues in Circuit, lies between *Porto Rico* and *St. Domingo*. Its Climate and Soil are faid to be excellent; there is great Plenty of good Water, and the Oranges that grow here are by much the largeft and fineft in *America*. It is well peopled for its Extent; and as it is under a particular Governor for the King of *Spain*, we thought it deferved particular Notice.

C H A P. X.

Of Peruviana, *or* South America *in general.*

THIS vaft Country is a kind of triangular Peninfula, joyned to *North America* by the Ifthmus of *Darien*, and on every other Side furrounded by the Sea. On the North it hath the *Antilles* and the *North Sea*, on the Eaft the *Spanifh America*, which is all that we have to deal with; hath befides the Sea the *Portugueze* Settlements in *Brafil*; on the South lie the Streights of *Magellan*, and on the Weft that vaft Ocean which we call the *Pacific* Ocean. On this Side of the *South Sea* the *Spanifh* Poffeffions reach from the

Ifthmus

Isthmus of *Panama* to the Streights of *Magellan*; but then they are far from reaching from the Sea Coast to the Heart of the Country. On the *North Sea*, their Territories reach no farther than the Equinoctial on one Side, and commence again at the *Rio de la Plata* on the other, the large Country of *Brasil* taking up the middle Space. From the *Rio de la Plata* the *Spaniards* claim rather than possess all the Coast to the Streights of *Magellan*.

The large Provinces of *Terra Firma*, *Quito*, and *Peru*, lie entirely within the Torrid Zone, and are consequently extremely hot. The Country of *Chili*, and the *Terra Magellanica* lie in the Southern temperate Zone. All the Provinces however are, in point of Soil, sufficiently fruitful; and, if we consider the immense Quantities of Silver and Gold which have been drawn out of its Bowels, it may well be reputed the richest Country in the Globe. Its Rivers we shall speak of in the particular Provinces through which they pass, as also of the Commodities in which it abounds; for here we intend to speak only of Things in general, that the Reader may the better apprehend what follows, and that we may not be under a Necessity of making frequent Repetitions.

The Countries which are already in the Hands of the *Spaniards* are of so great Extent, and afford such vast Riches, that they have

have no Temptation to make either Conqueſt or Diſcoveries; and as the ſame thing
may be ſaid of the *Portugueze* Settlements
in *Braſil*, ſo from thence we gather with the
utmoſt Certainty, that there is a very large
Country in *South America*, altogether undiſcovered, or at leaſt unpoſſeſs'd by any *European* Nation. If any one deſires to be more
particularly informed concerning this Point,
let him examine the beſt Maps of *South A-
merica* which have been publiſhed, and all
the credible Relations that have come from
thoſe Parts, and they will find that this undiſcovered Country, of which I ſpeak, muſt
be in Length near two thouſand Miles from
Eaſt to Weſt, and near a thouſand broad from
North to South. The People poſſeſſed of
theſe Parts are not only the original Inhabitants, but alſo vaſt Numbers of *Indians*, who
have fled hither from the Cruelties of the
Spaniards; and if we conſider their Multitudes, and the vaſt Advantages they have
from the Situation of the Countries in which
they dwell, we ſhall ſee no juſt Reaſon to
ſuppoſe they ever will be conquered, unleſs it
be by the Miſſionaries, in the Manner by
which they have ſubdued the People of *Paraguay*. However it be, this unknown Country contains a great deal more Land, as well
as many more People, than all the Provinces
of the *Spaniſh* Empire; and there is good
Reaſon to believe that it is infinitely more
rich

rich in Silver, Gold, Jewels, as well as in
Cattle, Corn, Sugar, rich Drugs, and fine
Fruits. Of this we can fcarce doubt, if we
reflect on what the beft *Spanifh* Writers affirm, that at the Time *Pizarro* made his firft
Irruption into this Country of *Peru*, he found
the Kitchen-Utenfils in the meaneft Houfes of
Gold, and their Roofs covered with Tiles of
the fame Metal ; but there are no fuch great
Quantities of Gold now to be had, whence
we ought to conclude, that this immenfe
Plenty of that precious Metal came from
the inland Parts of which we have been
fpeaking.

All the Provinces in *South America* are
fubject to one Governor, who is ftyled Viceroy, and Captain-General of *Peru*, whofe
Refidence is at *Lima*. Some Writers do indeed diftinguifh between thefe two Officers
and the Perfons poffeffed of them, but without any juft Grounds ; for though it be true
that the Commiffions, Salaries, and Powers
of thefe Offices are diftinct, yet it is certain
they are both in the fame Perfon, though it
muft be allowed that in *Mexico* there are
fometimes a Viceroy and a Captain-General.
But as it would be fimply impoffible for one
Man to govern abfolutely and by his own Direction, Territories fo far diftant from each
other, and of fuch vaft Extent, his Province
is divided into feveral Audiences, *viz. Panama, Terra Firma, Chuquifaca, Quito,
Lima,*

Lima, and *Chili*; fo that the Viceroy enjoys only a Pre-eminence, with a Refervation in fome Cafes of Appeals, and the fupreme Direction of military Affairs; in other Re-fpects thofe Audiences are in a manner inde-pendent of them.

Audiences differ not much from what the *French* call *Parliaments*; each of them confifts of a certain Number of Judges conftituted by his Catholick Majefty, with Officers dependent upon them, the whole un-der the Direction of a Prefient, who is fu-preme throughout his Jurifdiction. Every Au-dience is divided into four Chambers, or Royal Courts; the firft of thefe is ftyled *the Chamber of Juftice*; and in this all things are done which relate to the Adminiftration of publick Affairs. The next is the *criminal Court*. The third is in the Nature of the King's *Exchequer*, to which belong all Mat-ters relating to the Revenue. The laft is ftyled *the Chamber of Treafure*, or *Court of Aids*; and it takes Care of the Royal Funds, and whatever belongs to the Crown in Pro-perty, whereas the Exchequer meddles only with Rents, Duties, Fines, and in fhort with the current Revenue.

The Viceroy and the Prefidents are ufually conftituted for feven Years; the Governors of fome few Places of Importance for five Years; but the far greater part of the Go-vernors enjoy their Authority only for three
Years,

Years, and owe their Preferment entirely to
the Will and Pleasure of the Viceroys. This
Scheme of the *Spanish* Policy is plainly to
prevent thefe great Officers from making
many Creatures, and eftablifhing an extenfive
Intereft in their refpective Jurifdictions,
whence very mifchievous Confequences might
be feared in a Country at fuch a vaft Diftance
from the Seat of its Sovereign's Refidence.
But if in this Refpect there may be fome Advantages, there are alfo many and great Inconveniencies follow from it.

To fay the Truth, this very Rule which
may pafs for the Conftitution of the *Spanish
America*, is the Source of all the Evils complained of in that Government. For Magiftrates of all Ranks, knowing exactly how
long their Power is to continue, whether they
behave ill or well, think of nothing but pil-
laging the People, and raifing vaft Eftates.
It appears to them a kind of Harveft, with
this additional Circumftance, that a Man has
but one in his Life-time. Thus the King's
Servants are, generally fpeaking, a Race of
Thieves, and the Rulers of the People a Succeffion of Robbers. In fuch a Country what
can be expected but Corruption and Mifmanagement ? from whence it follows, that the
Government is weak and hated, and the Subjects in general uneafy and oppreffed. It may
be faid that the Court of *Madrid* muft fome
time or other think of a Reformation ; but
if

if they fhould, another Queftion would arife,
Whether, when they may think of it, it will be
practicable? For, when an evil Management
has prevailed for Ages, it is fometimes found
to be neither fafe nor prudent to attempt fetting Things right all at once ; and it is even
doubtful whether a gradual Amendment could
now be brought about.

The fettled Appointment of the Viceroy
of *Peru* is forty thoufand Pieces of Eight a
Year, befides occafional Salaries, which a-
mount to twice as much, and Perquifites
which exceed all Computation. I have feen
a *Spanifh* Hiftory of the Viceroys of *Peru*
from the Time of *Francis Pizarro* to 1720,
when the Prince *de Santa Bueno* had that
Title, who was the thirtieth. When this
high Office is vacant, as it frequently is by
Death, the Government is adminiftered by
the Royal Audience, that is, the Audience of
Lima. If I fhould attempt to fpeak of the
Number of People in *South America*, I muft
do it from very indifferent Authority, and
therefore I refer the Reader to the firft
Chapter of this Book. I fhall now proceed
to a diftinct Account of the feveral Jurifdictions within the Limits of *Peru*.

CHAP.

CHAP. X.

Of the New, *or* Golden Caftile; *called alfo the* Terra Firma.

THE frequent Alterations which the
Spaniards have made not only in the
Names, but in the Boundaries and Diftribution of the Provinces in *South America*, render it impoffible for us to proceed with the
fame Regularity in the Defcription of them
as we did in thofe of *Mexico*; all that we
can do, is to follow that Method which appears
to us the cleareft and the moft concife, and to
omit nothing which may contribute to the
Reader's obtaining a diftinct Notion of thefe
Parts.

The Province of *New Caftile* was difcovered by *Chriftopher Columbus*, in his third
Voyage, and was fo called by his Sailors,
who were moft of them Natives of *Old Caftile*. It afterwards obtained the Name of
the *Golden Caftile*, from the large Quantities
of that Metal found therein, particularly in
the Diftrict of *Uraba*. It is a very large
Territory, bounded by the Sea, on the North;
by *Caribana* and *Guiana* on the Eaft; by
Peru, and the Country of the *Amazons* on
the South; and by the *Pacific* Ocean on the
Weft. As to the Climate, it cannot be called either wholefome or pleafant, fince in one
Part of the Year they are fcorched with the
burning

burning Rays of the Sun, and in the other drowned with continual Rains. The Soil is very different, for in some Places, though there is a perpetual Verdure, yet the Trees produce little or no Fruit, and in other Parts there is a vast Plenty of all things, insomuch that they have two Harvests, and their Meadows feed prodigious Multitudes of Cattle. The Mountains abound with Lions, Tygers, and all sorts of wild Beasts. Rivers and Rivulets there are in abundance; but some of them are so far from being wholesome, that their Waters are dangerous, and not fit to be drank. There were formerly very rich Mines of Gold in this Province, but they are now in a manner exhausted, yet some Remains there are, as well as Silver and Iron Mines, which have been since open'd. On the Sea Coast there was formerly a very rich Pearl Fishery, but it is now in some measure wore out.

The Natives of this Part of *America* were never thoroughly conquered, and in all human Probability never will, for on the one hand they are a very warlike, gallant People, and on the other hand they hate the *Spaniards* to a Degree which Words can hardly express. Our Privateers have frequently made use of them in their Expeditions, and have observed this Aversion of theirs to the *Spaniards* to extend so far as not to give or to receive Quarter from them. It is not however to be expected that the *Indians* should

do

do much towards the entire Conqueſt of theſe Parts from the *Spaniard*; firſt, becauſe they are not very numerous or powerful; and, ſecondly, becauſe they are of a fickle inconſtant Diſpoſition, and in reality not cordially affected to any *Europeans*, as may be eaſily gathered, by a Compariſon of the many Relations we have of the Expeditions of the Buccaneers into this Province, which they have invaded more frequently than any other.

This extenſive Country is divided, for the Sake of its more eaſy Government, into ſeveral Diſtricts, of all which we ſhall treat in their Order, from that Part of the Country which borders on *North America*, to the great Country of *Guiana*, which lies to the South of the Province of which we are now ſpeaking. But in as much as entering into a particular Detail of the Circumſtances of each Diſtrict in Point of Soil, Climate, Commodities, *&c.* would extend this Tract much too far, we will ſpeak only of ſuch Places as are beſt known, and their Commerce.

The moſt Northern Part of the *New Caſtile* is that which is ſtyled *the Iſthmus of Darien*; and the principal City therein was that of *Nombre de Dios*. This City, which is now entirely abandoned, ſtood at the Diſtance of about twenty Miles Eaſt of *Porto Bello*. It was ſeated on the Shore in the midſt of a great Wood, which render'd it
extremely

extremely inconvenient, and exceſſively unwholeſome. Beſides this, there was a Marſh
on the Weſt Side of the Town, which in
the rainy Seaſon ſent up peſtilential Vapours;
the Road, for it cannot well be called a Harbour, was neither ſafe nor commodious; and
yet with all theſe Inconveniencies *Nombre de
Dios* would have continued a Place of great
Trade and Conſequence, if it had not been
deſtroyed over and over by the *Engliſh*, who
ſometimes burnt, ſometimes ranſomed it,
which compelled its Inhabitants to look out
for ſome Place with a better Port, and more
capable of being fortified than the City of
Nombre de Dios was.

The Place they fixed on was that which is
now called *Puerto Bello*, diſcovered, as we
have before obſerved, by *Chriſtopher Columbus* in 1507. It ſtands about the Middle of
the narroweſt Part of the Iſthmus, and not
above fifty Miles from *Panama*, which is on
the other Side. Its Situation is very agreeable, ſtanding about a quarter of a Mile from
the Harbour, in a fine Plain watered by three
Rivulets. It conſiſts of two good Streets,
and ſome little Outlets; in it there are two
good Churches, a handſome Houſe for the
Governor, an Exchange for the Merchants,
a Cuſtom-houſe, and a great Number of
Warehouſes. After all it is no very conſiderable Place, excluſive of the Trade carried
on there during the Fair, for it is an open
Town,

Town, without either Wall or Fortification;
all the Caftles and Forts, of which we fhall
fpeak hereafter, being intended to protect the
Harbour only.   The Air is as unwholefome
as that of *Nombre de Dios*, though there are
not fo many Marfhes about it.   The Sea,
when it ebbs, leaves a vaft Quantity of black
ftinking Mud upon the Beach, from whence
there exhales an intolerable noifome Vapour,
which is fuppofed to be the chief Caufe of
the Unwholefomnefs of the Place.   Be that
as it will, certain it is, that at every annual
Fair near four hundred People are carried off
by the Maladies which reign here, particularly a kind of peftilential Fever, which cau-
fing a Mortification in the Entrails, carries
off the Patient in three Days.   It is no wonder therefore, that except at this trading Seafon, *Porto Bello* is very thinly inhabited.   To
fay the Truth, there are none refide here but
what are obliged to it on account of their
Employments, either in the Army, or in the
Commerce : So that there are not reckoned
in it above two or three thoufand People, the
Garrifon included.

    The Harbour of *Porto Bello*, which very
well deferves that Name, is both large and
fafe ; it is formed by a Peninfula, about four
Miles in Length, joyned to the main Land
by a very narrow Ifthmus.   The Harbour is
about half a Mile over at its Mouth, but it
grows wider as you enter it farther, which
                                            renders

renders it very commodious, as well as very safe. According to a *Spanish* Plan, wherein the Soundings are very exactly laid down, there are about twenty Fathoms Water at the Entrance of this Port, towards the North Coast, and fourteen on the South, and about ten Fathom in the Midst of the Harbour all the Way. It is certain that most of our Geographers and other Writers have fallen into great Mistakes about this Place. To speak impartially, there are such wide Variations in their Accounts, that it is no easy Matter to distinguish the Truth. Some Authors place it in the Latitude of 9° 54', and in the Longitude of 82° 52', whereas in reality it lies in 9° 33' Latitude, and in 79° 45' Longitude, that is, West from *London.* As to its Fortifications, they have been so often ruined and rebuilt, and besides this have so frequently changed their Names, that it is a very difficult Matter to give a tolerable Account of them. On the North Side of the Harbour there stood formerly a strong Fort, called *St. Philip.* In my *Spanish* Map this is called *Fort de la Mare,* but of late it has been styled *Castillo del Hierro,* or the *Iron Castle.* Opposite to this, on the other Side of the Bay, stood the Fort of *St. Jago,* called in my Map *Forto Grande.* A little lower, that is, between this Fort and the Town, stood the *Castillo de la Gloria,* or *Castle of Glory,* an irregular Fortification, but the

strongest

strongeſt of them all. In the Town itſelf, but open towards the Sea, ſtood Fort *St. Michael*, which ſeems to be that which was lately ſtyled *St. Jerome's Caſtle.*

In ſpite of all the Pains taken to fortify it, there are few Places which have fallen oftner into the Hands of an Enemy than *Porto Bello.* In 1595, before it was half finiſhed, it was taken and ranſomed by the famous Sir *Francis Drake*, who died, and was thrown overboard in the Harbour. In 1601 it was taken again by Capt. *Parker*, though it had then as many Forts as it had lately. In 1669 it was taken, after a very obſtinate Defence, by Capt. *Morgan* and his Buccaneers. In 1678, Capt. *Croxon*, at the Head of another Body of Freebooters, ſurprized and plundered the Town, though they did not make themſelves Maſters of the Forts : And finally, in 1739, it was taken, and all its Fortifications demoliſhed by Admiral *Vernon*, with ſix Ships only. We have no Room to mention the Particulars of that glorious Action, nor indeed is it neceſſary, ſince all the World is well acquainted with it, and with the incredible Damage the *Spaniards* have received thereby : This Port being now laid entirely open, neither can it be ever refortified without our Permiſſion.

Before the Arrival of the *Galleons* in this Port, proper Expreſſes are diſpatched to *Panama*, requiring the King's Treaſure, and

the

the Merchandize from *Chili* and *Peru* to be conveyed thence to *Porto Bello*. This may be performed two Ways, by Land, which is a Journey of about fifty Miles, and a pretty good Road in Summer; or by Water, which is the only Method in Winter; and then the Plate and Goods are conveyed to *Venta de Cruz*, which is twenty-one Miles, by Mules, and thence down the *Rio Chiagro* to the Sea, whence they are tranfported to *Porto Bello*, which is about eighteen Leagues diftant. Thefe different Methods of Carriage are of vaft Utility, for in the Summer-time the *Rio Chiagro* is frequently fo low, that Boats cannot pafs; and on the other hand, in the Winter, when the Navigation by that River is free, the Road by Land is altogether impaff-able.

All the Country in this Neighbourhood, and indeed the greateft Part of the Ifthmus is of fmall Value and little regarded, the Climate being bad, the Soil a continued Bog, the Rivers muddy, and their Waters unwhole-fome. This Defcription may ferve as far as the Gulph of *Darien*, in the Neighbourhood of which there were formerly fome confide-rable Towns, but now they are ruined and decayed; fo that there is nothing remarkable, or worth defcribing, till we come to the Go-vernment of *Carthagena*, to which therefore we fhall proceed.

This

This Government of *Carthagena* is very confiderable, by Reafon of the great Trade of that City, for otherwife the adjacent Country cannot be ftyled rich, and is far from being populous. It was conquered about the Year 1532 by *Don Peter de Heredia*, whofe Succeffors, that they might run no Hazard of its being conquered again, made it their Bufinefs to ruin and root out the Inhabitants. Before they did this there were found confiderable Quantities of Gold, hidden in Caves, and Pits by the *Indians* ; but now thofe People are abfolutely deftroyed, there is very little or no Gold to be got.

The City of *Carthagena*, which is the Capital of this Province, ftands in the Latitude of 10° 30' and in the Longitude of 75° 21' Weft from *London*. It is a very fine City, as well as a very rich and a very ftrong one, confifting of five large Streets, each near half a Mile in Length, one larger and longer than the reft, in the Center of which there is a noble Square. The Houfes are moftly of Stone, very neatly built, and take it altogether, there is no City of its Bignefs that can make a finer Appearance ; fcarce any can boaft of fo happy a Situation. *Carthagena* is divided into the *Upper* and the *Lower* ; the *Upper* ftands on the Ifthmus, the *Lower* on a little Ifland, for fuch it feems to be, when the Sea flows. The *Spaniards* call this *Gafimani*, that is to fay, *the Suburbs*. Its Harbour

bour is excellent, but very hard to be defcribed. It is formed by an Ifland called *Varu*, and a Peninfula, which is called *Nave*, about four Miles in Length. The Coaft of both runs South by Weft, and North by Eaft; to the South of the Peninfula lies the Ifland, which on the North Eaft is feparated from the Land by a very narrow Paffage. There runs out from the North-weft Corner a Neck of Land which reaches within three Furlongs of the Peninfula of *Nave*. This fmall Diftance makes the Entrance of the Harbour thence ftyled *Boca chica*, i. e. *Littlemouth*. The Harbour lies behind the Ifthmus, between it and the Continent, and is one of the fineft and moft commodious Ports in the Univerfe, capable of containing not only one, but many large Fleets, which might ride fafely in many Parts of it; and therefore the Galleons winter here, whenever they are obliged to ftay in *America*. The Shore on which the City ftands, is fo fhallow and rocky, that though the Sea lies immediately before it, yet it is impoffible to approach it, at leaft fo as to land any Troops; but Admiral *Vernon* has lately thrown a great many Bombs into it, which have deftroyed abundance of fine Edifices, and done incredible Mifchief.

The Harbour is naturally ftrong, and in point of Fortifications, is better provided than any Place in the *Weft Indies*, the *Havana* only excepted. The Mouth of it is commanded

manded by the Fort of *St. Lewis.* Within, on an Ifland, ftands that of *St. Jofeph,* and two others, *viz.* the Forts of *St. Philip* and *James* ftand on the Shore three quarters of a Mile before you come to the Port.   On the Point of Land before-mentioned, within three Miles of the City, ftands the Caftle or Fort of *Santa Cruz* ; as alfo the *Caftillo Grande,* which is in a manner inacceffible, either by Land or Water.   Oppofite to this Fort ftands that of *Mancanillo* ; and befides thefe there is a Redoubt which commands the narrow Paffage between the upper and the lower City. Both Parts of the City itfelf are walled round, and regularly fortified : About a quarter of a Mile from thence, on the Continent, ftands the ftrong Fort of *St. Philip de Baraxas,* which commands both Cities ; and a Mile from thence the very rich and famous Monafte-ry of *Our Lady of the Candleftick,* which is likewife well fortified. It is not to be fuppofed that thefe Works were raifed all at once ; the contrary is certain, the *Spaniards* built them according to the Rules which their Neceffi-ties prefcribed them.

In 1585 this Place was taken by Sir *Francis Drake* with a Body of two thoufand three hundred Land Forces : they kept Poffeffion of it fix Weeks ; and having burnt a Part of the City, receiv'd thirty thoufand Pound Sterling in Specie for the Ranfom of the Re-mainder of it.   A very fhort Time after five

French

French Privateers took it again, and carried off
a Booty worth a hundred and fifty thousand
Ducats, but burnt the Place, which was newly repaired, to the Ground. In 1697 the
Sieur *de Pontis* undertook to plunder it with a
Squadron of *French* Men of War, on board
of which there were four thousand one hundred seventy five Men. At *St. Domingo* he
was joined by a Squadron of Buccaneers,
consisting of six Ships, and about fifteen hundred Men, without whose Assistance, in all
Probability, he had miscarried. The Place
made a vigorous Resistance, but was at length
taken, though not without considerable Loss
to the *French*. We have various Accounts
of the Plunder which they carried off; but
the most authentic Relations I have met with
compute it at two Millions Sterling at the
least. Besides, the Buccaneers being dissatis-
fied with their Share, returned again, and
retook Possession of the City, notwithstanding the former Composition, stripping the
Inhabitants of five hundred thousand Pounds
more.

Since this Time the City of *Carthagena*
has been thoroughly repaired, or rather rebuilt, and better fortified than ever. There
are in it five Churches, besides the Cathedral,
which is in itself a noble Structure, its Inside
being as richly furnished as its Outside is magnificent. There are also eleven Convents, a
fine Palace for the Governor, a sumptuous
Town-

Town-houfe and Cuftom-houfe; and a prodigious Trade is driven on by the Merchants
fettled here, efpecially in Pearls, Emeralds,
Indigo, Cochineal, and other rich Goods.
As to the Number of Perfons who inhabit
this City, it is not eafy to have an exact Account of them. A *French* Officer, who was
there in 1730, judged there might be about
twenty four thoufand Perfons, that is to fay,
about four thoufand *Spaniards,* and the reft
Creoles, Negroes, *&c.*

There are feveral other Places in this Government of confiderable Note, fuch as *St.
Sebaftian, de Buenavifta, Mopoxa, Cenu, Tolu,* and *Santa Maria.*

The Government of *St. Martha,* proceeding ftill towards the South, is the next Country we meet with; it is bounded on one Side
by the *Rio Grande,* or *River of St. Magda-
len;* and on the other by the *Rio de la Hacha.* The Country is for the moft part
mountainous, whence refults fome very confiderable Advantages to the Inhabitants; for,
in the firft Place, the Weather is cooler, and
much more wholefome than in the neighbouring Provinces, and the Land is notwithftanding extremely fruitful, efpecially in *Indian* Corn. Another Advantage is the Mines,
which in thefe Parts are of great Value, for
they not only find in them confiderable Quantities of Gold, but alfo precious Stones of
various kinds, fuch as Emeralds, Sapphires,
Jafpars,

Jafpars, Marble finely vein'd ; and on the Sea Coaft there is a very rich Pearl Fifhery : The Country alfo affords other rich Commodities, fuch as Indigo, Cochineal, Brazil, and Logwood.

The Capital of this Province is a City of the fame Name, excellently fituated on a Branch of the *Rio Grande*, near the Mountain of *St. Martha*, which is fuppofed by fome to be little, if any thing inferior, in Height to the Pike of *Teneriffe*. This City is the Seat of the Governor, a Bifhop's See, well built, and formerly well inhabited, tho' now upon the Decline ; tho' it has as many Conveniences to recommend it as any Place in *America*. It ftands in a healthy pleafant Country, in the Neighbourhood of a fine fruitful Plain ; it has a large, fafe, and commodious Port ; and there is a great deal of Trade carried on here in the richeft Conveniences, and befides all this, a great Manufacture of Cotton Cloth. There are two Caufes of its Decay ; the one, that the *Spanifh* Fleets feldom touch there now as formerly they were wont to do ; the other, that this Place has been taken fo often, that People are afraid to fettle there. In 1525 it was entirely ruined by Sir *Francis Drake* ; the next Year Sir *Anthony Shirley* plundered it. In 1630 it fell into the Hands of the *Dutch*, and fince then has been over and over taken by our Buccaneers, infomuch that in
1681

1681 they fcarce thought it worth the pilla-
ging.   This City lies in the Latitude of 11°,
and is fuppofed to contain about three thoufand Inhabitants.

There are fome other very confiderable
Places in this Government, fuch as *Baranca*,
in the Neighbourhood of which are Salt Pits,
which yield a vaft Profit ; *Ocanna*, *Ramada*,
and fome other Towns, which we want Room
to mention.

To the Southward of the Government of
St. Martha, lies the little Province of *Rio de
la Hacha*.   The Country is both pleafant
and fruitful, abounding with *Indian* Corn,
Herbs, and Fruits.   There are alfo Salt Pits,
fome Mines of Jafpar, and Chalcedonies; and
on the Coaft there is a very rich Pearl Fifhery, wherein, as the *Indians* are chiefly employed, fo they take Care to reap fome Part
of the Profit, notwithftanding all the Care
the *Spanifh* Infpectors can take to prevent it.
The principal Town is called alfo *Rio de la
Hacha*, from the River at the Mouth of
which it ftands, and was formerly both a rich
and a ftrong Town ; but having notwithftanding this been more than once taken by
the Buccaneers, the *Spaniards* were at laft
fo difheartened, that in 1682 they abandoned
it, but within a fhort Time after, they fettled
it again, and have fince fortified it in fuch a
Manner, as not to be any longer apprehenfive of fuch Vifits.   In the open Country
the

the *Indians* are free, not enduring the Yoke
of the *Spaniards*, though they willingly receive their Priefts, and for ought that appears
to the contrary, are very good Chriftians.
They fubfift chiefly by grazing their Cattle,
every Man marking his own, and thereby
fecuring his Property ; but as to the Ground
on which they feed, that is in Common, and
no Man hath a Property in it at all, except
fo much as his Houfe ftands upon, which is
furrounded with a little Fence.

The Province of *Venezuela* lies next on
the South, being divided from that of which
we fpoke laft, by the River or Lake of *Maracaibo*.   There is a great deal of Confufion
in moft of the Geographical Defcriptions of
this Country, occafioned by blending and
miftaking of Names.   In fome Books this
Province is called *Corana*, from the City of
Coro, which ftands upon the Lake ; and fome
again confound it with *Cumana* ; but the
beft *Spanifh* Writers ftyle it, as we do, *the
Province of Venezuela*.   It extends along the
Coaft of the *North Sea*, near four hundred
Miles, and extends alfo above three hundred
into the Heart of the Continent.   It is affirmed, that in the firft Conqueft of this Country, the *Spaniards* dealt very cruelly with the
Inhabitants ; but, however that might be,
certain it is that the Natives now live happily
enough, and that they are very numerous in
this Province, which enjoys a pretty good
Air,

Air, as alfo a very rich Soil. Some Writers
fay that the Number of *Indians* does not fall
fhort of a hundred thoufand. The old Capital of this Country was *Coro*, a City ftanding on the Shore of the *North Sea*, in the
Latitude of 11°. Thence the Land fhoots out
into a Peninfula about twenty-five Leagues
in Compafs, which is called *Paraguana*. Below the City of *Coro* lies the famous Lake of
Maracaibo, eighty Leagues in Compafs, the
Mouth of it half a League over ; and it extends into the Heart of the Country twenty-
five Leagues. As there are a vaft Number
of Rivers and Rivulets which run into it, the
Water is potable, but withal is very brackifh.
The prefent Capital of the Province is the
City of *Venezuela*, which is faid to derive its
Name from its Likenefs to the City of *Ve-
nice* in *Italy*. It is a Bifhop's See, fubject, as
we have before remarked, to the Archbifhop
of *St. Domingo*. In the Heart of this Province lie thofe famous Plains ftyled *Corora*,
where the Soil is wonderfully rich, and where
they feed vaft Numbers of *European* Sheep.
The only Difadvantage under which this fine
Country labours, is the Want of frefh Water, there being very few Rivulets, though
there are fome confiderable Lakes therein.
The Town of *Maracaibo on the Lake* is a
modern built Place, in refpect of the other
Towns of this Province, and yet it is in a
better Condition than any of them, being a
Place

Place of great Trade, and where feveral Ships are annually built by the Inhabitants, which is a rare Thing in this Part of the World, and therefore worthy of Notice. They like-wife cultivate Tobacco and Sugar in this Neighbourhood, which are famous through-out all *America.* Oppofite to the Coaft of *Venezuela* lie a great many Iflands, moft of them belonging to the *Spaniards*; as alfo *Curaço*, and two other lefs confiderable Ifles belonging to the *Dutch*, which gives them an Opportunity of carrying on a great deal of clandeftine Trade with the *Spaniards.*

Beyond this Province lies that of *New An-dalufia*, the Capital of which is *Comana*, or *Corduba*, which is no very confiderable Place; but the Port is called *Carvalleda*, near the Gulph of *Caraccas.* It is not eafy to affign the Bounds of this Province, fince to fpeak the Truth it is boundlefs; for though the *Spaniards* pretend to vaft Countries ftretch-ing along this Coaft to the South, yet in rea-lity they have fettled little farther than thefe Places of which we have been fpeaking, which however ought not to be efteemed fo great a Wonder as that other Nations fhould leave fo fine a Country as this to a Nation fo incapa-ble of making ufe of it.

All along this Coaft, from *Carthagena*, there are Pearl Fifheries, of which it may not be amifs to give the Reader fome Ac-count. In the firft Place then, let us obferve

that

that Pearls have been always efteemed, and
for ought we can perceive, in all Places, for
the *Indians* fet a great Value upon them, before any *Europeans* came amongft them. The
Beauty and Excellence of Pearls confifts partly in their Shape, and partly in their Water.
As to Shape, thofe that are perfectly round
are moft efteemed ; and next to thefe, Pear
Pearls. In *Europe* we efteem moft the white
or clear Water ; but the *Indians* and *Ara-
bians* prefer the yellow, provided the Pearls be
perfectly ripe. The great Diftinction between
oriental and occidental Pearl confifts in this,
that the latter have a Caft of Lead in their
Colour, however ripe or perfect, which a-
bates their Value ; and yet *Tavernier* fpeaks
of fix Pearls which came from the *Weft Indies* perfectly round and black, which one
with another weighed twelve Carrats, and
were efteemed at a high Rate. The Fifheries on this Coaft are ftrictly fpeaking five ;
the firft is at *Cubagna*, a fmall Ifland lying
off the Coaft of *New Andalufia*, about five
Leagues, in the Latitude of 10° 30'. The
Pearls here feldom exceed five Carrats, but
to balance this, they are found in great Quantities. Next is the Fifhery at the Ifland of
Margarita, or *Ifle of Pearls*, where there
are the largeft, fineft, and moft regular that
are to be found in the *Weft Indies*. The
Fifhery of *Comanagotta* is at the bottom of
the Gulph of *Caracca*, on the Coaft of *Venezuela*.

zuela. The Fourth Fifhery is that which
the *Spaniards* ftyle *la Rencheria*, at the
Mouth of the River *de la Hacha*. The fifth
is the Fifhery of *St. Martha*, at fixty Leagues
Diftance from the former. The Time of
Fifhing is from the Month of *October* to the
Month of *March*, at which Time there fails
from *Carthagena* ten or twelve Barks efcorted
by fome Men of War, ftyled *the Armadilla* ;
and thefe having made their Tour, return again
to the fame Port, which is the Center of the
Pearl Trade. Thefe Barks have an Admiral,
which is ftyled *la Capitana*, on board whereof
all the Oyfters that are taken in the Day are
depofited at Night. Some of the Slaves, who
are made ufe of in diving, will continue under Water near a quarter of an Hour, and
then bring up with them a little Bafket of
Oyfters. The Pearl-oyfter, or Mother of
Pearl, as it is ufually called, is three or four
times as big as another Oyfter, and contains
ufually ten or twelve Pearls of different Sizes.
The ripeft and largeft appear firft, the fmaller
and rawer lie deeper in the Shell. When the
Oyfters are brought on Shore, they bury
them in the Sand till by the Heat of the
Sun they corrupt and open of themfelves ;
and the Pearls are difcovered in fome more,
fome fewer, and in fome none at all ; then
they are taken out, cleaned, dried, and afterwards paffed through a kind of Sieve in order
to diftinguifh their Sizes. Such as are very

fmall,

finall, are fold for Seed-Pearl, and the reft according to their Sizes.

If I join to thefe Obfervations on the Pearl Fifhery fome Remarks on the Value of Pearl, the Reader muft make proper Allowances for the Vogue, which is fometimes greater, and fometimes lefs: All I pretend to give is the middle Rate. Seed-Pearls, for the Ufe of the Apothecaries, are worth about a Crown an Ounce; fmall Pearls, bored, are worth from one to three Crowns an Ounce. A round ripe Pearl of a Carrat Weight may be worth about ten Shillings; of two Carrats, about three Pound; of four Carrats, about fifteen Pound; and a very perfect Pearl of ten Carrats, or the largeft Size, is efteemed at about two hundred Pounds. When Pearls are very perfect, and much above this Size, they have no regular Price, but are eftimated merely by Fancy. Thus the fine Pearl which the King of *Spain* has called *la Peregrina*, which weighs fifteen Carrats, or fomewhat lefs, is faid to be worth twenty thoufand Pounds. Pear Pearls are about a third lefs in Value than round.

The Kingdom of *New Granada* is an Inland Province, and lies behind thofe which we have already defcribed. On the North it is bounded by the Governments of *St. Martha*, *Rio de la Hacha*, and *Venezuela*; on the Eaft by the fame Diftrict of *Venezuela*, and part which continue hitherto unconquered; on
the

the South by *Peru*, and on the Weſt by *Popayan.* It is in Length 130 Leagues, and in
Breadth twenty-five or thirty. It lies from
the firſt to the 9° of N. L. It is, generally
ſpeaking, a Champagne Country, though on
its Frontiers 'tis every where ſurrounded by
Mountains. There are abundance of Foreſts,
which contain excellent Timber; and large
Meadows, which feed prodigious Quantities
of Black Cattle and Horſes. Though it is
ſo near the Line, yet the Climate is very
temperate, inſomuch that many Writers tell
us, that as it always enjoys an Equality of Day
and Night, ſo on the other hand it is not diſ-
turbed by a Variety of Seaſons. But upon a
ſtrict Examination, this does not appear to
be the Caſe. The People in this Country
have, properly ſpeaking, two Summers and
two Winters, without either Autumn or
Spring. The firſt Summer begins in *December,* and ends with *February*; then follows a Winter, comprehending the Months
of *March, April* and *May*; the ſecond Summer takes in the Months of *June, July* and
Auguſt; and the ſecond Winter the Months
of *September, October,* and *November.* It is
true that all this Time there is little Difference between the Heat and Cold, which is
the Reaſon that ſome Writers ſay there is
here a continual Spring. But I think the
other the better Diviſion, becauſe in the Summer Months it is always fair Weather, where-

as

as in thofe which I call Winter Months, it conftantly rains all the Night.

This Country alone might fatisfy the De-
fires of any People, fince it is both pleafant
and rich, abounding with all things neceffary
to Life, and having befides very rich Mines
of Gold and Emeralds, but efpecially of the
latter, which are of prodigious Value, or at
leaft might be fo, if proper Care was taken
in the Management of this Trade.   We commonly diftinguifh between oriental, and occidental Emeralds, that is, between the Emeralds brought from the *Eaft Indies*, and
thofe brought from *Peru*.   But *Tavernier*,
who was a very good Judge, thought this
Diftinction altogether without Foundation ;
and I own I am of his Opinion.   I believe
there are no Emeralds but what do come
from *Peru*, except it be fuch as are found in
the Mines of *New Mexico*.   It is true, this
fuppofes a Commerce between the *Eaft* and
Weft Indies, before we difcovered *America* ;
and this fome think an Abfurdity ; but then
they ought to tell us where the *Eaft Indian*
Emeralds are found ; for their coming from
thence does not prove they grow there. Heretofore there were Emeralds of extraordinary
Hardnefs and Beauty, which were faid to be
of the old Rock ; and this has puzzled many
People ; but the Truth of the Matter is, thefe
were not oriental, but *Egyptian* Emeralds ;
and of thefe we have had few or none, fince
that

that Country fell into the Hands of the *Turks.* The Mines we are now fpeaking of produce vaft Quantities of different Degrees in point of Luftre and Value. Such as are perfect, and weigh from one to ten Carrats, are worth from ten Shillings to thirty Pounds or more. The *Spaniards* generally fend thefe to *Maracaibo,* and thence to *Carthagena ;* whence, with the other Commodities of this Country, they are tranfported to *Europe.*

The Capital of the Kingdom of *New Granada,* and indeed of the whole *Terra Firma,* is the City of *Santa Fé,* ftyled by way of Diftinction, *Santa Fé de Bogata :* It is the Seat of the Royal Audience, and of an Archbifhoprick, its Suffragans being the Bifhops of *Carthagena, Santa Martha,* and *Popayan.* The City is large, and well built, ftanding on the Banks of the Lake *Gutavita,* adorned with fine Buildings, and very populous. Befides this, there are a great many other large well built Towns in this Diftrict, but becaufe it is in an Inland Government, and Strangers can have no Intercourfe with their Inhabitants, we fhall omit their Names.

The Province of *Popayan,* which is the laft in this Audience, is of very large Extent. It is bounded on the North by the Province of *New Carthagena,* which is dependent on the Kingdom of *New Granada ;* as alfo a little Part of the Audience of *Panama.* On the Eaft lies the Kingdom of *New Granada ;*

on

on the South the Provinces of *Quito*, and *los Quixos*; on the Weſt it hath the *South Sea.* This Country is mountainous; and though all of it lies very near, and ſome of it immediately under the Line, yet the Air is very cool, and the Climate much better than one could expect. The Soil, wherever it is cultivated, appears to be rich and fruitful; but the Country is far from being thoroughly ſettled. All the Herbs, Flowers, and Trees, which grow in any Part of *South America*, are to be found here, eſpecially Cotton Trees, Cedars, Red Wood, and Trees which yield that ineſtimable Balſam which generally goes under the Name of *Balſam of Tolu.* Here are alſo very rich Mines of Gold, and precious Stones are found frequently, ſuch as Jaſpar, Chalcedony, and various kinds of Agates. The *Spaniards* call the Natives of this Country, *Indios Bravos*, or *Indios de Guerra*, that is, *Brave or warlike Indians*; and in truth they may well call them ſo, for in all this Time they have never been able to ſubdue them; but they remain free in the Mountains, though ſurrounded by the *Spaniſh* Dominions on every Side.

The Capital of the Province, or at leaſt that which is generally ſo ſtyled, is the City of *Popayan*, ſeated at the Bottom of the Mountains on the Banks of a River which in its Courſe falls into the *Rio Grande:* it is in the Heart of the Province, in the Latitude of

of 2° 30'. It is a Bishop's See, and the Prelate who resides there not only directs the Inhabitants in Spirituals, but governs them in
Temporals also; for the *Spanish* Governor
resides at *Cali*, which is a larger Town farther to the North, in the Latitude of 3° 40'.
The Bishop and his Clergy have done more
for the Crown of *Spain* than could have been
done by a large Garrison; for they have converted many of the *Indians*; and by bringing them into the City, and matching them
with *Creole* Families, they have introduced a
Commerce with the free Inhabitants of the
Mountains, which is of infinite Service, and
may be a Means of reducing the whole Country. It is remarked that the Inhabitants of
this Province are much more active and industrious, as well as much braver, than any of
the rest of the Natives of *New Spain*, which
is attributed to their continual Wars with the
free *Indians*, and their being obliged to make
long and hazardous Journeys for the mana-
ging their own Affairs.

There are in *Popayan* abundance of large
Towns, well built, and tolerably fortified;
but the open Country is much exposed to the
Courses of the *Indians*, who, whenever they
have an Advantage, use it cruelly enough a-
gainst the *Spaniards*, towards whom their
Hate is implacable. As the Northern Frontier of this Country joins the Isthmus which
is also inhabited by free *Indians*, the *Spaniards*

ards are extremely apprehenfive of the *Englifh* making fome Attempt this Way, and
thereby fecuring to themfelves a Settlement
on both Seas; but as this could not be undertaken but with a large Body of Land Forces,
much Hazard, and a vaft Expence, there is
Reafon to doubt they will never be difturbed
by any thing but their own Fears.

C H A P. XI.

Of the Audience of Panama.

THIS is a Territory of no great Extent, lying altogether on the Coaft of
the *South Sea,* from the Gulph of *Panama*
down to *Capo de Corintes,* that is, from about
9° to 5° of N. L. The Climate is far from
being wholefome, and yet it is much better
than in the Neighbourhood of *Porto Bello,*
on the other Side of the Ifthmus; but as to
the Soil, it is very good, and the *Spaniards*
either have, or might have, all Things in the
utmoft Abundance.

The old City of *Panama* was built very
early, as we have obferved in the former
Book, and became by degrees a very confiderable Place; for, befides a handfome Cathedral, there were eight Convents, a large Ho-
fpital, and feveral fine Buildings; but as for
Walls they had none; all the Fortifications
for the Defence of fo important a Place were
two

two forry Redouts, one on the Shore, and the other fronting the Road to *Venta Cruz*, mounted with fix Pieces of Cannon each. In 1673 the famous Sir *Henry Morgan* took this Place, and burnt it to the Ground; it confifted at that Time, if the *Spanifh* Writers may be believed, of between fix and feven thoufand Houfes, moft of them built of Rofe-Wood, and many of them more magnificent than any other in the *Indies*.

The new City of *Panama* ftands four Miles Weft from the Ruins of *Old Panama*, and is a very fair City, feated clofe by the Sea Side. It gives Name to a large Bay which is famous for a great many navigable Rivers running into it, fome whereof are very rich in Gold. This Bay is likewife fprinkled with feveral fmall Iflands, equally pleafant to the Eye of a Spectator, and profitable to the Proprietors. On the Land-Side *Panama* is encompaffed by a pleafant Country full of fmall Hills, verdant Vallies, and fine Groves of Trees, which appear like Iflands in the *Savannahs*. This City is furrounded by a ftrong and high Wall, well mounted on all Sides with Brafs Cannon. It has a Cathedral, eight Parifh-Churches, and thirty Chapels. The Prefident's Palace is a very grand Building, and all the publick Edifices may be juftly ftyled fo, confidering where they ftand. In point of Government, the King's Officers here are a Governor, Captain-General, and Prefident, four

four Counsellors, a Provost, and Procurator-
General; an Auditor of Accounts, a Trea-
surer, and a Commissary-General.

There are neither Woods nor Marshes near
Panama, but a fine dry champion Country,
little subject either to Fogs or Mists. The
rainy Season lasts here from *May* to *November*; but the Rains are by no means so heavy
as on the other Side the Isthmus; and yet
even here they are very unwholesome to all
but the Natives, or such as have dwelt very
long in the Place. As this is the great Center of Commerce from *Peru* and *Chili*, so
the Merchants who live at *Panama* are generally speaking rich; and the Port is never
without a considerable Number of Ships in it;
nay there is generally an *Armadilla*, that is, a
Squadron of small Men of War, either lying
before it, or cruising in its Neighbourhood.

There are not many Places in this Audience which deserve very particular Notice to
be taken of them, and therefore I shall take
this Opportunity of speaking of the Methods
made use of by the *Spaniards* for obtaining
Gold, out of the Rivers, of which there is
greater Plenty in this Audience, and in the
Mines of *Santa Maria*, not far off, than
within the same Space in any other Part of
New Spain, or perhaps in the whole World.

From the Mountains, in the Midst of the
Isthmus, there roll down several Rivers, with
a strong and rapid Current, during the rainy
Season

Seafon efpecially, and then tear away part of
the Soil, and therewith Abundance of Gold,
which afterwards is, with confiderable Pains,
feparated therefrom. The *Indians* are generally employed in this Work, as alfo the
Slaves of the *Spaniards*, that is, the Negroes:
the latter make about five Shillings a Day;
but the former, who fell what they get at a
Price agreed on, get confiderably more. They
take the Mud up in little wooden Difhes, and
after fuffering it to fettle, they wafh from it
as much of the black Earth as they can, then
it is put up into certain Bafons, called by the
Spaniards, *Lavaderos*, which are placed under a Pipe or Spring of running Water, and
is ftirred with an Iron Spatula, that as the
Water paffes through it may be the better a-
ble to carry off the Sand or Earth. After it
has gone through this Operation, it ftill retains its black Colour; but the Increafe of its
Weight, in Proportion to the Quantity that
is left, fufficiently indicates that all this Pains
is not taken without anfwering fome End.
This black Earth is next thrown into broad
wooden Difhes, either of a round or oval
Form, and hollow in the Middle, like a But-
cher's Tray, but not fo deep ; there, by repeated Wafhings and Rubbings, the black
Earth is entirely cleanfed away, and a fhining
Gold Sand is found at the Bottom. Though
there feems to be a great Trouble in this
Method, yet is it much the eafieft and the
cheapeft

cheapeft Way of coming at Gold, for there is neither a fourth Part of the Labour, nor of the Expence in thus feparating the Grains of Gold from the Soil, that there muft be ufed in extracting it from the Ore. In the dry Seafon they work at the Mines of *Santa Maria*, which lie not far from *Panama*, and are, as I have faid, exceedingly rich. It was taken about 1684 by our Buccaneers, and more than once fince; nay, *Dampier* tells us they had fome Thoughts of fettling there, and thinks they might have done it in fpite of all the Force the *Spaniards* had in *Peru*. They were tempted to thefe Thoughts by feeing the Mines abandoned to the *Spaniards*, as they were for a long Time, and by the Quantities of Gold, which from their own Experience they knew them to yield. For the obtaining of Gold from the Mine, they firft of all break to pieces the Mineray, or Marcafite which holds it, and then conveying it to the Mills, it is ground into a Powder as fine as can be imagin'd. This Powder being put into wooden Veffels, together with a proportionable Quantity of Quickfilver, is there wrought into a Pafte, which after being expofed to the Sun for forty-eight Hours, is wafhed in a particular Manner, till there is nothing left but the Quickfilver and Gold, and then the latter is feparated from the former by Diftillation. Such as are verfed in this kind of Bufinefs diftinguifh three kinds

of

of Gold; the firſt is called *Pepitas*, which is an *Indian* Word, though uſed by the *Spaniards*, and ſignifies the Seeds of an Apple. They uſe this to diſtinguiſh the pure Gold, which is either found in the Rocks, or waſhed down by the Rivers, already formed into little Lumps, which need no refining; theſe are of ſeveral Sizes, from the Bigneſs of a large Pin's Head to that of a Gooſe's Egg. The Second is the Grain Gold, obtained by waſhing only. The Third is Ingots caſt out of Gold, refined by the Help of Fire. The Inhabitants of *Panama* are ſaid to have gained formerly, by the Methods before-mentioned, ſome thouſand Pounds Weight of Gold a Year; but of late, though the Mine has not been diſcovered above ſixty Years, the Quantity is conſiderably decreaſed. Throughout all *America*, the King of *Spain* receives for his Duty a Fifth of the Silver, and a Twentieth of the Gold : This Duty is called the *Covo*, and when it is once paid, the Remainder belongs to the Subject; for he who finds a Mine, and will be at the Charge of working it, is the abſolute Proprietor, and has all the Encouragement given him that he could wiſh.

But this is a ſmall Article in the Profits of the Inhabitants of this rich City, who drive on a prodigious Commerce both in *North* and *South America*. As ſoon as ever the Galleons enter the Port of *Carthagena*, an
Expreſs

Exprefs is difpatched over Land to *Panama*, from whence he proceeds by Sea to *Lima*. In the mean time all the neceffary Preparations are made for conveying the Treafure as foon as it arrives, either by Sea or Land to *Porto Bello*. The Viceroy of *Peru*, on the other hand, makes all imaginable Difpatch in fending the *Lima* Fleet, efcorted by an *Armadilla*, or fmall Squadron of Men of War, to *Panama*, where, as foon as they arrive, they are unladen, and the Goods forwarded for *Porto Bello*. The *Lima* Fleet then fails to *Perico*, a little Port at a fmall Diftance from *Panama*, and there wait the Return of the *European* Goods from *Porto Bello* by the fame Carriage theirs was fent thither; and having taken this on Board, they immediately fail away for *Lima*.

Another Branch of Traffick, entirely managed by the Merchants of *Panama*, is that refulting from the *Englifh Affiento* Company, whofe Factors refide here conftantly in Time of Peace, receiving from *Jamaica*, by the Way of *Porto Bello*, thofe Negro Slaves which they afterwards fend into *Peru*, and *New Spain*. It is chiefly on Account of this extenfive Trade at *Panama*, that it was made the Seat of a Royal Audience; and indeed without this it would have been very hard to have regulated thofe Difputes which naturally arife among a mixt Body of Traders, all warmly

warmly concerned for their own Intereſt, and not over tender of other People's Concerns.

Although the Neighbourhood of *Panama* be pretty well cultivated, yet the reſt of the Audience is but very thinly inhabited, neither are there any tolerable Ports after you have paſſed the Bay of *St. Michael*, till you come to *Cape Corrintes*; though there are many Rivers which fall into the Sea along the Coaſt. What is ſtranger ſtill, this Country is abſolutely in the Hands of the Natives, with whom the *Spaniards* ſometimes trade for Gold, almoſt all of them bringing down more or leſs; but they have no Command over them, and are ſo much afraid to truſt them, that they never attempt to ſend ſo much as an Expreſs by Land from *Panama* to the Audience of *Quito*.

From *Cape Corrintes*, which, as I have obſerved, is in 5° N. L. to *Rio de Jaga*, which is in the Latitude of 2°, extends the Coaſt of *Popayan*, on which there are ſeveral ſmall Harbours; but the moſt conſiderable is the Bay of *Bonaventura*, by which is carried on all the Trade to *Cali*, which, as I have before obſerved, is very conſiderable. On this Coaſt lies the little Iſland of *Gorgona*, in the Latitude of 3°. It is about two Leagues long, and a League broad, four Leagues from the Coaſt, hath a good Road, is well wooded and watered, though but an indifferent Climate, it being commonly reported that it rains here

more

more or lefs every Day of the Year, which
however is not ftrictly true. It is uninhabited, though very remarkable for being the
only Place (except on the Coaft of *California*) in the *South Seas*, where Pearl-oyfters
are found. It is true, there are fome little
Iflands in the Bay of *Panama*, which are
called the *Pearl Iflands*; and perhaps a
Fifhery might be there formerly; but
there is none now. Our Privateers, who
have frequented the Ifland of *Gorgona*, report the Pearl-oyfters to be neither pleafant
nor wholefome, as having a copperifh Tafte,
very apt to difguft the Stomach, and make
Men fick, The Pearl here are generally
fmall, and of little Value, though now and
then there have been very large and valuable
Pearls found here by the Fifhing Barks fent
from *Panama*, with which we have now
done, as well as with its Dependencies, and
are to pafs on to the next Province beyond it
and *Popayan*.

CHAP.

C H A P. XII.

Of the Audience of Quito.

Uthors differ pretty much in the Boundaries they affign to this Province, and not a few comprehend it under the general Title of *Peru* ; but, according to the beft Accounts I have met with, its Boundaries may be thus affigned. To the North it hath the Government of *Popayan* ; to the Eaft an undifcovered Country, inhabited by barbarous Nations; to the South the Audience of *Lima* ; and on the Weft the *South Sea.* It extends from two Degrees North Latitude to about fix Degrees South, and is properly divided into three Diftricts, that is, thofe of *Quito proper*, *Los Quixos*, and *Pacamores.* The Climate is immoderately hot, and far from being wholefome, fubject to great Rains, and thick Fogs, efpecially in the Vallies, and towards the Sea Shore, which makes thefe Parts miferably unhealthy. The Soil again is fandy and barren, though here and there are fome Spots of tolerable Ground, which are pretty well cultivated. Notwithftanding all thefe Inconveniencies, the Province of *Quito* is tolerably inhabited, for Reafons that will prefently appear. In this Country there are abundance of that kind of Sheep which the Natives call *Llamas* ; the *Spaniards, Carne-*

ros

ros de la Tierra. They have a fmall Head,
a long ftraight Neck, the upper Lip divided before ; they are very large and ftrong, capable of carrying from fourfcore to a hundred
Weight, with which they will travel four or
five Leagues in a Day; but they will not ftir
a Step in the Night. They have a Spur behind their Heel, which enables them to travel through Rocks, and down Precipices,
where no other Creature could do, with the
utmoft Security, and even without ftumbling.
Of thefe camel Sheep, as fome Writers call
them, there are four Sorts. The *Llamas,*
the *Vigognes,* whofe Wooll is finer than that
of the *Llamas* ; the *Guanacos,* and the *Al-
pacas,* thefe laft yield a very fine black Wooll:
and indeed all their Fleeces are very valuable.

The Capital of this Province is the great
City of *Quito,* feated in 45 Minutes of South
Latitude, at the Foot of exceeding high
Mountains, and at the Diftance of 60 Leagues
from the Sea. It is very large and populous ;
the Country about it naturally the beft in the
Province, and well cultivated. It is the Seat
of the Prefident and King's Courts for this
Audience, as alfo a Bifhop's See. The Revenue of the Bifhop confifts in eighteen thoufand Pieces of Eight, which he receives annually from the Royal Treafury, and in a-
bout four times as much, which he draws
from the People by various Methods. There
are

are in *Quito* about three thoufand *Spaniards*, and upwards of thirty thoufand *Indians*. They have a grand Manufacture here of coarfe Cloth and Serges, which make the Clothing of the common People all over *Peru*. Befides this, the Inhabitants draw immenfe Riches from the golden Mountains in their Neighbourhood, wherein, however, there are no Mines, but Lavaderoes only; yet as thefe are frequent indeed in every Brook, and are alfo very rich, the Quantities of Metal taken out of them are prodigious. To balance all thefe Advantages, this Audience, as I faid, is extremely unwholefome, infomuch, that when the Inhabitants grow very rich, they ufually quit the Province, and go and fettle at *Maracaibo*, or *Venezuela*.

There are abundance of great Towns in this Country, fuch as *St. Michael de Ybarra*, *Sevill del Oro*, or *Golden Sevil*; *Loxa*, *Zamora*, &c. neither is it deficient in Ports. *Puerto Viejo*, or the *Old Port*, lies in 1° 15′ S. L. and was formerly a Place of fome Note; but it was fo often plundered by the Buccaneers in their Paffages from the *North* to the *South Seas*, that it funk at laft into a Village. But the great Port of *Quito*, by which all its Trade is carried on, is *Guiaquil*, a very confiderable Place. It ftands in the Latitude of 2° 30′, about four Miles up a River of the fame Name, Part on the Side, and Part on the Foot of a Hill of eafy Afcent. The Port

is

is a very good one, and the Town makes a very handſome Figure, having ſeveral Churches and fine Buildings. The Trade carried on here in Cocoa, Hides, Tallow, Sarſaparilla, and other Drugs, beſides *Quito* Cloth, and Serges, is very conſiderable; and indeed it is one of the moſt flouriſhing Places in the *South Seas.* The Inhabitants are active and induſtrious, and they build the beſt Ships here both for War and Trade that are to be met with in *Peru.* Yet no Town has ſuffered more than this from our Privateers, who have taken it frequently; the laſt time in 1710, under the Command of the Captains *Rogers* and *Cook,* when, after making a vaſt Booty, they burnt a Part of it, and ranſomed the Remainder for twenty two thouſand Pieces of Eight. Authors differ as to the Wholeſomeneſs of this Place; for ſome report it to be very healthy, others ſay that it is extremely ſickly; and both ſpeak Truth according to their Apprehenſions of the Matter. Healthy it is in compariſon of *Quito,* and other Inland Towns; but very ſickly in reſpect to *Maracaibo, Venezuela,* and other Places. Before we leave this Place, we muſt obſerve, that as there is very little Wood in this Province, the Timber which is made uſe of in building of Ships is brought thither from other Places, particularly from the Iſland of *Gallo,* which is not far diſtant.

The

The Province of *los Quixos* lies behind *Quito*, having *Popayan* on the North, the River of *Amazons*, which rifes in this Province, on the Eaft; the Country of *Pacamores* on the South, and *Quito* on the Weft. It is very far from being thoroughly fettled; but as both the Air and Soil are better here than in *Quito*, and as great Advantages are drawn from the Commerce carried on with the numerous Nations of *Indians* inhabiting to the Eaft, the *Spaniards* efteem it of great Confequence. There are fome good Towns in it, fuch as *Anate*, immediately under the Line; *Baeza*, which is the chief Town in the Province; *Avila*, and *Archidona*. The Country of the *Pacamores*, fo called from the *Indians* who inhabit it, is divided from this Province by a high Ridge of Mountains, which I take to be Part of the *Andes*.

That Province which is of equal Extent with *Los Quixos*, is bounded on the Eaft by the River of *Amazons*; on the South by part of the Province of *Peru*; and on the Weft by *Quito*. The Inhabitants are very induftrious, and confequently rich : They have various Woollen and Cotton Manufacturies; and befides, make no inconfiderable Profit of their Lavaderoes. The Capital of the Province is *Valadolid*, a Place fo confiderable, that it is a Bifhop's See; *Loyola*, and *St. Jago de las Montanas*, i. e. *St. Jago in the Mountains*, which lies on the Frontiers of the Province,

on

on the Banks of a pleafant River, in a healthy and fruitful Soil. The chief Intent of thefe Settlements is to keep the *Indians* in Awe; for, as this Province borders on a vaft undif-covered Country, neither *Quito* nor *Peru* would be fafe, if there were not fome good Towns here, partly to bridle, and partly to entertain a Trade with the *Indians.* Thefe are far from being fo bafe and barbarous a People as fome reprefent them ; on the con-trary, as they are ftrong and robuft in their Perfons, fo they are brave and generous in their Difpofitions, eafily wrought upon by kind and gentle Ufage, but fierce and intrac-table if any Attempts be made upon their Free-dom. The miffionaries however preach amongft them with Succefs ; and it muft be owned that they take a very proper Method to con-vert them, for they protect them from the *Spaniards,* form them into civil Societies, and take all imaginable Care that no body fhall have the fleecing them but themfelves; yet even this is very advantageous to the *Spa-nifh* Provinces, as it fecures them from thofe Invafions which were formerly frequent, in-fomuch that they were fometimes difpoffefs'd of large Tracts of Country, and all their Set-tlements deftroyed. But enough of this Au-dience of *Quito* ; let us now proceed to that Province which may be called *Peru proper.*

CHAP.

C H A P. XIII.

Of the Audience of Lima.

THIS is generally called by the *Spaniards*, the *Royal Audience*, not only becaufe the Viceroy hath his Seat there, but by reafon of its having the fole Direction of all the Affairs of *South America*, during the Vacancy of the Viceroyfhip. This Audience of *Lima* is bounded on the North by that of *Quito*; on the Eaft by that unfettled Country we have fo often mentioned; on the South by the Audience of *Los Charcas*; and on the Weft by the *Pacific* Ocean. It extends from 5° 20′ to 18° of S. L.

It is not eafy to imagine any thing more various or uncertain than the Climate and Soil of this Country. In fome Places it is exceffively hot, in others very cold; at *Lima*, and on the Coaft, always temperate. The Seafons vary within the Compafs of a few Miles, and in fome Places all the Varieties of Weather are experienced within the Compafs of twenty-four Hours: But what is moft fingular in this Refpect, and hath exercifed the Wits of curious Perfons moft, is the Want of Rain, and in a great meafure of Rivers on the Sea-Coaft. The Soil differs in like manner; on the Shore it is barren, and looks as if it was burnt up: Farther up the
Country

Country there are Vallies clothed with perpetual Verdure, and Plains of a rich and
fruitful Soil. By this Mixture it falls out,
that taking the whole Audience together, we
may fay it is extremely rich, fufficiently fruitful, and wonderfully pleafant. The Seat of
the Viceroy, the Beauty of the Country, the
Conveniency of the Ports, and above all, the
Abundance of Gold, and other rich Commodities, renders this Territory extremely populous, and full of confiderable Cities and great
Towns, that is, in comparifon of other Countries under the *Spanifh* Government.

The City of *Lima*, which is not only the
Capital of this Audience, but of all *South
America*, is fituated in 12° 1' S. L. and in 76°
34' of Longitude Weft from *London*, at the
Diftance of two Leagues from *Callao*, which
is its Port on the *South Sea*. It ftands in a
pleafant Valley, and owes its Foundation to
the Conqueror of *Peru*, *Francis Pizarro*,
who called it *Cividad de los Reyes*, i. e. *the
City of Kings*, and who began to build it in
January 1535. The Plan of this Place is extremely well contrived, the Streets perfectly
ftraight, and of a convenient Breadth. In the
Midft of the City is a grand Square, which
may be juftly accounted one of the fineft in
the World. On the Eaft Side of it ftands
the Cathedral; on the North the Palace of
the Viceroy; on the Weft feveral publick
Edifices; on the South Piazzas, and handfome

fome Shops of all Sorts. In the Midft there
is a curious brazen Fountain. The River of
Lima runs on the North Side of the City,
and divides it from a very confiderable Sub-
urb, which is however joined to the City by
a very beautiful Stone Bridge, confifting of
five Arches. This River is generally fordable except in the Midft of Summer, when
the Snows being melted on the Mountains,
where there alfo falls at that Seafon a great
deal of Rain, it is thereby raifed to a confiderable Height. In point of Fortifications,
there is very little to be faid, notwithftanding what we find in fome Books of Travels.
It is indeed furrounded with Walls eighteen
or twenty Foot high ; and thefe again are
ornamented with Baftions; but then what
are thefe Walls? nothing but Brick dried in
the Sun, fo thin and fo ill built, that they
cannot fupport the Weight of Cannon ; neither is there fo much as a Ditch ; fo that except it be the *Indians*, no Enemy could be
kept out an Hour by them. In point of
Magnificence, we are told that the Inhabitants keep about four thoufand Calafhes,
which are the only kind of Vehicles here, and
are drawn by Mules. A ftronger Teftimony
we have from the Difplay the Merchants of
this City made of their Wealth in 1682, when
on the Entry of the Duke *de la Palata*, their
Viceroy, they paved two of the Streets, thro'
which he paffed, with Ingots of Silver, to the
Amount

Amount of eighty Millions of Pieces of Eight, which is about eighteen Millions Sterling. But it is not conceived to be near fo rich at prefent. Befides the Court of the Viceroy, and of the Royal Audience, this is the Seat of an Archbifhop, and Metropolitan fince the Year 1546. His Suffragans are the Bifhops of *Panama, Quito, Truxillo, Guamanga, Ariquipa, Cufco, St. Jago,* and the *Conception.* It hath alfo eight large Parifhes, a great many Hofpitals, and fo many Monafteries and Nunneries, that it is a difficult thing to reckon them. There is likewife a Tribunal of the holy Office, or of the Inquifition here, which however is not very terrible, becaufe both the Viceroy and the Archbifhop have Seats therein ; and, to crown all, there is a Univerfity. As to the Number of Inhabitants, it is not eafy to fay any thing with Certainty ; the modefteft Computation I have feen reckons eight or nine thoufand white Families, and about eight and twenty thoufand other Inhabitants ; though fome would perfuade us that here are double the Number.

It is impoffible to imagine a more pleafant and delightful Climate than that of the City of *Lima,* though it ftands in the Midft of the torrid Zone. Notwithftanding it never rains, yet the Sky is generally overcaft, which defends the Inhabitants from the fiery Beams of the Sun, and renders the Weather cool and pleafant.

fant. Add to this, that they enjoy the Advantages of all the Seafons at once; for, as
we obferved before, that they vary throughout the Province; fo the Produce of all Parts
being brought hither, there are in the Markets of *Lima* all forts of Fruits in full Perfection the whole Year round. It is true, the
Sea-Coaft is generally barren and bare to the
laft degree, but in the Neighbourhood of this
City there are Variety of pleafant Valleys,
watered either naturally or artificially by living Streams, adorned with Orange-Groves,
and whatever elfe can render them elegant
and pleafing. But with all thefe Bleffings,
the Citizens are not without continual Apprehenfions, which muft fufficiently qualify
their Enjoyments, fince there is no Place in
the World more fubject to Earthquakes. On
the 17th of *June*, 1678, a great Part of the
City, and feveral of its Churches, were thrown
down in a quarter of an Hour; yet this was
a flight Misfortune to what happened on the
19th of *October*, 1682, when the City fuffered two hundred Shocks in the Space of twenty-four Hours, infomuch that it was wholly
overturned, and the Inhabitants deliberated
for fome time whether they fhould rebuild
their City on the fame Spot where it ftood
before, or endeavour to find out fome other,
where they might have at leaft a Probability
of being fafer. On this Account their Buildings are far lefs magnificent than otherwife
they

they would be, the Climate too favouring this flight kind of Building; for where it never rains, almoft any Houfes will laft long, and anfwer all other Purpofes tolerably well.

Callao, which is as I have faid the Port of *Lima*, lies on the Coaft of the *South Sea*, in the Latitude of 12° 10′. Its Road is by much the largeft, faireft and moft fecure in the *South Seas*. Ships anchor there in what Depth of Water they will, and without any Apprehenfion of Danger. The Town makes a good Figure from the Sea, having abundance of publick Edifices, feveral Churches, and five Monafteries; though the Number of Inhabitants does not exceed four or five hundred Families at moft. It is furrounded by a Wall fortified with ten Baftions, and is believed in *Spain* to be a Place of great Strength, for it cofts the King annually great Sums for the Garrifon, Fortifications, and Squadrons of Men of War, which are fuppofed to lie in this Port. Yet fuch is the Vigilance, fuch the Integrity of his Officers, that the Soldiers at *Callao* are hardly enough to mount Guard; the Walls are in many Places fallen down; and it would take fome Months to repair the Ships, fo as to be fit to go to Sea. It is neverthelefs a Place of prodigious Confequence, and of very extenfive Trade, as the Reader will perceive from the concife Account we fhall give him of its Commerce. There are two Flota's annually fail from hence, one

for

for *Arica*, the other for *Panama*. The former fails about the End of the Month of *February*, and having received at *Arica* the
Silver fent from *Potofi*, returns towards the
End of *March*. In the beginning of *May*,
the Flota fails for *Panama*, having on board
the Wealth brought from *Potofi*, the Silver
from *Chili*, which comes in the *Valparaifo*
Fleet, the King's Revenue and Merchandizes
from all Parts of *Peru*, and the Audience of
los Charcas; and on the Return of this Fleet,
laden with *European* Commodities, they are
difpofed of from hence, Part by Sea, Part by
Land, to all the different Places to which
they are deftin'd. Befides thefe Fleets, there
fail annually two Ships for *Acapulco*, of which
we have already given an Account; and the
Indian Commodities which they bring back,
are all depofited in the Magazines here, and
fent from hence to all the Southern Provinces
of *America*.

Befides *Callao*, there are fome other Ports
in this Province, though none comparable to
that. To the Northward lies the little Harbour of *Guanchaco*, neither fafe nor commodious, yet however ferves for the Traffick
carried on by the Inhabitants of *Truxillo*,
which lies fix Leagues above it, and is a very
rich and flourifhing Place. Twenty-fix
Leagues South from *Lima* lies the Port of
Sangalla, in the Latitude of 14°, and near
it the Ifle of *Lobos*, and fome other little Ifles,
where

where formerly the Natives of *Peru* went to sacrifice to their Idols. Some other Roads and Creeks there are of little Confideration, till you come to *Ariquipa*, which is the moft Southern Port. The Entrance of it is narrow, but when you are once in, there is good Anchorage in eighteen Fathom Water. It ftands about a hundred Leagues from *Lima*, in the Valley of *Quilea*, and is without Controverfy the pleafanteft City in *Peru*, and enjoys a very pure wholefome Air. It is a Bifhop's See, but not very populous, there not being above four or five hundred Houfes in it at moft, yet there is a wonderful fine Country about it, exceedingly fruitful, and well ftocked with Cattle ; but though it is a very important Place, there are few or no Fortifications round it ; and it is the Obfervation of a *Spanifh* Writer, that the Safety of its Inhabitants confifts in the Ignorance of Foreigners of their wretched Weaknefs.

The Inland Towns of *Peru* are alfo very confiderable. *Guanuco* is a large Town feated in a pleafant Valley in 10° of *South* Latitude. In the Country adjacent all Sorts of *Spanifh* Fruit grow in the higheft Perfection. *Guamanga*, or, as the *Spaniards* call it, *St. Juan de la Vittoria*, ftands in the Midft between *Lima* and *Cufco*. It is feated on a fine River, furrounded with beautiful Gardens ; and the Air is remarkably pure and frefh. It is a Bifhop's See, erected chiefly for the Sake of of the *Indians*, the Miffionaries, who are employed to convert them, making it their principal Station. From thence to *Cufco* it is about forty-five Leagues, travelling all the Way on the Royal Road fo called, becaufe it was made by the *Yncas* of *Peru*. This famous Metropolis of the *Peruvian* Empire ftill retains fome Marks of its former Magnificence, and fuch as will always ftrike intelligent Strangers with a juft Idea of the Power and Wifdom of the antient Monarchs of that Country, notwithftanding all the Pains the *Spaniards* have taken to pull down and deftroy the *Ynca's* Palace, and the reft of the publick Edifices. Out of the Ruins they take thofe large Stones of which their Houfes are here built, as they owe a great deal of their Riches to the Difcoveries they daily make of the hidden Treafures of the *Indians*. The Air of *Cufco* is fo remarkably pure and wholefome, that fick People come thither from all Parts of *Peru* in order to recover their Health.

The mountainous Country about *Cufco*, and throughout the Middle of *Peru*, is well inhabited by the *Indians*, who are better treated here than elfewhere. The *Spaniards* demand of them a fmall Tribute, which is paid half yearly; in all other Refpects they are not only free, but alfo at Liberty to gain their Bread as they think fit; and as their Mafters are not much addicted to Labour, fo

the fe

thefe People being induftrious, exercife all
kind of Manufactures ; and, befides addicting
themfelves to a kind of peddling Trade, they
live much at their Eafe, and fometimes acquire a good deal of Wealth.   They likewife
trade with thofe *Indian* Nations who have no
direct Commerce with the *Spaniards*; and
by furnifhing them partly with Neceffaries,
partly with Baubles, obtain from them confiderable Quantities of Gold Duft, and other
rich Commodities, which they again barter
with the *Spaniards* for fuch Tools and Orna-
ments as they ftand in need of.

Before we quit the Audience of *Lima*, it
is neceffary for us to obferve, that within its
Bounds there are found almoft all kinds of
Mines. Of Gold there are feveral, befides
very rich Lavaderoes: thofe particularly in
the Diftrict of *Guanuco* near *Lima*, will be
for ever famous for two extraordinary *Pepitas*, or Lumps of pure Gold that were found
in them, and are by far the largeft that were
ever heard of, the one weighing fixty-four
Marks, the other forty-five ; the Mark is
eight Ounces ; and what is ftill more fingular, the laft of thefe contained Gold of different Degrees of Finenefs, *viz.* of eleven,
eighteen, and twenty-one Carrats. There are
alfo feveral Mines of Silver ; and there were
more efpecially in the Neighbourhood of
Cufco, before thofe of *Potofi* were difcovered,
which are much richer, and are wrought
with

with far lefs Expence. However, in 1713, they opened here at *Cufco* the rich Mine of *St. Anthony*, of which they had great Hopes.

But there is another Mine, which though it yields neither Gold nor Silver, is more confidered than all the reft in the Province. It is in the Neighbourhood of *Guancavalica*; it lies in the Latitude of 14°, at the Diftance of about 180 Miles from the Sea. This Mine is of Quickfilver, of which it is fuppofed to contain an inexhauftible Quantity. At leaft this we know for certain, that it yields fufficient for the Service of all the Mines in this Audience. It is managed with a great deal of Caution, for it is neither opened nor fhut but by the exprefs Direction of the Viceroy of *Peru*. The Mine is about 100 Foot broad at the Mouth, and fix or feven hundred Foot deep. The Mineral is of a reddifh Colour, like a half burnt Brick. When it is taken out of the Mine, they break it to pieces, and by the Help of a quick Fire, and proper Furnace, they extract the Quickfilver much in the fame way that our Chymifts ufe in making *Lac Sulphuris*. It is dug out of the Mine, and purified at the Expence of private Perfons; but then they are obliged to bring it to the King's Warehoufes, on the Pain of perpetual Slavery, where they fell it for fixty Pieces of Eight the Quintal. The King fells it out again for the Ufe of the Gold and Silver Mines at the Rate of Eighty Pieces of Eight.

Eight.   As foon as there is a fufficient Quantity drawn out of the Mine, the Mouth of it is fhut by order of the Viceroy; and Quickfilver is a Commodity no private Man can deal in under the higheft Penalties.

The Quickfilver from the Mine of *Guancavalica*, as well as all the Commodities and Manufactures of the City of *Guamanga*, and thereabouts, are tranfported by Land to the Port of *Pifco*, of which I forgot to fpeak when I enumerated the Harbours on this Coaft. It lies in 13° 40', and the Road before it is equally fafe and commodious.   This Place heretofore ftood clofe by the Sea-Side; but on the 19th of *October*, 1682, there happened an Earthquake, which occafioned the Sea to retire half a League, whence returning with prodigious Violence, it fwept away the whole Town.   The new one was built about a quarter of a League from the Sea, and contained about three hundred Families, moft of them Meftizos or Negroes: But on the 3d of *February*, 1716, this too was demolifhed by an Earthquake; but inafmuch as the Harbour is very good, and there are great Conveniencies of wooding and watering here, we may fuppofe that by this Time it has recovered its former State.

CHAP.

C H A P. XIV.

Of the Audience de los Charcas, *or as some call it, the Audience* de la Plata.

THIS Province is not only known by the Names mentioned in the Title of this Chapter, but also by that of the Audience of *Chuquisaca*, from a City of the same Name, of which we shall presently take Notice. It extends from 18° to 24° S. L. and from 63° to 75° of Longitude, West from *London*. It is bounded on the North by the Audience of *Lima*; on the East by *Paraguay*; on the South by *Chili* and *Tucuman*; and on the West by the *South Sea*. The greatest Part of it lies in the Torrid Zone; but the Frontier, towards *Chili* and *Tucuman*, lies in the South temperate Zone, yet the Climate is but indifferent throughout. On the Shore it is excessively hot, and the Inland Parts of the Country partake so much of the other Extreme, that it is said the *Spanish* Ladies, when pregnant, are compelled to seek a warmer Climate before they can be delivered. The Soil however is generally speaking fruitful; on the Coast it is made so by Art, but the Valleys among the Mountains in the Inland Part, are from Nature luxuriously fertile, being every where sufficiently watered; whereas there are no Rivers

at

at all upon the Coaft. As to the Commodities of this Country, though it may be juftly
ftyled one of the richeft in the World, yet
they may be reduced to two, *Pimento*, which
grows upon the Coaft, and is a kind of Pepper little different from that which we call
Jamaica Pepper, and which produces to
the Inhabitants fix hundred thoufand Pieces
of Eight *per Annum*. The other Commodity is Silver, of the Value of which, for the
Space of fifty Years, we fhall prefently fpeak,
from the Authority of the beft *Spanifh* Writers, and the Records of *Potofi*.

Throughout the whole Extent of this Province there are very rich Mines, fome near
the Coaft, fome at a greater Diftance, fome
very lately difcovered, and fome which have
been wrought ever fince the *Spaniards* fettled
here. We will begin our Defcription with
the Capital of this Country, which is *La
Plata*, or, as the *Indians* call it, *Chuquifaca*,
a large, populous, and well built City, erected
by Pope *Paul* V. into an Archbifhoprick,
having for its Suffragans the Bifhops of *La
Paz*, or *Chuquiaca*, *St. Miguel el Eftero*,
Santà Cruz de la Sierra, *Santa Trinidad de
Buenos Ayres*, the *Affumption* in *Paraguay*,
and the *Affumption* on the *River of Plate*.
It was formerly very confiderable on account
of the rich Mines in its Neighbourhood, many
of which are now neglected; however, it is
ftill the Capital of the Audience, and one of
the

the moft confiderable Cities in the *Spanish* Dominions. It lies in the Latitude of 20°, at the Diftance of near three hundred Miles from the Sea Coaft, one hundred and fifty Leagues S. E. from *Cufco*, about two hundred from *Lima*, and about fifty N. E. from *Potofi*. This laft Place, fo famous for its inexhauftible Treafures, lies in the Latitude of 21°, toward the Extremity of the torrid Zone, in a Climate much colder than ours, though according to the Latitude in which it lies, it ought to be exceffively hot. The Reafon of its Coldnefs is its great Height, expofed to Winds, and particularly one they there call *Tomahavi*, which is fierce and cold, and prevails from *May* till *Auguft*. The Mountain is naturally dry, cold, barren, bare, and uncouth, producing neither Fruit nor Grafs, and fcarce habitable; and yet the Plenty of Silver has caufed it to be inhabited, and afford Plenty of all Things. The Colour of the Earth is a dark red, the Shape of the Hill is like a Sugar Loaf, rifing above all the other Hills about it; the Afcent fteep, yet fo as that they go up it on Horfeback, about a League in Compafs at the Bottom, and a quarter of a League from the Top to the Foot. From the bottom of it rifes another Hill called *Guanapotofi*, that is, *Young Potofi*, where there were formerly Mines, but the Veins were not fixed. At the Foot of the great Hill lies the Town of *Spaniards* and

and *Indians*, which is about two Leagues in Compafs, where is a prodigious Trade. The *Ingas* wrought at the Mines of *Porco*, but never knew thefe, which were found by an *Indian*, called *Gualca*, of the Nation of the *Chunbibilcas*, in the Territory of *Cuzco*, who following fome Deer, they ran up the Hill, and he purfuing up the fteep Part, laid hold on a Bufh that grew in a Vein, and being torn up, difcovered the Metal which the *Indian* knew by being acquainted with the Mines at *Porco*. He carried fome Pieces of it to *Porco*, to be affayed by Fire, and privately melted the Silver he drew from thence, till another *Indian* of the Vale of *Xauxa* obferving that he throve better than he had done before, and had larger Pigs of Plate, preffed him to impart the Secret. *Gualca* told him, and they agreed to divide the Mine, but foon fell out, becaufe he of *Xauxa* knew not how to refine his Silver, and *Gualca* would not tell him how he managed his; fo that being incenfed on this and other Accounts, he difcovered the Matter to his Mafter, whofe Name was *Villareal*, refiding at *Porco*, who finding the Treafure his Servant had told him, obliged *Gualca* to regifter, and ftake out the Vein jointly with him, which is marking out the Number of Yards the Law allows to thofe that difcover or work Mines; by this Means, and notifying the fame to the proper Officers, they became Proprietors of the Mine,

to

to work it as their own, paying the King the fifth Part of the Product. This first Regifter of the Mines of *Potofi* was in *April* 1545. From that Time new Entries were made, as new Mines were difcovered ; and that we may form fome Idea of the immenfe Wealth accruing from the Difcovery of thefe Mines to all *Europe*, I fhall fet down from the Regifter, the King's Fifth, from the Year 1545 to the Year 1595, which amounted to one hundred and eleven Millions of *Pefos*. This Term has led many Writers into Miftakes, who have computed them as Pieces of Eight, whereas it is certain that the *Pefo* is an imaginary Denomination, like our Pound Sterling, and is worth thirteen Reals and a quarter, which makes a vaft Alteration in fo large an Account. The King's annual Fifth then for that Time was about eight hundred and eighty thoufand Pound *per Annum*, which is indeed a prodigious Sum ; and therefore I am apt to think that this Account is not the King's Fifth, but the Silver of which he received the Fifth, and even at this Rate, thefe Mines in fifty Years produced upwards of forty four Millions Sterling. They are ftill wrought to an immenfe Profit, though not to near fo great as formerly.

The Town of *Potofi*, which ftands at the Foot of the Hill, is very large, and the Buildings very magnificent, efpecially the Churches. The Number of its Inhabitants is computed

at

at 60,000, of which 10,000 are *Spaniards*,
the reft *Indians* and Slaves. The neighbouring Cantons of the *Indians* are obliged to furnifh annually fuch a Number of Labourers as
are demanded. This is done about *Chriftmas*;
and though the *Indians* go with little Spirit
to *Potofi*, yet it is obferved that many of
them fettle there, and never return home, as
they might do at the End of the Year. It is
a great Miftake we are under in our Notion,
that Negroes are employed in working thefe
Mines, fince it is certain that though they are
much ftronger and more robuft than the *Indians*, yet they are not able to bear the Exhalations of the Mines, which ftifle them as
foon as they are let down ; neither would the
Indians be able to work, if they were not
frequently refrefhed with *Paraguay* Tea.

Weft from *Potofi* ftands *Porco*, in the
Neighbourhood of which there are Mines
much richer than thofe of *Potofi*, but harder
to work by reafon of the Water which is
found in them, whereas there is none in the
Mines of *Potofi*, even at a very great Depth.
Nearer to the Coaft are the famous Mines of
Lipez, in the Latitude of 23°; they are numerous, and were formerly very rich : they
are now wrought to great Profit, and without doubt would be more minded than they
are, if fo many new Mines were not daily
difcovered, which yield ftill more Silver, and
with lefs Trouble ; as for Inftance, thofe
that

that *Oruro*, a little Town eighty Leagues from *Arica*, whence they draw a fifth Part of Silver from the Ore, befides many others. It may not be amifs to obferve here, that when Mines are fhut up, and no longer wrought, we muft not fuppofe that they are totally loft, for after a confiderable Space, they open them again, and draw from them frefh Riches, fometimes in greater Quantities than at firft. The very Drofs, and Refufe of the Mines of *Potofi*, after being thrown into the River, and raked from thence, hath been found to yield large Quantities of Silver, which pro- bably grew therein, after it was firft wrought.

Though we hear very little faid of the Gold of this Country, yet it is not deftitute of that precious Metal. At *La Paz*, on the Frontiers of the Audience of *Lima*, there is one of the richeft Mines in *America*, whence the *Indians* call it *Chuquiago*, or the *Golden Grange*. About the Year 1680, there hap- pened a violent Storm of Thunder and Light- ning thereabouts, which ftruck down a Piece of the Mountain *Ilimana*, the Shivers of which flew all over the City, and being picked up were found full of Grains of Gold, though that Mountain is fo high as to be al- ways covered with Snow. At the other Ex- tremity of the Audience of *los Charcos*, to- wards the Country of *Chili*, in the Neigh- bourhood of a Town called *Tarya*, there are alfo Gold Mines which are very rich.

The

The moſt conſiderable Places in this Audience, beſides thoſe which we have already
mentioned, are *Santa Cruz la Nueva, Santa Cruz de la Sierra, Oropeza,* &c. of all
which we have not Room to ſpeak here. But
as to the Ports in this Province, it is neceſſary
we ſhould ſay ſomewhat. *Ilo,* or as the *Spaniards* call it, *Ylo,* is the moſt northern Port
in the Lat. of 17° 37′. It has but an indifferent Road, and the Village in its Neighbourhood is far from being conſiderable. The
French, during the late War, made a kind of
Settlement here, and carried on a great contraband Trade, notwithſtanding the Climate
is ſo unwholeſome, that it frequently carried
off one half of a Ship's Crew.

Arica is the proper Port of *Potoſi* and *la
Plata.* It is an indifferent good Road, if it
were not open to the South. Formerly it
had ſome Fortifications, but they are now
decayed, and the Place is very little better
than a Village, occaſioned chiefly by its being extremely ſubject to Earthquakes, and
withal exceſſively unwholeſome. One great
Cauſe of this is the Stench of Cormorants
Dung, which the Inhabitants call *Guana :*
this they gather with great Care, and thereof they make a great Profit. It is uſed
to manure the Earth, and is ſaid to fertilize
it ſo much, as to make it yield four or five
hundred Buſhels for one.

This

This Port of *Arica* ſtands in the Lat. of 18º 29′, at the Diſtance of about 70 Leagues from *Potoſi*. In the Month of *March* they begin to bring the Silver from thence to *Arica*, and in *June* the Flota from *Lima* comes to fetch it. There is a conſtant Intercourſe between *la Plata, Oruru, Lipes,* and this Port, by Land, for the Conveniency of which there are Inns at every four Leagues, inſomuch that it is computed there are two thouſand Perſons employed in the Management of theſe Inns, and as Carriers : Yet this is nothing in compariſon of the Numbers employed in the ſame Way, with reſpect to the Inland Commerce with the Mines ; for, as this extends through the whole *South America*, there are not leſs than ten thouſand People concerned therein, who are continually in Motion. Beſides all this, there is a Communication both by Land and Water between *Potoſi* and *Buenos Ayres*, by which, if the Crown of *Spain* thought fit, the Silver might with great Eaſe be brought into *Europe*. But it is time to quit *Los Charcas*, and to proceed from this Country of Silver to that which of all others abounds moſt in Gold.

CHAP.

C H A P. XV.

Of the Audience of Chili.

THIS very rich Country lies along the Coaft of the *South Sea*, from the S. Lat. of 26° to that of 47°; and from 61° to 72° of Longitude Weft from *London*, that is, taking in the whole of the Country fo called by the *Spaniards*, and not confining ourfelves to that only which is fettled and conquered. On the North it is bounded by *Peru* ; on the Eaft by *Tucuman, Paraguay*, and the *Terra Magellanica* ; on the Weft by the *South Sea* ; through the Midft of it, from North to South, run thofe prodigious high Mountains, called by the *Spaniards, Sierra Nevada de los Andes*, to which, fome Writers tell us, the *Alps* themfelves are but Hillocks, and in paffing over them, the Air is found to be fo pure and light, as not to ferve, at leaft conveniently, for Refpiration. Some, who have travelled over thefe Mountains, have been feized with fuch violent Vomitings, as forced them to bring up vaft Quantities of Blood ; nor could they poffibly have furvived a very few Minutes, on the Summits of thefe Mountains.

The Climate of *Chili* is differently fpoken of by different Writers ; fome commend, and fome condemn it, according, probably, to the Seafons in which they were there ;

but,

but, according to the Accounts we have from the beft Writers, fome of them Natives of this Country, its Summers are not hotter than thofe in *Spain*; but the Winters are more rigorous by far; whence the Name of the Country, for *Chili*, in the Language of the Natives, fignifies *Cold*. Towards the Mountains particularly, it is fo fharp, that Cattle, and even Men, are frequently frozen. Befides, in the Winter, towards the Coaft efpecially, there fall prodigious Rains; and during this Time the Country is accounted unwholefome, as well as very unpleafant. The Soil is wonderfully fertile, producing not only *Indian*, but *European* Corn, Wine, Fruits, and all the Neceffaries of Life in Abundance; whatever Herbs, Fruits, or Flowers grow in *Spain*, are cultivated with Succefs here: And we learn from the Accounts of the lateft Travellers, that in the Gardens of the Cities near the Coaft, Orange-Trees are kept bearing all the Year.

But the Products of *Chili*, which are moft valuable in the Eyes of the *Spaniards*, are not fuch as grow on, but are found in the Earth, in which it is, without comparifon, the richeft Country hitherto known in the whole World, its Mountains every where abounding with Gold, Silver, Copper, Lead, Mercury, Saltpetre, and Sulphur. From fuch Parts of it as the *Spaniards* have thoroughly fettled, they reap immenfe Profits, and

and yet the richeft Part of *Chili* is ftill in the Hands of the Natives, and like to remain fo, their mountainous Situations affording the *Indians* fuch Advantages, as the *Europeans*, confidering their fmall Number, can hardly ever furmount. In the mean time, the Governors run away with the greateft Part of the Wealth accruing from this important Settlement, the King on the one hand being daily cheated of his Revenues, and on the other, paying prodigious Salaries, which are ftiled here, *Real Situado* ; fo that fmaller Returns are made to *Spain* on the King's Account from hence than can well be imagined. It muft however be owned, that within thefe twenty Years, fome Pains have been taken to remedy thefe Abufes. After the Difgrace of the great Duke *de Ripperda*, fome of the *Spanifh* Nobility advifed King *Philip* to have fent him Governor hither, and as he was a Man of great Parts, well fkilled in Trade, and of a Temper not to be difcouraged by crofs Accidents, it is very probable he might have done great Things here, both for himfelf and for the *Spanifh* Crown; but being difappointed of this Preferment, he is faid in Revenge to have formed fome Schemes for the taking away *South America*, entirely from its prefent Mafters. However, this perhaps may not be fo certain as fome have pretended, for that Nobleman was wont to fpread Re-

ports

ports of himfelf, which had not always the beft Foundations.

The Natives of *Chili* are of a kind of Copper Colour, tall, well made, robuft Perfons, extremely active, very ingenious, and withal brave, and Lovers of Liberty: At leaft fuch they were when the *Spaniards* broke in upon them, about the Middle of the fixteenth Century. The Marquis *Pizarro* gave this Government to *Peter de Valdivia*, a great Politician, and a good Officer, unfortunate only in not having a fufficient Body of Men. He founded the prefent Càpital *St. Jago*, as well as a City of his own Name; but when he once difcovered that the Country was full of Gold, he attempted fo many Eftablifhments, that he gave the *Indians*, whom he had treated alfo harfhly, Opportunity, as he had before given them Inclination to revolt and to recover their Country. They conducted this Defign with equal Boldnefs and Addrefs. Before they took up Arms, they confidered attentively the *Spanifh* Manner of Difcipline, the Ufe of Fire-Arms, and the Advantages refulting from them. They then fell upon fome ftraggling Parties, and having defeated and deftroyed them, feized their Arms, and made ufe of them, as well as if they had been accuftomed to the Soldiers Trade from their Infancy. *Peter Valdivia* faw his Error too late, and endeavoured to rectify it as foon as was pof-fible.

sible. He collected with the utmost Expedition, a very considerable Body of Troops, with which he marched against the *Indians*, who did not engage him immediately, as he expected, but by attacking several Places of the utmost Importance, forced him to make Detachments, and then fell upon the Body commanded by himself, and cut him and them to pieces. This was in the Year 1552, and by this Defeat the *Spaniards* had well nigh lost the Country. His Lieutenant, *Don Francis de Villagra*, was a Person, in Favour of whom a Digression will seem pardonable. As soon as the News reached him of the Governor's Misfortune, he immediately slighted the advanced Posts, and even abandoned some of the new Towns, that he might preserve the rest. The Inhabitants were so well satisfied both of his Capacity and Integrity, that they refus'd no Service upon which he put them, which saved the Province. The Government however at *Lima* thought proper to remove him, merely because he had acted without their Authority, directing the Magistrates of Cities to govern till they took farther Order; but they wisely represented against so ruinous a Scheme, and at their Intercession *Villagra* was constituted first Magistrate, and Commander in chief. While he acted in this Capacity, he obtained several great Victories over the *Indians*, and made considerable Conquests, though they carried

on

on the War regularly, fortified their Camps with Intrenchments, and erected several Forts in order to cover the open Country. In all Probability he would have reftored the Colony to its former State, but the Viceroy of *Peru* wifely fent his Son to take from him the Command, and to fend him Prifoner to *Lima*, which was accordingly done ; but the *Spanifh* Inhabitants ftill preferve the Memory of his glorious Atchievements, and own him for the Conqueror of *Chili*, or at leaft fo much of it as hath remained in their Hands ever fince.

This Country extends not lefs than three hundred Leagues from North to South, but then its Breadth is nothing proportionable ; it is entirely under the Government of its Prefident, for lying at fuch a Diftance from *Lima*, the Viceroy feldom interferes. For the Sake of the more eafy Diftribution of Juftice, it is divided into three Diftricts, *viz.* thofe of *Chili proper*, *Imperial*, and of *Cuyo*. As to the Number of Inhabitants, they are not according to the lateft and beft Accounts any way agreeable to fuch a vaft Extent of Territory. The *Spaniards* throughout the Whole are not accounted above twenty thoufand Men capable of bearing Arms ; of Meftizos, Mulattos, Negroes, *&c.* there may be between feventy and eighty thoufand ; but the Bulk of the Inhabitants are *Indians.* Of thefe, fome are ftyled *free*, and others *fub-jetted.*

jected. The former own'd the Dominion of
the King of *Spain*, but they pay him no
Tribute; whereas the latter belong to the
Spaniards, live amongst them, and serve them;
not however as Slaves, but as Servants: they
are divided according to their Habitations into little Lordships of so many Families more
or less, styled *Commanderies*, which the King
gives to whom he pleases. If the *Indians*
live with their Lord and serve him, he must
not only maintain them, but give them each
thirty Pieces of Eight a Year. On the other
hand, if the *Indians* are not inclined to live
with their Lord, they are exempted, paying
him an annual Tribute of ten Pieces of Eight.
The Number of these subjected *Indians* may
be about fifteen thousand. There are also
some *Indian* Slaves which are sold to the
Spaniards by the free *Indians*, yet by the
Laws they cannot be sold a second Time, but
by their own Consent.

The free *Indians* amount to many thousands,
and inhabit the greatest Part of the Country,
especially towards the Mountains. About the
Year 1690, they made their last Treaty of
Peace with the *Spaniards*, by which on the
one hand they acknowledge the King of *Spain*
for their lawful Sovereign, and on the other
he granted them to live peaceably according
to their own Manner, and their own Laws.
They are governed by their respective Chiefs,
whom the *Spaniards* style *Caciques*; but the
Indians

Indians themfelves do not acknowledge that Title. Thefe Chiefs, like the Judges of *Ifrael*, claim no Authority, but in adminiftering Juftice, and commanding their Tribes in time of War, having neither Palaces nor Revenue, nor any great Marks of Refpect paid them, except in the Execution of their Office. They alfo manage the whole Affairs of their Nation in certain general Affemblies, where each has a Seat, and free Liberty of Speech; after Debate, the Queftion is decided by Plurality of Voices. Every free *Indian* is bound to have his Horfe and Arms always in order, fo that on the Sound of a Trumpet, they immediately mount and repair to their refpective Pofts, where their Chiefs form them into order: Their Arms are Pikes, Bows and Arrows, with Swords. When they engage, they do it regularly, in Squadrons and Battalions, never fighting but with a Morafs in their Rear, into which, in cafe of the worft, they retreat, and fortify themfelves fo effectually, that it is rarely found advifeable to attack them. They have very little Religion, and yet are very unwilling to receive the Inftructions of the Miffionaries, chiefly becaufe the Chriftian Religion forbids Drunkennefs and Poligamy, to both which Exceffes they are, generally fpeaking, extravagantly prone. Notwithftanding this, they are commonly very healthy, and live to great Ages. It is obferved that by degrees they accuftom
them-

themfelves to the *Spanifh* Manners, which gives that Nation great Satisfaction, though perhaps it is not very well founded; for as thefe People are very brave, and very far from being Barbarians, they may fome time or other quarrel with the *Europeans*, and once again expel them their Country.

The Reader will fee the Probability of this, when we have told him what happen'd here fo lately as in the Year 1715. During the long Wars, on Account of the Succeffion to the Crown of *Spain*, great Inconveniences arofe in *America*, from the Want of due Attention to the Conduct of the Viceroys and Governors in that diftant Part of the World. The Governors of the *City of Conception* in *Chili* were feveral of them of this unruly fort; a Defire of getting hindered them from attending to the Confequences, even of the moft violent and unjuft Proceedings, efpecially towards the *Indians* of the Plain, who were divided into Commanderies, and of confequence fubject to the *Spaniards*. This had rendered them moody and difcontented, though they are naturally the moft docile People in the World. The Son of the firft Prefident of the Audience of *St. Jago*, a Youth of about two and twenty Years of Age, coming to have the fupreme Command there, drove them into an open Rebellion, in preparing for which they acted with fuch Addrefs, that the Confpiracy was upon the

Point

Point of breaking out before it was fufpected. The young Governor behaved worfe upon this Occafion than he had done before, obliging the Inhabitants to fend many of their *Indians*, who were innocent, to Prifon, and even proceeding fo far as to execute feveral of them in order to ftrike, as he pretended, Terror into the Rebels.

At the Time this happened, there were a great many *French* Ships in the Road, and upon this Occafion the Officers went in a Body to offer the Governor their Service. He received them with the utmoft Contempt, told them the *Spaniards* never needed any Affiftance either to fecure or to inlarge their Conquefts; nay, threatened to punifh them for carrying on an illicit Trade, though a third Part of the Squadron were able to have taken and burnt the Town if they had fo pleafed. Upon this the *French* failed away, and within a few Days after this modern *Don Quixot*, having firft privately fent to *Peru* his moft valuable Effects, would willingly have fled himfelf, and have left the Town to the Mercy of the inraged *Indians*; but the Inhabitants prevented him. By a feafonable Supply of Forces from *St. Jago*, the Rebellion was quafhed, partly by fair means, and partly by Force. On this Occafion the *Indians* of the Plain had demanded Affiftance of the free *Indians*, but were refufed it, only they were content to intercede for them, when

when these Troubles were composed. From
hence it may be easily judged, that of all the
Spanish Provinces in *America*, this is in most
Danger; and yet such is the Luxury and
Corruption of this infatuated Nation, that
they go on oppressing the *Indians* and neg-
lecting their Fortifications, as if they had no-
thing to fear either from the Fury of their
Enemies, or from the Resentment of their
Master.

After having said so much of the Inhabitants, it is now time to speak of the Places
they inhabit; and, in order to do this with
some Method, we will treat of the Districts
before-mentioned, in the Order in which they
lie.

In order then to proceed regularly in the
Description of this great Country, we shall
advance from North to South, mentioning all
the considerable Ports, and other great Towns
as they are found in the Maps, taking in
thereby the two maritime Provinces of *Chili
proper* and *Imperial*, and then we will
speak of the District of *Cuyo*, which lies
quite behind these, and hath not hitherto
been fully settled, though the *Spaniards* pro-
mise themselves great future Advantages therefrom.

The first Place we meet with then in pas-
sing from *Peru* is *Copiapo*, in 27° of S. L. to
which belongs the Port of *Caldera*, which
has a Road tolerably safe, and would probably

bly be much frequented, if Wood and Water were not exceſſively ſcarce and dear. *Copiapo* lies fourteen Leagues to the Eaſtward of Port *Caldera*, and twenty Leagues according to the ordinary Road, over a miſerable Country, deſtitute of all things either pleaſant or convenient. Until of late Years it hath paſſed for a Place of no great Importance; but ſince 1710, it has been conſidered in another Light. A *Spaniſh* Author ſays it is the richeſt Place in the World; and the Reaſon he aſſigns would induce one to think him in the Right. Its Foundations are of Gold, that is, the Village of *Copiapo*, for ſo it originally was, ſtands upon a Gold Mine exceſſively rich. This however is not wrought at preſent, becauſe at about ſix Miles Diſtance, they have diſcovered Mines of Gold ſtill richer. What theſe Mines, well managed, might produce, is uncertain; but, by an Account given by a *Fleming*, who in the Year 1720 was employed in working them, the Reader may form ſome Computation; and therefore from his Account we will ſtate the Facts.

The Inhabitants of *Copiapo*, according to his Apprehenſion, might be ſeven hundred, the Perſons employed in the Mines a thouſand at leaſt. Their Mills were twelve in all, and one Day with another they extracted from the Mineral, one hundred and fifty Ounces of Gold, or about thirty thouſand Ounces

Ounces in a Year, as appear'd by the Infpec-
tor of the Mines Account. This Gold
might be fold on the Spot for fifty Shillings an
Ounce, confequently thefe Mines yield better than eighty thoufand Pounds *per Annum.*
The Neighbourhood of this Place, though
nothing can be more miferable in Appearance, is however rich beyond Expreffion.
Saltpetre lies, or rather ftands upon the
Ground two Feet high in many Places ; and
any where elfe this alone would be fufficient
to attract a Trade. About fixty Miles South
from *Copiapo* are Lead Mines, neither wrought
nor thought of; yet fome intelligent Perfons
think them more valuable than the Gold
ones, becaufe fome who have vifited them,
have picked up on the Surface of the Earth
feveral Pounds of *Lapis Lazuli,* one of the
moft valuable Commodities in the World;
nay, it is affirmed that this *Peruvian* Stone
is not at all inferior to that which comes from
the *Eaft Indies,* but is rather of a deeper
Blue, and has fewer Veins. In the *Cordil-
leras* Mountains, which lie Eaft-fouth-eaft
from this Town about a hundred Miles,
there are Mines of Sulphur, which in their
kind furpafs all others. The Vein here is
two Foot broad at leaft, whence the Sulphur
is drawn perfectly pure, fo that they have
nothing to do but to carry it away and expofe
it to Sale. Such are the Riches of *Copiapo,*
which notwithftanding hardly affords Bread
and

and Roots to the fcanty Number of its Inhabitants.

In moving South towards *Coquimbo*, you pafs through an hundred Leagues of the worft Country in the World, without meeting with either Village or Town, Tree or Shrub, River or Brook; fo that frequently the Cattle upon the Road perifh for Want of Refrefhment. In this Journey, however, you fee many Mines of Copper and Tin; and in a Mountain on the South-eaft there have been found very fine *Turkey* Stones; though, for Want of any Settlement near it, the farther Search of them has been abandoned. The Cold of this Country is fcarce to be expreffed : the *Indians* of *Peru* are frequently killed by it.

The River of *Coquimbo* gives Name to an agreeable Valley through which it rolls into the Sea. The Bay at the Mouth of it is a very fine one, and Ships lie there very fafely as well as commodioufly, though the Coaft is rocky; but fome Iflands fo effectually keep off the Winds, that there is no fort of Hazard in lying as clofe to them as poffible. The Town is commonly called *Coquimbo*, but the Name of it is properly *la Serena*. It lies in the Lat. of 29° 53', and boafts of one of the fineft Situations in the Univerfe. The few Streets it has are ftraight, and well laid out; there is a reafonable Plenty of Water, tho' the River of *Coquimbo* is generally fordable.

Every

Every Houſe has a large Garden filled with Oranges, Olives, &c. An endleſs Verdure reigns here without Storms, without parching Heat, or any Cold that is inconvenient. The Soil is fruitful, and all the Country about it abounds with the Neceſſaries of Life, eſpecially Corn, Wine and Oil, exquiſite in their kind, and exceſſively cheap ; there is the ſame Plenty of Cattle, tame and wild Fowl ; and in the adjacent Valleys there is ſo plentiful a Breed of Horſes, that one which would coſt thirty or forty Pounds in *England*, may be had here for half as many Shillings. After all this, the Town of *la Serena* is a very pitiful Place; there are indeed five or ſix Convents, which make a tolerable Appearance, but except the Governor's, all the Houſes in the Town are mere Cabbins, and the People who inhabit them, are far enough from being at their Eaſe, I mean in the *Spaniſh* Senſe of the Word, that is, they are not rich. There are no Mines of Gold in this Neighbourhood, and though there are many of Copper, yet they are little wrought. We muſt not however imagine that they are altogether deſtitute of rich Commodities, for, in the Winter Seaſon, when the Rains are violent, all the little Brooks bring down Gold, of which, if they had Hands enough, a great Profit might be made ; but as all the Inhabitants do not exceed twelve or fifteen hundred Perſons at moſt, they do not get much.
The

The Trade of this Place confifts in fending four or five Ships yearly to *Lima* laden with Flower, Wine, and other Provifions, in return for which they receive all forts of *European* Goods, which are tranfported from hence into other Parts of *Chili*. This Place has been often plundered heretofore by our Buccaneers. The *Spaniards* have now fecured it effectually ; they have render'd it fo poor, that it is not worth plundering.

The next Port on this Coaft of any Confequence is that of *Valparayfo* ; it lies in 32° 15′ of S. L. and is by much the moft confiderable Haven in thefe Seas, being conftantly frequented by Veffels from *Callao* and *Panama*, which come hither to lade Corn : they are of confiderable Burthen ; and therefore there is no doubt of meeting here with experienced Pilots for any Part of the Coaft, efpecially to the Northward. The Harbour is tolerably good, in the Summer Months efpecially, but in the Winter it is infecure, by reafon of its lying open to the North Wind, which blows then with great Force. Some Pains has been taken to fortify this Place ; and the *White Caftle*, or *Caftillo Blanco*, as the *Spaniards* call it, makes a formidable Appearance ; but then there are rarely above two or three Guns in a Condition of firing. Befides this, there is another Fort which covers the Road. The Port of *Quintero*, which lies about five Leagues to the North, and is

is very near as good as this, has no Fortifications at all. Ships fometimes lie there for
Conveniency till they can get a Lading from
Valparayfo. This confifts chiefly in Corn,
of which fuch vaft Quantities are fent to
Market, that the Magiftrates have a difcre-
tionary Power of ordering as much as they
think proper to be thrown into the Sea, that
the Remainder may fell the better ; and this
they have fometimes pufhed fo far, as to deftroy many thoufand Loads at once; which,
confidering the extraordinary Scarcity many
Cities in the *Spanifh* Dominions frequently
experience, muft be regarded as a very ftrange
Stroke of their Policy, much like that of
their *Lima* Merchants, who fo overlade their
Veffels with Corn, that they founder at Sea.

At the Diftance of 28 Leagues from *Valparayfo* to the South-eaft, lies the great City
of *St. Jago,* or rather, as I take it, *the City
of St. James the Great,* whom the *Spaniards* call *San Jago* ; for *St. James the Lefs,*
they call *San Diego.* This City, which is
the Capital of *Chili,* ftands in 33° 40′ S. L.
at the Foot of the Mountains, having a very
fine Plain before it, watered by no lefs than
three Rivers. It is very regularly built, and
makes a fine Shew, every Houfe having a
Court before, and a Garden behind it. The
whole City is fo happily watered, that, by
the Help of Canals, they not only fupply
their Gardens plentifully, but can alfo, whenever

ever they think fit, turn a Stream of Water through each of the Streets, keeping them thereby continually clean and cool. In the Center of the Place there is a very fine Square. The Eaſt Side of this is taken up by the Cathedral and Archbiſhop's Palace. On the North ſtands that of the Preſident, the Courts of Juſtice, and the Priſon. On the South there is a Row of Piazzas, with very commodious Shops under them ; and the Eaſt Side is taken up by rich Merchants Houſes. The Number of Inhabitants may be about eight thouſand Whites, and between twenty and thirty thouſand *Indians* and Mulattos. In ſome Authors we have very pompous Deſcriptions of this City, much ſurpaſſing any thing I have ſaid, or indeed can ſay ; but the Miſchief of it is, that theſe are taken entirely from Report ; what I have ſet down is from an Eye-Witneſs, and a Perſon who is an Engineer by his Profeſſion, who owns, that the City of *St. Jago* is pleaſant and pretty ; but as to Streets of Stone Buildings, he ſays not a Word ; nor ſhould I have copied him, if he had, ſince in a Country frequently troubled with Earthquakes, and in a City twice ſubverted by them in fifty Years, Stone Houſes would be far from deſirable Habitations. In truth, they are no better than Lath and Plaiſter ; but the Plaiſter being extremely white, and painted ſo as to reſemble Stone, might poſſibly give Occaſion to this Report.

The

The Citizens of *St. Jago* are rich, and live much at their Eafe, many of them retiring hither from *Baldivia*, the *Conception*, *Valparayfo*, and other Places, when they have acquired Eftates by Trade; and fome again grow very rich even here by being concerned in the Gold Mines at *Tiltil*, which are about half way between *St. Jago* and the Sea, and in feveral Lavaderoes nearer the City, which are very rich, and in which they fometimes find Pieces of Gold of an Ounce Weight, twenty-three Carrats fine. In the Mountains immediately behind the City, particularly in that called *St. Chriftopher Lampanquio*, there have been within thefe thirty Years Mines of all forts of Metals difcovered, clofe together; *viz.* of Gold, Silver, Iron, Copper, Lead, and Tin; but, for Want of Hands, and becaufe they do not yield quite fo great a Profit as fome others, they are neglected. As for the *Indians*, they deal little in thefe Metals on their own Account; they content themfelves with raifing Corn, and feeding Cattle; and though they have Plenty of both, they are very far from being rich, fince even in a Country where Money is fo plenty, their Wheat, which is very good, will not yield more than a Groat a Bufhel.

We have now gone through the Province of *Chili proper*, and are next to enter that of the City of *Imperial*. The firft Place we meet with of Confequence is the Town and
Port

Port of *Conception*, which lies in 36° 42' S. L. The Port is good, and the Town very neat, feated clofe on the Side of the Bay, whence it makes a fine Shew. The *Indians* call this Place *Penco*, i. e. *I have found Water*. The *Spaniards* look upon this as a Place of great Confideration, as indeed it is; and therefore his Catholick Majefty allows three hundred and fifty thoufand Pieces of Eight *per Annum* for maintaining a Garrifon here of three thoufand five hundred Men: There are alfo fome Fortifications and Forts on the Land-Side, in order to defend the Place againft the *Indians*, but all miferably out of Repair; and the major part of the Garrifon fleep in the Governor's Pocket, that is to fay, he keeps up fifteen hundred or two thoufand Men poorly clothed and fadly paid, putting the reft of the King's Money into his own Coffers. Yet is this City of *Conception* a Bifhop's See, which was transferred thither when the *Indians* took and deftroyed the City *Imperial*; and here likewife was the Royal Chancery, till out of mere Fear of the *Indians*, they thought fit to remove it to *St. Jago*. The Force of the Town confifts in its Trade, for this keeping always a confiderable Number of Ships in the Bay, the *Indians* are afraid of attempting any thing; and from a Confidence of this, the *Spaniards* live lazily and without Care, though it is more
than

than probable that they may fome time or
other repent it.

Before we leave this Place, it may not be
improper to take Notice of a beneficial Trade
carried on by the Inhabitants of the City of
Conception with the *Indians* behind them,
who, though they are not Subjects of the
Crown of *Spain*, nor have ever negotiated a
Peace with the *Spaniards*, yet trade with
them, and this in a very particular Manner.
Thefe *Indians* are ftyled *Peulches*, and inhabit the *Cordillera*, or *great Chain of Mountains* at the Back of *Chili*, for a Space not
certainly known, and who retain exactly the
fame Manners and Cuftoms they had before
the *Spaniards* arrived here.   When a Perfon
goes to trade with them, he addreffes himfelf to the Cacique or Chief.   No fooner this
little Prince fees a Stranger, than he cries out,
What ! are you come ? The *Spaniard* anfwers,
Yes, I am come.   The Cacique's next Queftion is, *Well ! what have you brought me ?*
The Merchant anfwers, *A Prefent.* To which
the Prince replies, *Then you are welcome.*   A
Lodging is inftantly provided him, near that
of the Cacique's, whither all his Family go
to vifit the Stranger, in hopes he will make
them fome Prefents.   In the mean time a
Horn is founded, to give Notice to the *Indians* who are abroad, that a Merchant is arrived.   Upon this they all run to the Place,
where the Stranger exhibits his Treafure,
confifting

consisting of Knives, Sciffars, Pins, Needles, Ribbands, small Looking-glasses, &c. All these the *Indians* carry away without giving any thing for them, only a Price is settled; and thus the Merchant credits Folks he never saw, and whom, for ought he knows, he may never see again. After a certain Time is elapsed, the Horn, by the Direction of the Cacique, is sounded a second Time, when immediately the Savages return, and exactly perform their respective Promises. The Goods they deal in are Cattle, Skins of wild Beasts, and some Gold; but this they bring only in very small Quantities, knowing well how dear the Possession of that Metal hath cost their Neighbours and their Ancestors. As for the other *Indians*, who were formerly subdued, and have now recovered their Freedom, they have little or no Intercourse with the *Spaniards*.

The Port of *Baldivia*, of which we are next to speak, lies in 39° 36′ S. L. This Place is very advantageously situated, three Leagues within a spacious Bay, and is defended by four pretty strong Castles, mounting in all above a hundred Brass Guns, of a considerable Size. The Garrison too is or ought to be very considerable, the King allowing yearly three hundred thousand Pieces of Eight for their Pay, and for keeping the Fortifications in Repair. It is however very oddly composed, for all the Soldiers, and
most

moft of the Officers, are Criminals fent hither from *Peru*, as in other Places they are
fent to the Gallies. It is, it feems, a Maxim in
the *Spanifh* Government, feldom or never to
punifh any white Perfon with Death, but to
content themfelves with placing them as they
are here in a Frontier Garrifon. But whatever the Officers and Soldiers may be, the
Governor is always a Man of Quality, and
one who pays pretty roundly for that Poft,
purely that he may have the Honour of paying that large *Situado* above-mentioned, or
elfe have a good Reafon fhewn why it is not
paid. Some Perfons of good Intelligence
fay, that a very honeft Viceroy of *Peru* contents himfelf with ftopping only a Third,
and that a Governor of a fcrupulous Confci-
ence puts no more than a Fourth of what remains in his Pocket : Such honeft People,
however, do not come often to the *Indies*.
This Place is not only threatened by domeftick, but alfo by foreign Enemies ; and there
have been Times, in which the *Spaniards*
equally dreaded the *Indians* and the *Dutch*.
The latter, in 1643, actually made themfelves Mafters of the Place, and intended to
have kept it, but that Famine and Sicknefs
compelled them to retire, which gave the
Spaniards an Opportunity of refettling it. I
muft however take Notice, that the Viceroy
of *Peru* acted upon this Occafion like a true
Spanifh Governor ; he delayed fending Supplies

plies till the Place was taken ; but being then apprehenfive he might be punifhed for this ill Conduct, he affembled fuch a Body of Troops, and made fo much hafte to *Baldivia*, that the *Dutch* were obliged to quit it in great Confufion, being, as I faid, attacked before with Famine and Sicknefs, and left therein thirty Pieces of Cannon, and all their Baggage. The prefent Number of Inhabitants in this City may be about two thoufand, or rather more. Heretofore its Commerce was more confiderable than at prefent, becaufe of feveral Gold Mines in its Neighbourhood, which are not wrought now; yet there are ftill eight or ten Veffels of between four and five hundred Tons each, which are employed in carrying on the Trade between this Port and *Lima.* The Cargoes they carry are Hides, Goat Skins tanned, *a la Cordovan*, Salt Meat, Corn, and fome Gold : They bring back Chocolate, Spices, Sugars, and all Sorts of *European* Goods.

Farther to the South the *Spaniards* have a Garrifon of five hundred Men, at a Place called *Aranca* ; as alfo a Settlement in the Ifle of *Chiloe*, which is a very pleafant and fruitful Place, and the utmoft Boundary of *Chili*, towards the South ; confequently we have fulfilled this Part of our Tafk, and are to fpeak next of the inland Diftrict.

This Diftrict is ftyled *Chicuito :* it lies to the Eaft of *Chili*, on the other Side of the Mountains,

Mountains, from the thirtieth to the thirty-
eighth Degree of South Latitude, being in
Length about two hundred Miles, its Breadth
very uncertain.   The whole Country is famous for its prodigious Fertility, owing chiefly to the numberlefs Rivulets of melted Snow,
which run down from the Mountains which
furround it.   Its Products are Corn, Wine
and Oil, of which the Plenty in Quantity,
is not greater than the Excellence in Quality.   The Towns here are few, and not very
confiderable : The Capital of the Province is
the Town of *Mendoza*, feated at the Opening of the Mountains from *St. Jago :* In its
Neighbourhood there are excellent Copper
Mines.   *St. Juan de la Frontera* is now the
moft populous Place in the Country : it ftands
about fixty Leagues North-eaft from *St. Jago*,
and in the Mountains near it there are Silver
Mines exceffively rich.   There is nothing
farther remarkable in this Part of *Chili*, except what is common to the whole Audience,
and that is, the being free from all venomous Creatures ; for though there are in fome
Parts Toads, in others Serpents, and in many
Places Spiders of an enormous Size, yet it is
certain that none of thefe are poifonous, no,
not even the Scorpions, which are fometimes
found in the Grafs, but were never known
to do any Mifchief.   The Days in the Summer are very fhort in *Chicuito*, the high
Mountains

Mountains intercepting the Light of the Sun within a few Hours after Noon.

C H A P. XVI.

Of the Province of Tucuman.

I Thought it unneceſſary to go farther South in order to ſpeak of the *Terra Magellanica*, becauſe, though the *Spaniards* claim it, they have no Settlement there; and I have ſaid enough in the firſt Book to prevent the Reader's being led into any Miſtakes about it. In quitting *Chili* therefore I proceed Eaſtward, in order to reach again the oppoſite Ocean, and ſo to ſpeak of the *Spaniſh* Settlements to the South of *Brazil*, on the River of *Plate*, which falls into the *North Sea*. I could not do this without taking Notice of the large Country of *Tucuman*.

It lies in the midſt, between *Paraguay* and *Chili*; nor is it eaſy to ſtate its Boundaries; however, we will do it in the beſt Manner we may. On the North there are none but barbarous Nations, the Names of which it would be needleſs to repeat. On the Eaſt lies *Paraguay*, and the River of *Plate*; on the South the unknown Country called *Terra Magellanica*; on the Weſt, part of *Chili*, and part of *Peru*. Where it begins, we cannot ſay with any Certainty; but the beſt Writers own it does not extend to above 37°

S. L.

S. L. As it lies for the moſt part in the temperate Zone, we need not ſay much of its Climate; only this is remarked, that ſo much of it as lies in the torrid Zone is exceedingly cold, which is occaſioned by the Height of the Mountains. Farther South there are vaſt Plains, and great Foreſts. When the *Spaniards* invaded it, about the Year 1558, they found it very populous, but they found means to deſtroy an infinite number of People, tho' they did themſelves little Good. The Cities of *St. Jago* and *St. Michael* are now the moſt conſiderable of thoſe poſſeſſed by the *Spaniards* in theſe Parts; but they owe any Dominion they have over the Natives, rather to the Pains taken by their Prieſts, eſpecially the Jeſuits, than to the Force of their Arms, or the Wiſdom of their Government. The principal Thing aimed at in ſettling Towns and Garriſons in this Country for the Space of three hundred Miles, is to ſecure a Communication between the Plantations on the *North* and *South Seas*; not but that there reſults ſome Benefit from the Trade carried on with the *Indians*, of which we ſhall ſay more hereafter, in diſcourſing of the Commerce of *Buenos Ayres*.

Since the Acceſſion of *Philip* V. to the Crown of *Spain*, the Miſſionaries in theſe Parts have had their Privileges much augmented, which has enabled them to make many thouſand Converts, and to extend their

own

own Power confiderably, though perhaps they have not done much to increafe that of the Civil Magiftrate, for which they generally make this Pretence, that whenever their Converts come to converfe with the *Spaniards*, they begin to lofe their Refpect for the Chriftian Religion ; which, if true, is furely a little extraordinary, and not much to the Honour of this Catholick Nation.

C H A P. XVII.

Of the Spanifh *Settlements on the River of Plate, particularly* Buenos Ayres.

IT is an old Obfervation, that Names are not always impofed according to the Reafon of Things. The new World, of which we have been fpeaking, did not receive that of *Columbus*, who difcovered it, but was called *America* from *Americus Vefpufius*, who defcribed it, or at leaft firft publifhed his Defcriptions to the World. In like Manner the *Spaniards* call that great River which falls into the Ocean in 35° S. L. *Rio de la Plata*, though in truth it is the leaft of three Rivers which compofe that Stream. The firft of thefe is the great River of *Paraguay*, which rifes in the Weftern Part of *Brazil*, in the Latitude of 60°, or thereabouts ; running Southward, it paffes through the great Lake of *Charafis*; and about fifty Miles below the
City

City of *Affumption* it joins the *Rio de la Pla-*
ta, in the Latitude of about 30°. About
fixty Miles lower, the great River *Parana*
joins them, and rolls in Conjunction towards
the Sea. Befides thefe there are many other
leffer Rivers, which concur in forming fo
vaft a Body of Water in fo long a Courfe,
fuch as the *Rio Vermejo, Rio Blanco, Rio*
Salado, Rio Tercero, &c.

The River of *Plate* receives its Name from
the City of *la Plata* in the Audience of *los*
Charcas, in the Neighbourhood of which it
rifes, and runs two thoufand Miles before it
falls into the Sea, below *Buenos Ayres,* its
Mouth being little fhort of fixty Leagues
broad. By the Help of this noble River,
there is a quick and ftraight Paffage from *Po-*
tofi to *Buenos Ayres,* and a good Road thither
alfo by Land, though thefe Cities are diftant
five hundred Leagues from each other, an immenfe Tract of Territory, all faid to be under
the Dominion of the King of *Spain.* As it
would take up much Room to defcribe thefe
inland Countries, and to mention the feveral
Eftablifhments made by the *Spaniards* for
the Sake of fecuring a Communication between the feveral Provinces of *Peru, Los*
Charcas, Chili and *Tucuman,* with the City of
Buenos Apres, I fhall content myfelf with
giving an Account of this laft mentioned
Place, which is, on many Accounts, one of
the

the moſt important Settlements which the *Spaniards* have in the *Weſt Indies*.

The City of *Buenos Ayres* is ſeated on the South Side of the River of *Plate*, about ſixty Miles above the Mouth thereof, the oppoſite Shore of the River belonging to the *Portu-gueze*. It lies in 35° S. L. and is ſuppoſed to receive its Name from the Excellence of its Climate, which is indeed indiſputable, there being few Places on the Globe comparable therewith, in point of Pleaſantneſs of Situation, or Fertility of Soil. The City is built on the Side of a Hill, at the Mouth of a little River which falls there into the *Rio de la Plata*. It conſiſts of about four thouſand Houſes (if *Coreal*, from whom we take this Particular, was not miſtaken in his Computation) built for the moſt Part of Earth, tho' ſome Perſons of Diſtinction live in Brick Buildings. There is a Fort, and ſome other Fortifications, with a Garriſon, but, if we may truſt the Writer laſt mentioned, a Native of *Spain*, zealouſly affected to his preſent Catholick Majeſty, and who reſided in this Place ſix Months, very ill provided.

The Importance of *Buenos Ayres* conſiſts chiefly in its convenient Situation for Commerce, indeed for ſuch a Commerce as no Port in the *Spaniſh Weſt Indies* can boaſt of the like. Hither come, even from the moſt diſtant Provinces in the *Spaniſh* Empire, the moſt valuable Commodities in order to be
exchanged

exchanged for *European* Goods; such as *Vigognia* Wooll from *Peru*, Copper from *Coquimbo*, Gold from *Chili*, and Silver from *Potoſi*. From the Towns of *Corientes*, and *Paraguay*, the former two hundred and fifty, the latter five hundred Leagues from *Buenos Ayres*, there are brought thither Tobacco extremely valuable, Sugar, Cotton Thread, Yellow Wax, and Cotton Cloth, moſt of which is uſed at *Buenos Ayres*, and in its Neighbourhood, by the Slaves and other Domeſticks, being cheaper, and anſwering their Purpoſe full as well as either *French* or *Dutch* Linen. Theſe are the Merchandize of the Town of *Corientes*. As for the Trade of *Paraguay*, it conſiſts almoſt intirely in the Herb ſo called, which in theſe Countries is of prodigious Value. The Uſe made of it is to compoſe a certain Draught, Infuſion, or Tea, which recovers ſuch as work in the Mines from thoſe grievous Cholicks and intolerable Diſorders in the Stomach, cauſed by the Exhalations in ſuch Places. The Herb of *Paraguay* is of two ſorts, *Camini*, and *Yerva con palos*, one eſteemed of twice the Value of the other; but it is uſually mixed as Congo and Pekoe Tea with us. Thoſe who go to *Paraguay* to buy it, are obliged to ſtay two Years before they return. The firſt Crop being always beſpoke, and in a manner abſolutely diſpoſed of, ſo that theſe Traders muſt content themſelves with making the beſt

Bargain

Bargain they can for the next, in order to which, Prefents to the Governor, and many other Articles of that Sort are neceffary. The Amount of this Trade is at leaft a Million of Pieces of Eight *per Annum*, all paid for in Goods, thofe who have the Government of *Paraguay* fuffering no Money to pafs there. Thefe Goods are Knives, Sciffars, Ribbands, Taffaties, Silk Stockings, *Englifh* Bays, Hats of all Sorts, and coarfe Cloth from *Quito*. All thefe Merchandizes are carried through this vaft Extent of Country in little Waggons; though between *Buenos Ayres* and *Corientes* there are not lefs than fifteen or fixteen great Rivers, in paffing which the Cattle are made to fwim, and the Goods are paffed over on Floats made by taking the Waggons to pieces.

The Merchants do not bring any more of thefe valuable Commodities to *Buenos Ayres* than are abfolutely neceffary for the Supply of the Inhabitants, but fend them to the Town of *Santa Fé*, in order to avoid double Carriage, and double Duties. Thence they tranfport the Herb of *Paraguay* to *Potofi*, partly in Waggons, and partly on Mules: This they do at all times of the Year with equal Facility; and though it be a Journey of five hundred Leagues, yet they common-ly perform it in a Month. They difpofe of the Herb of *Paraguay* for ready Money, and generally gain upon it *Cent. per Cent.* having

fometimes

sometimes made three hundred *per Cent.* of
the Goods by which they purchased it in Exchange. The Journey to *Chili* is much more
troublesome, though not above fifty Leagues
farther, because the Passage through the Mountains, which divide that Country from the
inland Parts of *America*, is passable only
from *December* to *March*. As far as the
Town of *Mendosa*, which is three hundred
Leagues from *Buenos Ayres*, the Goods are
carried in Waggons drawn by Oxen, thence
they are transported on the Backs of Mules
to *St. Jago de Chili*. The Pass in the Mountains is about sixty Leagues in Length, and
takes up commonly six or seven Days. What
makes it the more troublesome, is the Necessity which the Merchants find themselves
under of carrying Provisions for themselves,
and Forage for their Mules, as well as their
Goods; but from *St. Jago* to the Mines the
Way is altogether easy and pleasant.

The Commerce between *Buenos Ayres* and
Peru is chiefly for the Sale of Cattle, and of
Mules; such as are concerned in the former,
go first to the Governor, and ask his Leave
to drive a Herd of Cattle into *Peru*, which is
never refused, if the Petition be backed by a
Present of some thousand Pieces of Eight.
The next thing to be done is taking thirty or
forty thousand wild Cows out of the King's
Pastures, which is performed by Persons who
apply themselves to that Business for their
Livelihood,

Livelihood, and who deliver thefe Creatures at about three Pieces of Eight *per* Head. At this Rate thirty thoufand Cattle may come to about a hundred thoufand Pieces of Eight, and at Market they fetch about two hundred and fifty thoufand. The Commerce in Mules is carried on in quite a different Manner, for the Merchants of *Peru* and *Potofi* fend Factors annually to *Buenos Ayres* for this Purpofe. The firft Step with them is obtaining the Governor's Licence, by the Help of a very confiderable Prefent. They next addrefs themfelves not only to the Inhabitants of *Buenos Ayres*, but to all fuch as have Farms in the Neighbourhood, and enter into Agreements with each, fpecifying the Times when, and the Number of Beafts that fhall be delivered to them. At the appointed Time they receive thefe Mules, and mark them with a hot Iron on the Shoulders, being thenceforward to be maintained at their Expence. Thefe Creatures coft them between two and three Pieces of Eight each, and are driven by pretty quick Journies to *Salta*, which is about two thirds of the Way to *Potofi*. There they winter, and are fatted with all imaginable Care. When they are in full Flefh, they carry them to *Potofi*, where they are fold for feven, eight or nine Pieces of Eight *per* Head ; but fuch as are carried into *Peru*, or farther, fetch forty or fifty Pieces of Eight at leaft, and fometimes much more.

The

The Trade carried on between *Buenos Ayres* and *Europe* ought to be only by the Regifter-Ships from *Spain*, and the *Affiento* Ship, fent by the *South-Sea* Company from *England*; but befides thefe they are faid to carry on a great contraband Commerce; in refpect to which, as I have no authentick Memoirs, I do not think it proper for me to treat of it. When I fay this, I would be underftood only of the contraband Trade to *Spain* and *England*; for there is a third Sort of illicit Commerce to which I can very well fpeak. This is carried on with the *Portu-gueze*, who, as I obferved before, poffefs the oppofite Shore of the *Rio de la Plata*. Thence they take Occafion to fend from time to time little Veffels laden not only with their own Commodities, but with fuch as they receive from *Europe*; and this in Spite of all the Care the *Spanifh* Governor can or at leaft will take; for it is Intereft governs every thing in the *Indies:* I wifh it was in my Power to fay that its Influence was felt only there.

From this Account of *Buenos Ayres* it appears, how well Governor *Pulleyn*'s Project lately publifhed under the Title of, *A Pro-pofal for humbling* Spain, was grounded, and to what excellent Purpofes it might be carried into Execution. By taking this Place alone, or even by making a good Settlement in its Neighbourhood, we fhould have the *Spaniards* at our Mercy.

BOOK

B O O K. III.

C H A P. I.

Of the Trade between Spain *and the* Weſt
Indies.

IT has been always the ruling Maxim in
the *Spaniſh* Councils to preſerve by all
means poſſible the Commerce with the *Weſt
Indies,* not only to the *Spaniſh* Nation, but
to the Crown of *Spain.* On this Principle
they reſtrained, with great Punctuality, all
Strangers from paſſing into their *American*
Dominions; and though there have been formerly ſome Inſtances of Foreigners paſſing
through the *Spaniſh* Settlements, and even
reſiding in them, yet they are ſo rare, and
attended with ſuch extraordinary Circumſtances, that inſtead of admiring that ſuch
things have happened, we ought rather to
wonder that they have not happened more
frequently, conſidering the ſtrong Paſſion that
Strangers have always had for penetrating unknown Countries, eſpecially ſuch Countries
as *Mexico* and *Peru,* rich in themſelves, and
repreſented much richer than they were. It
is true, that of late Years the *Spaniards* have
found themſelves in ſome manner obliged to
relax in this Point, eſpecially during the long
Controverſy

Controverſy about the *Spaniſh* Succeſſion, when they laboured under a Neceſſity of being protected by the *French* Fleets. But as ſoon as *Philip* V. was acknowledged by the Maritime Powers for King of *Spain*, they returned immediately to their old Notions, and Orders were diſpatched to the *Weſt Indies* to compel the *French*, who were ſettled there, to return into *Europe*, and to break off all Commerce with them for the future, which in the *South Seas* at leaſt were punctually obeyed. Thus we ſee that the lawful Commerce between *Europe* and *Spaniſh America* is intirely in the Hands of the *Spaniards*, and abſolutely ſubject to the Direction of the Crown.

The Method in which this Trade is carried on is well enough known in general, but few enter far enough into its Particulars. In order to give as diſtinct an Account of this Matter as poſſible, we ſhall ſpeak of the Galleons, the Flota, the Flotilla, Regiſter-Ships, and Guarda Coſtas ; and when we have done this, the Reader will perfectly comprehend the Myſtery of the *Spaniſh* Policy in this Point.

A Galleon is, properly ſpeaking, a very large Man of War, of three or four Decks, built in a Manner now altogether out of Faſhion, except in *Spain* ; and the Reaſon why it is ſtill uſed there, is, that it affords a great deal of Room for Merchandize, with which the King's Ships are generally ſo much crowded, ed, as to be in no Condition of defending themfelves. That Fleet which we call the *Galleons,* confifts of eight fuch Men of War. Of thefe there are three very large ones, ftyled *la Capitana, la Admirante,* and *Il Governo;* two others which are lefs, *la Patacha,* and *la Margarita,* each of fifty Guns; and an Advice Frigate of forty. The Merchant-men which fail with this Fleet, and purchafe their Licences at a very high Rate, are in Number from twelve to fixteen, and in Burthen at leaft a third Part bigger than is exprefled in their refpective Schedulas. Thefe Ships are intended to carry all that is neceffary, either of Warlike Stores, or Merchandize for *Peru:* and this is the fpecific Difference between this Fleet and the Flota, which is intended for *Mexico.* In Time of Peace, the Galleons fail regularly once a Year from *Cadiz,* at no fet time, but according to the King's Pleafure, and the Convenience of the Merchants. From *Cadiz* the Galleons fteer directly for the *Canaries,* where, if the Flota fails with them, as it fometimes does, they anchor together in the Haven of *Gomera.* Thence they bear away for the *Antilles,* and when they arrive at that Height, the Flota feparates, and the Galleons bear away for *Carthagena.* As foon as they double *Cape de la Vela,* and appear before the Mouth of *Rio de la Hacha,* Advice is fent to all Parts, that every thing may be got ready for their Reception.

Reception. In the Harbour of *Carthagena* they remain a Month, and land there all the Goods defigned for the Audience of the *Terra Firma*. Then they fail to *Porto Bello*, where they continue during the Fair, which lafts five or fix Weeks; and having landed the Merchandize intended for *Peru*, and received the Treafure and rich Commodities fent from thence on board, they fail again to *Carthagena*, where they remain till they return to *Spain*, which is ufually within the Space of two Years. When they have Orders to return, they fail firft to the *Havana*, and having there joined the Flota, and what other Ships are returning to *Europe*, they fteer through the Gulph of *Florida*, and fo to the Height of *Carolina*, where meeting with the Weftern Winds, they fhape their Courfe then for the *Azores*. They take in frefh Water and Provifions at *Terçera*, and thence continue their Voyage to *Cadiz*.

The Flota confifts, as well as the Galleons, of a certain Number of Men of War, and of a certain Number of Merchants Ships. The former are feldom more than three, *la Capitana*, *la Admirante*, and *la Patacha*. The latter are ufually about fixteen, in Burthen between five hundred and a thoufand Tons. This Fleet fails about the Month of *Auguft*, that by the Favour of the Winds which reign about *November*, they may the more eafily purfue their Voyage to *la Vera Cruz*. In
their

their Paſſage they call at *Puerto Rico*, to take in freſh Water and Proviſions, then paſs in Sight of *Hiſpaniola, Jamaica,* and *Cuba* ; and, according to the Seaſon of the Year, and the Nature of the Winds, paſs either by the Coaſt of *Jucatan,* or higher thro' the Gulph, to *la Vera Cruz,* which lies at the bottom of it. The Run of this Fleet, according to the Courſe we have mentioned, hath been thus computed. From *Cadiz* to the *Canaries,* two hundred and fifty Leagues in about ten Days ; to the *Antilles* eight hundred Leagues in twenty Days ; to the moſt Weſtern Point of the Iſle of *Cuba,* five hundred Leagues in twenty Days ; to *Vera Cruz,* two hundred and ſixty Leagues in twelve Days, or thereabouts ; in all eighteen hundred and ten Leagues in about ſixty-two Days. As the Flota is deſigned to furniſh not only *Mexico,* but the *Philippine Iſlands* alſo, as we have before remarked in ſpeaking of the Trade of *Acapulco,* with *European* Goods, they are obliged to remain there for a conſiderable Space; and, when it is neceſſary, they winter in that Port. The Cargo with which they return, is not ſo rich as that of the Galleons; but ſome Writers ſay, that it increaſes annually in its Value, which muſt be owing to the Progreſs made in ſettling what the *Spaniards* call the Kingdom of *New Mexico.*

It is uſually in the Month of *May* that the Flota leaves *La Vera Cruz,* though ſometimes

times it is detained in that Harbour till *August*. Then the Ships that compose it, sail for the *Havana*; for though the Galleons and the Flota seldom leave *Spain*, yet they generally return, together. As soon as they are safely arrived in the *Havana*, they detach a few of the lightest and cleanest Ships to *Europe*, who, besides Money and Merchandize, carry also an exact Account of the Contents both of the Galleons and Flota. These Ships are called by the *Spaniards*, with Propriety enough, the *Flotilla*, i. e. *the Little Fleet*. The principal Reason of sending them in this Manner into *Spain*, is to give the Court of *Madrid* an Opportunity of judging what Convoy may be necessary, in case of any Alteration of Affairs, to be sent to escort the Grand Fleet, as also to regulate the Indulto which may be levied on the Merchants in proportion to their Interest in the Galleons and Flota. But the Reader may possibly incline to enquire what obliges this great Fleet to remain so long at the *Havana?* to which two Causes may be assigned, *viz.* waiting for a Wind, or for the Register-Ships which they are to convoy home.

A Register-Ship is so called, from its being registered with all the Effects embarked in *Spain*, in the Books kept for that Purpose in the Chamber of *Seville*. As this general Account will not probably appear satisfactory, I shall endeavour to state the Matter more fully. A Company of Merchants

chants having, as they conceive, juft Grounds
to imagine that *European* Goods are greatly
wanted at fome particular Ports in the *Weft
Indies*, they draw up a Memorial or Petition,
containing thefe Reafons in the cleareft and
concifeft Terms, and lay it before the Council of the *Indies*. The Prayer of this Petition
is, That they may have Leave to fend a Ship
of three hundred Tons Burthen, or under, to
the Port they mention. When Leave is obtained, they pay a certain Sum to the Crown,
which is generally between thirty and fifty
thoufand Pieces of Eight, befides Prefents,
and thofe no fmall ones, to the King's Officers, from the greateft to the leaft. That
this however may not induce any Sufpicion of
Fraud, they regifter their Ship and Cargo,
that it may appear confiftent with their Petition and Licence, and yet (fuch a Fatality
there attends on all Cuftom-houfe Cautions)
this Ship of under three hundred Tons generally carries upwards of fix hundred Ton of
Goods, and affords Accommodation for Paf-
fengers befides. Copies from the Regifter are
tranfmitted to the Governor and Royal Officers at the Port, to which the Regifter-Ship
is bound; and fuch is their Diligence, fuch
their Integrity, that when the Ship comes
to an Anchor in the Port, they make a very
narrow Enquiry, and yet there is feldom or
never any Fraud difcovered, but, on the
contrary, this Ship of fix or feven hundred
Ton

Ton returns into *Europe* with an authentick Certificate from all the King of *Spain*'s Offi-cers, that she does not carry quite three hun-dred, together with a Bill of Lading in the same Strain of Computation. By these Re-gister-Ships there is sometimes a Gain of two, or three hundred *per Cent.* which enables the Owners to pay so bountifully for cheating the King, having first got the Money by robbing his Subjects.

These Register-Ships go to *Buenos Ayres, St. Martha, Porto Cavallo,* and other Places, to which neither the Galleons nor Flota come; yet, generally speaking, they return with those Fleets, as they sometimes go out with them, and so leave them in a certain Latitude. The *Spanish* Grandees often inte-rest themselves in procuring such Licences; and some People do not stick to say that they find their Account in it. What surprizes me more, is the bold Declaration of a certain *French* Writer, that our *Assiento* Company enter'd readily into these *Spanish* Customs, and even out-did the *Spaniards* themselves in a Craft which they had both studied and practised for many Years, and by making ex-traordinary Presents to Governors, Com-ptrollers, Inspectors, and other *Spanish* Offi-cers, they amply rewarded them for the Jus-tice they did their Master, and the Kindness shewn by them to Strangers; which no doubt were equally great. The Profits accruing by
                                            this

this Sort of Commerce making thofe concerned therein extravagantly rich in a fhort Space
of Time, the *Englifh* and *Dutch* in the *Weft
Indies*, who are known to be a fort of People
quick in their Tempers, and not over nice in
point of Manners, have always had a ftrong
Defire to be dealing this Way without the
Ceremony of a Licence; and for many Years
they fucceeded to their Wifh, partly by the
Connivance of *Spanifh* Governors, and partly by employing Force. At length this Evil
grew fo flagrant, that the Court of *Spain* de-
termin'd to put an End to it, and, in order
thereto, fent new Governors into *America*,
with very precife Orders on this Head, de-
claring at the fame time, that they fhould be
carried fully into Execution.

Thefe Inftructions gave Rife to the Guarda
Coftas, or Guard-Ships, which have fince
made fo much Noife in the World, and of
which I think it neceffary to fpeak more particularly. It cannot be denied that there was
originally good Grounds for equipping them,
fince the *Englifh* in fome meafure, and the
Dutch more openly, began to carry on an
illicit Trade by Force. The *Dutch* Veffels
were from twenty to thirty-fix Guns, and
therefore valued nothing the Governor of
Carthagena could do, to prevent their trading on his Coaft; but when the Guard-
Ships were ftationed here, they for fome time
put an End to the Evil; for, falling in with
fome

fome of thefe Interlopers, they funk one, and took two, the Cargoes of which were worth upwards of a hundred thoufand Pounds; nay finding on board them fixteen *Spanifh* Merchants, who on a fignal given were come off to trade, they hanged them all without Mercy. So far all was right, for, without queftion, thefe Smugglers not only prejudiced the King of *Spain*, but even the fair Traders of their own Nations, by the clandeftine Commerce they carried on, as the Reader will eafily apprehend, after perufing our next Chapter. The Captains of thefe Guard-Ships however foon altered their Conduct, and inftead of taking contraband Traders, infefted the *Englifh* Commerce, and took without Diftinction all they were able, at firft under very frivolous Pretences, and at laft without any Pretence at all. As the Governors reaped a confiderable Profit from the Prizes thefe Privateers, or rather Pirates, brought into their Ports, they were ready to fend deceitful Accounts to the Court of *Madrid*, which produced that Spirit of Obftinacy, whereby they drew on themfelves the prefent War, which, as it is certainly juft and neceffary, will, I doubt not, end fuccefsfully and glorioufly in Refpect to the Adminiftration by whom it is conducted, as well as the Admirals and other Officers who have the Honour to command His Majefty's Forces and Fleets. Whenever this fhall happen, thefe Guard-

Ships

Ships muſt be put under new Regulation, and all Captures examined by a mixed Tribunal of *Engliſh* as well as *Spaniſh* Judges ; and if in ſpite of all Expedients this haughty and ill judging Nation, who have often intrigued themſelves into ill Circumſtances, and fought away fine Provinces, which they might have kept by doing Juſtice, ſhould be mad enough to provoke us again, there will need nothing but ſending an Admiral of the Name of *V E R N O N*, into the *Weſt Indies*, to bring them to their Wits. The Lectures he has read at *Porto Bello*, and *Carthagena*, have, I dare ſay, made ſuch deep Impreſſions on their Memories, that, as in a Century they will ſcarce be able to repair the Ruins he has left, ſo in leſs Time they will hardly forget, that the ſame Nation produced *V E R N O N* and *B L A K E* ; and may poſſibly chaſtiſe them by a third Commander of equal Valour, and leſs Clemency. —— But I forbear inſulting a beaten, though boaſting Enemy, and return from their piratical Guarda Coſtas, to ſpeak of their ſinking Trade, and to ſhew how it comes to paſs, that with the richeſt Territories the *Spaniſh* Monarch is one of the pooreſt, as well as proudeſt Princes in Chriſtendom. A Paradox I ſhall not find it difficult to explain.

Previous to this, it will be neceſſary to give the Reader a ſhort View of the true Value

Value of the Money and Effects annually returned to *Spain* from her *American* Dominions.   That this cannot be done exactly, the
judicious Reader will easily believe ; but that
it may be guessed nearly, he may without
Trouble apprehend, especially when we tell
him, that the Computation which follows,
was found among the Papers of a *French* Mi-
nister, who had the Superintendency of the
French Commerce to the *South Seas* during
the War.

He states the Account thus :

Pieces of Eight

In Gold, of which the Galleons
bring home between two and
three Millions, and the Flota,
generally, about one.   4,000,000

In Silver, by the Galleons, from
eighteen to twenty Millions,
by the Flota, from ten to
twelve.   30,000,000

In precious Stones. By the Galleons in Pearls two hundred
thousand ; in Emeralds, three
hundred thousand ; in Bezo-
ars, Turkoises, Amathists, &c.   600,000
thirty thousand ; and of late,
by the Flota, some Turkoises which may render the A-
mount of this Article.

In

In *Vigognia* Wooll, by the Galleons, fifty thoufand, by the Flota none.	50,000
Quinquina, by the Galleons, twenty thoufand ; by the Flota as much.	40,000
In Raw Hides, by the Galleons, feventy thoufand, by the Flota as much.	140,000
By Hides from *Buenos Ayres* in a Regifter-Ship.	200,000
In Logwood, by the Galleons, fixty thoufand, by the Flota none.	60,000
In Cochineal by the Flota and Regifter-Ships.	1,000,000
In Indigo about	200,000
In Sugars, Tobacco, and other Drugs, about	2,000,000
	38,290,000

CHAP. II.

Of the Means by which Spain *is drained of the Effects brought from the* Indies.

THERE is nothing more common than to hear *Spain* compared to a Sieve, which, whatever it receives, is never the fuller. How common foever the Comparifon may
be,

be, moft certainly it is a very true one; but the Means by which all this immenfe Wealth, or at leaft the far greateft Part of it is drawn from the *Spaniards*, and conveyed to other Nations, and in what Proportions, is neither fo well, nor fo generally underftood. To account for this fhall be our prefent Tafk; not that we have much Hopes of doing it exactly, but that we are defirous to provoke fome better Pen to fupply our Omiffions; and, by ftriking the Outlines for the prefent, afford the World fuch a Likenefs, as may invite an abler and better inftructed Painter to finifh the Piece. Befides, what we have to fay of *Spain*, may poffibly fuit fome other Nation; and there is a great Pleafure in ftating to the Publick intricate and important Truths in fuch a Light, as may render them bearable. This is an Age in which Flattery and Calumny fo much abound, that few Writers know how to mention our own Affairs in Terms acceptable to all Parties. But, with refpect to the *Spaniards*, we may certainly fay what we pleafe, and be fure of an attentive Hearing.

If after the Difcovery of the new World, as the *Spaniards* juftly enough called it, the Government had encouraged Trade or Manufacturies, there is great Probability that the fupreme Direction of the Affairs of *Europe* would have fallen into the Hands of the Catholick Kings. For, if all the Subjects of
Spain,

Spain, without Reftraint, had traded to thefe far diftant Regions, this muft have created fuch a maritime Force, as no other Nation could have withftood : Or, fuppofing the Trade had been reftrained as it is at prefent, yet, if Manufactures had been encouraged, fo as that the greateft Part of the Trade of the *Weft Indies* had been driven without having Recourfe to Foreigners, fuch prodigious Sums of Money muft have refted in *Spain*, as would have enabled its Monarchs to have given Law to all their Neighbours. But, by neglecting thefe obvious, and yet certain Rules for eftablifhing folid and extenfive at leaft, if not univerfal Dominion, her Kings had Recourfe to thofe Refinements in Policy, which, however excellent they may feem in Theory, have never yet been found to anfwer in Practice. They were for fixing their Commerce by Conftraint, and for eftablifhing Power by the Sword ; the firft, Experience has fhewn to be impracticable, and the latter, perhaps, was the only Method whereby they could have miffed that End they ufed it to obtain. In fhort, by repeated Endeavours to fecure the Wealth of the *Indies* to *Spain* abfolutely, they fcattered it throughout *Europe*, and, by openly grafping at univerfal Monarchy, they alarmed thofe they might have fubdued ; fo that in Procefs of time, fome of thofe they intended for Slaves, became their Equals and Allies, and fome their Mafters.

Yet

Yet the Princes that took thefe Steps were not either rafh and hafty, or voluptuous and profufe, but, on the contrary, were efteemed by all the World the wifeft Monarchs of their refpective Times, and, in many Things deferved to be fo efteemed. They erred, not through Want of Capacity, or Want of Application, as their Succeffors did, but for want of confidering Things in a right Light, occafioned purely by their fixing their Eyes on that dazling Meteor, univerfal Empire. *Ferdinand* the Catholick, in whofe Reign *Columbus* difcovered *America*, was a Prince in the Flower of his Age, too wife for all he had to deal with ; and, in the Decline of his Age, he proved too wife for himfelf. Living, he by his Arts deftroyed his Neighbours ; and, if the beft Hiftorians may be believed, his Death was the Confequence of his own Arts. Inftead of confiding in *Columbus*, who, of all Men living, beft deferved his Confidence, he, by an unaccountable Stroke of Policy, inclined to truft any other Man in the Management of the new found World, merely becaufe *Columbus* found it. We have fhewn in the firft Book how by thefe Projects he broke that worthy Admiral's Heart, and prejudiced his own Affairs. *Charles* the Vth, who fucceeded him, minded little any of the *Spanifh* Concerns, farther than he could render them fubfervient to his other Views ; of which there cannot be a ftronger

Inftance,

Inftance, than his granting a whole Province in *South America* to the Citizens of *Augsburgh* in *Germany*. *Philip* II. was fo much taken up in endeavouring to reduce the *Netherlands*, inflave *Italy*, conquer *England*, over-run *France*, and in annexing *Portugal* to his Dominions, that he never confidered his Subjects in the *Spanifh America* farther, than as they enabled him by Supplies of Money to carry on thefe his vaft Defigns.

From what has been faid it is evident, that however wife, however penetrating thefe Princes might be, they certainly overfhot themfelves in their Schemes concerning the *Weftern Indies.* Inftead of looking upon it as an Eftate, they feem'd to think it only a Farm, of which they were to make prefently the moft they could. In doing this, it muft be owned, they acted with Skill and Vigour, for they drew immenfe Sums from thence, which they wafted in *Europe* to difturb others, and in the End to deftroy their own State. Mr. *Lewis Roberts*, Author of *the Map of Commerce*, an excellent Book for the Time in which it was written, tells us, that it appeared by the Records in the Cuftom-houfe of *Seville*, that in the Space of feventy-four Years, computing backwards from the Time in which he wrote, the Kings of *Spain* had drawn into that Country from *America*, two hundred and fixty Millions of Gold, which make about ninety-one Millions Sterling. He
alfo

alſo obſerves, that this very Prince, *Philip* II.
of whom we have been ſpeaking, ſpent more
in his Reign than all his Predeceſſors in the
whole of their reſpective Reigns; tho' no leſs
than 62 Kings had reigned before him. Yet
this cunning, this ambitious Monarch left his
Subjects in a Manner quite exhauſted, and,
by eſtabliſhing a moſt pernicious Syſtem of
Politicks, left the total Ruining of his Dominions by Way of Legacy to his Succeſſors,
a Point which with wonderful Obſtinacy
they have purſued ever ſince.

All who are in any degree acquainted with
the Hiſtory of *Europe* know, that for a long
Courſe of Years *Spain* maintained Wars in
Flanders, Germany, Italy, and ſometimes in
Ireland, which created a prodigious Expence
of Treaſure and of Troops; neither of which,
from the Death of *Charles* V. they were in
any Condition to ſpare. As Families were
reduced by the Expence of ſerving in the
Army, they were inclined to ſeek new Fortunes in the *Weſt Indies :* and thus Numbers
went over thither, not to cultivate the Country, or to improve Trade, but to ſtrip and
plunder thoſe who were there before them.
Other great Families again concurred with
the Meaſures of the Crown, in hopes of Vice-
royalties, and other valuable Offices in its
Conqueſts: but if ever their Schemes were
beneficial to their Families, which may admit of Doubt, certain it is that they contributed

buted more and more to the Ruin of the *Spanish* Nation. For, though his Catholick Majefty once poffeffed *Naples, Sicily, Sardinia, Milan,* with other Territories in *Italy,* befides all the Low Countries, and fome other Provinces which are now loft ; yet, for want of attending to Commerce, and by having no fort of Oeconomy, all this turned to his Prejudice ; and it plainly appeared towards the Clofe of the laft Century, that with all their boafted Sagacity and Firmnefs, the *Spaniards* had ruined themfelves by acquiring too great Power, and rendered themfelves Beggars by mifufing their immenfe Riches. With fwelling Titles and wide Dominions, they were defpicably weak, and fcarce any but Copper Money was to be feen in a Country, which received above twenty Millions annually from its Plantations.

Before I quit this Topick, I muft take Notice of another Thing, which is certainly very extraordinary. This wrong Turn in the *Spanish* Policy had a wonderful Effect; it made all the Enemies of that Nation rich, and all its Friends poor. Every body knows that the United Provinces not only made themfelves free and independent, but rich and powerful alfo, by their long War with *Spain.* Our Maritime Power was owing to the fame Caufe. If *Philip* II. had not difturbed Queen *Elizabeth,* our Fleet might have been as inconfiderable at the Clofe of her Reign as it

was

was at the Beginning, when we were pester-
ed with Pirates even in the narrow Seas. Our
Plantations abroad were in a great measure
owing to Expeditions against the *Spaniard.*
Our Manufactures at home were the Consequence of affording Refuge to the King of
Spain's Protestant Subjects. When Queen
Elizabeth's Successor closed with *Spain*, he
suffered by it, while *France*, the only Country then at War with *Spain*, was a Gainer.
I say nothing of *Cromwell*'s Breach with
Spain, and the Advantages he drew from it,
because the World seems well enough apprized of all I could say on that Subject already;
but I cannot help observing, that both the
Dutch and We were at vast Expences after
the Restoration, to preserve the *Spanish Flanders*, while the *Spaniards* themselves were
inactive, and left all to be done by their Allies.
As soon as the Tables were turned, by the
Accession of King *Philip* V. the *French* became great Losers by siding with this Nation,
though they had always got by fighting a-
gainst them, insomuch that all the true Pa-
triots in *France* complained, that while *Lewis*
the Fourteenth shewed himself an excellent
Parent in his Family, he discharg'd but indifferently his Trust, as the Father of his
People. But to what End should I look a-
broad, when it is plain from our own Situation, that we were never Friends with her,
but at our Cost, and never Foes but at her's.

By

By fo long a Series of Mifmanagement the *Spaniards* have brought their Affairs into fo wretched a Situation, that they neither have, nor can have any very great Benefit from their vaft Dominions in *America*. They are faid to be Stewards for the reft of *Europe*; their Galleons bring the Silver into *Spain*, but neither Wifdom nor Power can keep it there; it runs out as faft as it comes in, nay, and fafter; infomuch that the little Canton of *Bern* is really richer, and has more Credit, than the King of *Spain*, notwithftanding his *Indies*. At firft Sight this feems to be ftrange and incredible; but when we come to examine it, the Myftery is by no means impenetrable. The Silver and rich Commodities which come from the *Indies* come not for nothing (the King's Duties excepted) and very little of the Goods or Manufactures for which they come, belong to the Subjects of the Crown of *Spain*. It is evident, therefore, that the *Spanifh* Merchants are but Factors, and that the greateft Part of the Returns from the *Weft Indies* belong to thofe for whom they negotiate. Let us next enquire who they are, and what their Shares may be.

The Goods and Manufactures ufually fent to the Provinces of the *Spanifh America*, are Gold and Silver Stuffs, Silks of all Sorts, as well Stockings and Gloves, as Piece Goods; Woollen Manufactures of all Kinds, Linens, Laces

Laces and Thread, Hats, and all other Manufactures of Felt; Spices, Drugs, Colours
for Painters, Materials for Dying; all Sorts
of Perfumes, Green and White Wax, Ha-
berdashers Ware, Toys of all Kinds, Copper,
Brafs, and Iron Goods, *Ruffia* and other Kinds
of dreffed Leather ; Paper for Writing, Printing, and Packing; Playing Cards, Mafts, Rig-
ging, Pitch, Tar, Cordage, *&c.* Pipe Staves,
Veffels for Wine, Oil, and other Liquors; and
almoft all Sorts of Domeftick Utenfils; with
various Kinds of Provifion.   Befides,   the
Spanifh Settlements muft be fupplied with
Negroes, which is a prodigious Article.   Our
South Sea Company ftipulated to furnifh at
leaft four thoufand eight hundred every Year.
It is plain that of all thefe Articles the *Spaniards* themfelves can furnifh little or nothing.
It is true, they may fend Wines, Oils, Olives,
and fome fort of Sweetmeats, which are liked
in the *Indies*; but then the Value of thefe
Commodities is inconfiderable,   when compared with the reft of the Cargoes which they
fend out.   The prime Coft of thefe Goods
amounts to a vaft Sum, and the Profits upon
them to a greater.   The very Probity of the
Spanifh Merchants is deftructive to their
Country; for, as they are never known to
betray their Truft, confequently the Foreigners who make ufe of their Names to cover
their Commerce in the *Indies*, reap the
intire Advantage of the high Price at which
                                             their

their Goods fell. All then that refts in *Spain*
is the Silver and Gold on the King's Account,
the Profit upon fuch Goods as were actually
fent by *Spanish* Merchants, and the Commiffions which *Spanish* Factors receive ; all
befides is prefently drawn away.

The *French*, *English*, *Dutch*, and fome
other Nations in the North, fupply the *Spaniards* with the neceffary Affortments for
their *Weft India* Cargoes : we fhall fay fomething of what is furnifhed by each. The
French, fince the Succeffion of King *Philip*,
have a very large Share in this Commerce,
fupplying all forts of Gold and Silver Stuffs,
rich Silks, Velvets, flower'd and plain ; Hats,
Silk and Worfted Stockings, Slight Woollen
Stuffs of the Fabrick of *Amiens* and *Reims* ;
but chiefly of *Lile* and *Arras* ; vaft Quantities of Linen, Paper, Cards, Toys, and
many other Things. It is impoffible to guefs
nearly at the Value of what they furnifh ;
but we may form fome fort of Idea of it,
from the Article of Linens, which a Perfon,
well acquainted with their Trade, computed
at three hundred thoufand Pounds Sterling
at leaft. During the laft general War, almoft the Whole of this Commerce was in
the Hands of the *French*, which in a great
meafure enabled them to fupport it. They
managed it however very injudicioufly, glut-
ting the Markets with *European* Commodities to fuch a Degree, that for three or four
Years

Years before the Peace they were Lofers. Experience, however, has made them wifer fince ; and if we eftimate their Gains at three Millions, it cannot be thought too much.

The *Dutch*, for about twenty Years before the breaking out of the laft War, managed the beft Part of the *Spanifh* Trade, that is to fay, they fupplied alone what is now furnifhed both by them and the *French*. They have ftill, however, at leaft as great a Share as any other Nation, and fome think a better. The Commodities they fend are Spices, fuch as Nutmegs, Cloves, and efpecially Cinnamon, of which vaft Quantities are ufed in making Chocolate in *America*. Linens of all Sorts, Callicoes, Ribbands, Silk Twift, Cloths, Serges, Camblets, Shalloons, Slight Silks, *German* Toys, Hemp, Tar, Pitch, Copper, and Iron Ware, dried Fifh, *&c.* Linen and Woollen, however, are the two great Articles, the latter efpecially, contrary to the common Opinion, at leaft in this Country, where it is fuppofed, that our moft formidable Enemies in this Trade are the *French.* It is, however, a thing pretty certain, that our Goods are fuperior in Value to the *Dutch* Manufactures ; but the Traders of this Country afford better Pennyworths, and have befides an Art of fcruing themfelves into the Confidence of the *Spaniards*, beyond what other People can pretend to, infomuch, that fince the Peace of *Utrecht*, they have in
fome

some measure beat out the *French* even in Gold and Silver Lace; though these have always been esteemed the prime *French* Manufactures. On the whole, the best Judges are of Opinion, that the *Dutch* draw annually out of the Effects imported from the *Spanish West Indies*, at least five Millions of Pieces of Eight; and when *Spain* is at War with us, much more.

The Goods supplied by the *English* are Pepper, all sorts of Woollen Goods, especially Bays, Perpetuanas, Flannels, *&c.* Hats of all Sorts, fine and coarse, Silk and Worsted Stockings, several Sorts of rich Silks; Copper, Brass, and Iron Ware; Toys, Clocks, Watches in vast Quantities, dried Fish, Salt Provisions from *Ireland*; with other less considerable Articles, which, taken altogether, amount to a vast Sum, besides what was annually sent directly to the *Indies* in the *South Sea* Ship, and the Negroe Trade, which is of mighty Consequence. To balance this, it must be allowed that we took a large Quantity of their Produce; yet the Balance in our Favour is generally esteemed to have been between four and five Millions. Add to this, what the *Spaniards* receive from other Parts of *Europe*; and it may well be reckoned at two Millions more: so that in the whole not less than fifteen Millions in every such Cargo from *America* may be reckoned to belong to Strangers, on account of their
Interest

Intereft in the Goods exported thither. But, befides all this, we muft confider that *Spain* itfelf hath great Wants, much beyond what its native Commodities will purchafe; and thefe muft of confequence create farther Demands on the Effects brought from the *Weft Indies :* fo that on the whole there are good Grounds to fuppofe that between twenty and twenty-five Millions are conftantly taken either in Money or Effects, out of what the *Spaniards* receive, which clearly explains the Intereft that other Nations have in preferving to her all that fhe poffeffes in the new World.

As long as the Court of *Spain* perfifts in this Kind of Policy, her Affairs muft grow worfe and worfe; and while fhe vainly fancies that fhe aggrandizes herfelf by difturbing the Peace of *Europe*, fhe will abfolutely beggar her Subjects, and, in the Courfe of a few Years, will be obliged to abandon, through Poverty, the Places fhe undoes herfelf to conquer. We may poffibly be miftaken in the foregoing Computations; but, if we are, it is very probably on the Right Side ; but fuppofe it otherwife ; fuppofe that 15 Millions of Pieces of Eight reft in that Country after all Accounts are balanced. Out of thefe, the Civil and Military Expences of the Government are to be paid, large Sums to be fent *Don Carlos*, and abundance of coftly Intrigues to be carried on in *Germany* and other Places. Thefe Expences, and indeed all Expences in *Spain*,

Spain, differ from the Expences of any other Court in *Europe*, becaufe fooner or later the greateft Part of the Money difburfed goes out of the Kingdom. A great Part of their Troops, and at leaft a Moiety of their Officers, are Foreigners, who fend their Effects away, if ever they are fo happy as to have any. The greateft Part of the Artizans, Pedlars, and fmall Shop-keepers, are *Frenchmen* or *Italians*, who either retire in the Decline of Life, or leave what they are worth to Relations in their own Country. Nay, the very Labourers and Harveft-People come thither annually by thoufands out of the Provinces of *France* next to *Spain* ; and when they have done their Bufinefs, and received their Wages, go home again till the next Year. Whenever the Galleons are ftopt, and thereby the Supplies from *America* cut off for one or more Years, it is eafy to difcern what Troubles and Diftreffes this muft occafion, and what irremediable Evils fuch Difappointments bring along with them ; for, as thefe never fall out but in time of War, an Increafe of Expence meets with a Deficiency of Funds, and thofe who are at the Head of Affairs have at once both thefe oppofite Mifchiefs to deal with.

When thefe Things are thoroughly confidered, no body can wonder at the Advices we receive from *Spain*, or conceive what is related in them to be incredible. Under fuch a

Govern-

Government the meaner People muft ne-
ceffarily want Bread, the better Sort fcarce
have more in their Power, Money will be
very feldom feen, the Publick muft be always
diftreffed, and equally in Want of Cafh and
of Credit. It is impoffible then that a *Bri-
tifh* Adminiftration fhould be at all afraid of
fuch a defpicable Enemy ; nay, if *France*
fhould, in her prefent Circumftances, join
with her, the War muft be fatal to both ; we
may command the Trade, and confequently
the Wealth of the *Spanifh Weft Indies :* and
whoever attentively weighs this, will certainly fall into my Sentiments, that how loud
foever the *French* may bark, they will never
attempt to bite, for fear of beating out their
Teeth.

C H A P. III.

Of the Contraband Trade carried on by the
Spaniards *in the* Weft Indies.

THE Methods taken by his moft Catholick Majefty for effectually fecuring
the Commerce of his *American* Dominions
to the Inhabitants of *Old Spain*, is the grand
Source of the little Refpect paid him in the
Indies, and of the great Weaknefs of his Government at home. The Inhabitants of the
Spanifh America confider Gold and Silver as
Commodities, which they have, and would
willingly

willingly barter for fome other Commodities, which they have not, and which would be more ufeful to them than large Heaps of either of thofe Metals. It feems therefore to thefe People a great Hardfhip, that either proper Care is not taken to furnifh them with what they want from *Spain*, or that they fhould not be allowed to fupply themfelves fome other Way. The Native *Spaniards*, who have the Government of the *Indies* intirely in their Hands, treat fuch Complaints with the Haughtinefs natural to that Nation, which renders them univerfally odious and infupportable. Men, whatever Climates they dwell in, of whatfoever Complexions they be, have the fame Inclinations, and the fame Refentments, if once you trefpafs on their natural Rights ; and this all Governors ought to confider, becaufe both their Glory, and their Safety depend upon it. Yet fo little is this a *Spanifh* Viceroy's Concern, that Sir *John Narborrough* tells us the Soldiers in Garrifon at *Baldivia* had Silver hilted Swords, and their Officers Gold ones ; and yet there was not a whole Coat, or a good Pair of Shoes amongft the Corps.

When Folks are in fuch a Situation, there needs be no Wonder at their endeavouring to carry on a clandeftine Trade, as, on the other hand, one cannot think it ftrange that their Neighbours, who live under better Governments, who have at cheap Rates all that thefe

Spaniards

Spaniards want, and yet ftand in need of the Silver and Gold with which they abound, fhould be very willing to commence fuch an Intercourfe as might take away all their Wants. Sometimes Governors have winked at this, not from a Principle of Avarice only, that they might fhare in the Profits refulting from fuch a Trade, but alfo from a Senfe of the Neceffity of difpenfing with Laws fo ill executed as to deferve no Refpect. For, to be fure, that Rule of Juftice, which connects the *Spanish* Plantations to *Spain*, requires that the Government of *Spain* fhould have a reciprocal Regard for thofe Plantations; and a Neglect on one Part infers a Licence on the other. Upon this Principle it was, that before the Treaty of *Utrecht*, and the *Affiento* Contract, the *Englifh* at *Jamaica* furnifhed the *Spaniards* at *Porto Bello* with Negroes, with the Knowledge at leaft, if not by the Permiffion of the Governors. The Inhabitants of *Peru* never could be without Slaves. The Government of *Old Spain* never could, indeed never attempted to fupply them, but permitted fometimes the *Genoefe*, fometimes the *French* to carry on this Trade ; and when they did not do it effectually, the Deficiency was made good by fuch a Commerce as I before mentioned with the *Englifh*, though without any formal Licence, but by a Connivance, the lefs criminal for its being abfolutely neceffary.

The

The Situation of the Ifland of *Jamaica*, together with the Conveniencies of building and freighting Sloops from thence, engaged the Inhabitants in this, and in other Branches of Traffick. Such as settle themselves in these distant Parts of the World, do it generally from a Spirit of getting, and therefore the grand Point with them is always how to get most. They therefore for a long Tract of Time, and by various Methods, not neceffary to be infifted on here, fupplied the *Spaniards* at *Carthagena*, *Porto Bello*, *Rio de la Hacha*, and other Places with *European* Commodities of all Sorts, notwithstanding the mighty Hazard they ran in the Management of so dangerous a Bufinefs, their own Lives, and those of their Customers, being alike expofed, and frequently forfeited to what the *Spaniards* call Justice. They likewife carried on a Trade with the *Indians* of *Darien*, to their great Profit, but with equal Rifque, for the *Spaniards* were wont to fhew no Mercy either to *English* or *Indians* that fell into their Hands; which is so much the harder, fince the latter never were their Subjects, nor ever will have any Intercourfe with them. By degrees the Gains by this Commerce tempted so many Perfons to be concerned in it, and the Ships made use of were so well manned, and of fuch Force, that the *Spaniards* grew less timorous than formerly; so that at last the Commerce by the Galleons

was

was greatly affected; for, knowing where to buy Goods cheaper, the Merchants would not give the Prices ufually demanded at the Fairs of *Carthagena* and *Porto Bello*: and this, as I have faid, gave Rife to the Guarda Coftas. Some, however, who pretend to be well acquainted with thefe Parts of theWorld, fay pofitively, that this clandeftine Trade was carried on in fpite of thofe Ships, and even by the Connivance of the Governors, who, while they made Prize of fair Traders, protected Smugglers: If fo, their Proceedings were indeed extremely flagrant; nor is it altogether incredible, Thirft of Money being the predominant Paffion in all *Spanish* Officers.

It feems, however, to be our Intereft to put an End to this contraband Trade, if thereby we could fecure effectually the Friendfhip of *Spain*, and a due Return of Kindnefs in what regards the Trade of *Cadiz*, and of the *South Sea* Company. There is a certain Proportion of our Goods and Manufactures neceffary to the Inhabitants of the *Spanish America*, and which they will have fome Way or other. Now it is certainly preferable in refpect to us, that they fhould have them in a fair, than in a clandeftine Manner; yet we ought not to be more tied up in this Refpect than the *Dutch*, who have as flourifhng a fair Trade with *Spain* as we, and yet are much the greater Smugglers of **the**

the two; which leads us to speak of their Manner of carrying on this Trade, which turns so largely to their Profit.

The *Hollanders*, in 1632, dispossessed the *Spaniards* of three little Islands off the Coast of *Venezuela*, viz. *Curaçao*, *Bonnairy*, and *Aruba*. Altogether they are of very little Consequence in respect either to their Extent or their Product, and yet the *Dutch* draw from them an immense Profit. *Curaçao* is the nearest to the Continent, and therefore well fortified, and thoroughly peopled, tho' its Soil does not afford so much as will subsist its Inhabitants for one Day; but they are constantly furnished with Provisions from the other two Islands, which in truth are good for little else. As this Island is not above seven Leagues distant from the *Spanish* Coast, a more convenient Station cannot be wished for carrying on a clandestine Trade. It was first introduced by the Sale of Negroes brought thither by the *Dutch* from their numerous Settlements on the Coast of *Guinea*. These the *Spaniards* formerly bought in a Manner openly, and have transported in their own Vessels fifteen hundred at a Time; but since the *English* from *Jamaica* have interfered in this Trade, it is sunk very considerably; tho' they still supply the neighbouring Provinces, and reap a great Profit thereby, because no body understands the Management of this Business better than they do, can bring Slaves at a

cheaper

cheaper Rate, or vend them at a higher Price. Some Writers have afferted, that in its moft flourifhing Condition the Slave-trade alone drew from the *Spaniards* a Million of Pieces of Eight *per Annum*.

The Dealers at *Curaçao*, and their Correfpondents in *Holland*, were too knowing, too converfant in Bufinefs to let the Declenfion of the Slave-trade rob them of the Benefit of this Ifland. In order to replace what was loft by the *Englifh* interfering with them, they built vaft Magazines, and ftored them with all Sorts of *European* Goods, which had a very good Effect. In the firft Place it preferved to them the Remainder of their Slave-Trade; for the *Spaniards* knowing that this of all others was moft winked at by their Governors, refolved to keep up a Pretence of buying Slaves, in order to have an Opportunity of purchafing other Things. Secondly, it tempted the *Spaniards* to run all Hazards, that they might, at a reafonable Price, obtain any Sort of *European* Merchandize they wanted, and that too whenever they pleafed. It is incredible what vaft Sums have been annually traded for in this Way. Befides, the Inhabitants of *Caraçao*, to keep up a good Correfpondence with their Neighbours, and, as far as poffible to fix their Affections, refufed to fuffer any Privateers to enter their Ports, nor would upon any Terms purchafe their Plunder, which at the fame time was publickly

lickly fold in *Jamaica*, where the Privateers
ufually fpent their Money. This Spirit of
Self-Denial, however, did not hinder the
Traders of *Curaçao* from directing the Privateers to put into the Ifland of *St. Thomas*,
whither they inftantly fent Sloops with Money and Agents on board them to purchafe
what the Privateers had to fell, taking Care
to fend the Effects as foon as poffible to *Europe*, that the *Spaniards* might have no Intelligence of this Contrivance.

It has been before obferved, that in refpect
to this clandeftine Commerce it was chiefly
carried on by the *Spaniards* themfelves, who
ran all Hazards, came in Perfon to the Ifland,
and carried away whatever they bought in
their own Ships. In Procefs of time, however, fome Merchants devifed another Way
of carrying on the fame kind of Commerce,
by Ships fent directly from *Europe* on the
Spanish Coafts. Thefe Veffels were of fuch
Force, that thofe on board them ftood in no
Fear of any Precautions the Governors could
take; and, on the other hand, as their Cargoes paffed immediately from their original
Owners to the *Spaniards*, they could be afforded confiderably cheaper than fuch as were
configned to Factors in *America*. The Method of trading was by a Signal from the
Ships, or from the Shore. The Long-Boat
was then fent off well manned, brought the
Merchants on board with their Money, and
carried

carried them back with their Goods. The Reader has been already told, with what Obſtinacy one of theſe Ships was defended a-gainſt two Guarda Coſtas, and to ſay the Truth, thoſe on board them chuſe rather to ſink than be taken ; a very extraordinary kind of Courage ; for which, however, it is not impoſſible to account ; and as it may be uſe-ful as well as pleaſant, I think it not amiſs to enter into the Particulars thereof.

At the Time one of theſe Ships is fitting out, Notice is given to all Sailors, that they may have an Opportunity of entering, which they do with great Alacrity, there being, ge-nerally ſpeaking, twice as many who offer themſelves as can be made uſe of. When the Proprietors have their Compliment of picked Seamen, they not only allow every Man his proper Cargo, to a certain Value, but alſo furniſh it themſelves on Credit at prime Coſt. By this means every private Man on board becomes a Proprietor, and, if the Ship is attacked, fights for his own Pro-perty, which is the Reaſon that he will drown rather than part with it, and is one Cauſe why Guarda Coſtas are not over fond of meeting with theſe Veſſels, but chooſe rather to prey on fair Traders, who have fewer Men, and are of leſs Force. The Scheme I have mentioned is certainly a right one, though in a wrong Cauſe. The only Way to ſupport the Spirits, and fix the Affections of ordinary

People,

People, is to confult their Intereft; and thofe who imagine that Juftice, Honour, or any thing elfe will anfwer the fame End, without a due Regard to this, muft not expect much Pity when they find their Miftake. So true in all Senfes is that divine Maxim, *That the Children of this World are wifer in their Generation than the Children of Light.*

But to return once more to our Subject.

The little Ifland of *St. Thomas,* which lies in the *North Seas,* about fourteen Leagues off *Porto Rico,* is the fole Colony poffeffed by the *Danes* in the *Weft Indies;* nor would it be worth the keeping, but as it ferves to maintain an illicit Trade with the *Spanifh* Iflands in its Neighbourhood. We may form fome Idea of the vaft Advantages flowing from this contraband Commerce, from this very Particular, efpecially if we confider that the *Hamburghers* have likewife a Factory in this little Ifle purely on the fame Score. In order to maintain this Correfpondence, they tranfport from the *Danifh* Colonies in *Africa* a confiderable Number of Slaves for the Supply of *Porto Rico,* and fometimes of the *Spanifh* Part of the Ifland of *St. Domingo.* Under Colour of this Trade, a Commerce in *European* Goods is carried on; and we may eafily difcern how hard the *Spaniards* are put to it for the Neceffaries, or at leaft the Conveniencies of Life, when we find them trading to a Place which is a free Port to

Privateers

Privateers and Pirates of all Nations, who there vend openly, and in the very Sight of the *Spaniards*, what they have taken from them in the bafeft and moft barbarous Manner poffible; and yet fo tame are they, that they not only bear this with Patience, but will even purchafe Commodities from thefe very Buccaneers. Of late Years other Nations have made an Advantage of this free Port, and keep Warehoufes there of all forts of Commodities, for the Service of fuch Cuftomers as will run the Hazard of coming at them; and in time of War the Privateers never want a Market in this Place.

The *Portugueze* at *Rio Janeiro* entertain alfo a very beneficial Correfpondence with their *Spanifh* Neighbours. The Goods with which they fupply them, are Sugars, Indigo, Tobacco, Wines, Brandies, and Rums, with fome *European* Goods, and fometimes Slaves. The Inhabitants of this Colony are far more induftrious than the reft of the *Brazil* Planters; and this gives them an Opportunity of gaining confiderably by the Inhabitants of *Buenos Ayres*, and other Places on the *River of Plate*. Of late Years the *Spaniards* are grown exceffively jealous of this Colony, and, when the late Difputes happened between the Crowns of *Portugal* and *Spain*, both Parties were preparing to have acted vigoroufly on this Side, and nothing could have hindered them but their mutual Apprehenfions

henfions of becoming thereby a more eafy Prey to Strangers. They are the more jealous of this, becaufe confcious of their own Weaknefs; and yet one may fafely fay they are more fufpicious than they need; and this for feveral Reafons. For, firft, few foreign States have either an exact Information of the State and Importance of thefe Colonies, or any Difpofition to make Difcoveries or Conquefts at fuch a Diftance. Secondly, The Thing itfelf is not fo eafy as themfelves believe it; for Strangers, when they land on thefe Coafts, may well enough take and burn Towns; but they would find it extremely difficult to keep them, as well on Account of their Want of Experience, as of their being fubject to epidemical Diftempers, which carry them off fuddenly in great Numbers. Thirdly, The Weaknefs of the *Spaniards* is, properly fpeaking, the Weaknefs of their Government. There wants not People, there wants not a Capacity of Defence, if the Governors, and other Royal Officers, were not wanting in their Duty, and did not thereby fet fo ill an Example as corrupts and effeminates all who are fubject to them.

Befides thefe Methods of trading, which we have hitherto fpoken of, there is another common to all Nations; with the Mention of which we fhall conclude. Ships frequently approach the *Spanifh* Coafts under Pretence of wanting Water, Wood, Provifions,

or more commonly, in order to ftop a Leak.
The firft Thing that is done in fuch a Cafe, is
to give Notice to the Governor of their great
Diftrefs, and, as a full Proof thereof, to fend
a very confiderable Prefent.   By this Means
Leave is obtained to come on Shore, to erect
a Warehoufe, and to unlade the Ship; but
then all this is performed under the Eye of
the King's Officers, and the Goods are regularly enter'd in a Regifter as they are brought
into the Warehoufe, which when full is fhut
up, and the Doors fealed.   All thefe Precautions taken, the Bufinefs is effectually carried
on in the Night by a Back-door, and the
European Goods being taken out, Indigo,
Cochineal, Vinellos, Tobacco, and above all
Bars of Silver and Pieces of Eight are very
exactly packed in the fame Cafes, and placed
as they ftood before.   But then, that fuch as
have bought may be able to fell publickly, a
new Scheme takes Place.   A Petition is prefented to the Governor, fetting forth the
Stranger's Want of Money to pay for Provifions, building the Warehoufe, Timber for
repairing the Ship, and a proportionable
Number of fuch like Items; in Confideration of all which, Leave is defired to difpofe
of fome fmall Part of their Cargo, in order
to difcharge thefe Debts.   This being obtained in the ufual Manner, fomething of each
fort of Goods which had been privately fold,
is now publickly brought to Market, and
purchafed

purchased by those Persons respectively who had larger Quantities in their Warehouses before. Thus the whole of this Scene of Iniquity is transacted with all the formal Solemnity which could attend an Act of Justice and Compaffion.

We have now accomplished all that we intended in this Work; and, if in treating so many Things in so concise a Manner, we have been guilty of any Omissions or Mistakes, they are submitted to the Censure of the Reader, who, it is to be hoped, will be the less severe, when he reflects on the Difficulty of the Task, and on the great Variety of curious and entertaining Particulars which are here drawn together. It would have been easy to have extended this Performance to a much greater Length, but as the saving Time and Expence to the Peruser was next to the giving him a just Idea of the Subject, our principal Aim, we flatter ourselves that small Imperfections will not deprive us of that Reward, which is dearest of all other to honest Men, the Approbation of the Publick.

The A P-

THE

APPENDIX.

THE following Memoir feemed to me fo curious in itfelf, and to have fo near a Relation to the Subject of this Book, that I thought there could be nothing more agreeable to the Reader, or more confonant to my Defign of giving a full Account of the *Spanifh* Settlements in the *Weft Indies*, than the adding it by Way of Supplement to this Work. The Author of it was a *French* Officer, who, in the Year 1708, was wrecked in the Entrance of the *River of Plate*, and who remained for fome time in the Country which he defcribes. He drew up this Memoir at the Inftance of a *French* Statefman, who intended to have tranfmitted it to the Court of *Spain*, but dying foon after, this, with fome other Papers relative to the *Spanifh Weft Indies*, came into private Hands, which is the Reafon that many Copies of it are extant, not only in *France*, but here, and in *Holland*.

* A.

* A. S. E. M. L. C. D. B.

M E M O I R *concerning the Settlements of the Jesuits in* Paraguay.

I T is a Liberty generally taken by, as well as ascribed to Travellers, that they paint pretty strongly, and take a Pleasure in representing Things a little beyond the Truth, as if thereby they meant to indemnify themselves for the Dangers run, and the Fatigues by them endured. It is very probable that I might have fallen into this Error myself, if I had written for the View of the Publick; but, addressing myself to a Person of so illustrious a Rank, and at the same time of such distinguished Abilities, I shall be very careful to advance nothing, of the Truth of which I am not thoroughly convinc'd; neither shall I presume to add any Reflections, but content myself with barely stating Matters of Fact with as great Exactness as I am able; being thoroughly, sensible that you want to be informed as to such Things only as you have not seen, without needing any Helps in discovering the Lights that may be drawn from them.

It has been the Misfortune of the Christian Church in *America* for this last Century, and

* This is the Address in the Original.

perhaps

perhaps longer, that except the Jefuits, nei-
Priefts nor Monks have taken any Pains either
to convert the *Indians* by their preaching, or
to influence them by the Regularity of their
Conduct. The natural Confequence of this hath
been, the throwing intirely into the Hands of
the *Jefuits* an Affair of the laft Importance, *viz.*
the propagating the Faith amongft the *Indians*, for which it muft be allowed, that they
have fhewn themfelves extremely well qualified; of which more convincing Evidence
cannot be had, than the Progrefs they have
made in thefe their Miffions. This of *Paraguay*, concerning which I have undertaken
to write, is by far the moft confiderable, and,
if attentively confidered, will appear almoft
as remarkable an Event as *Pizarro*'s Conqueft
of *Peru*, or *Mendoza*'s fubduing *Chili*.

The Country, under the Government of
the Fathers, lies about two hundred Leagues
South of *Brazil*, about the fame Diftance
from the Province of *Buenos Ayres*, one hundred and fourfcore Leagues from *Tucuman*,
and about a hundred Leagues from the Province of *Paraguay*. The Country, which is
of vaft Extent, is as pleafant and as fruitful
as can be defired, watered with Variety of
Rivers, and pleafant Streams, abounding with
Timber and with Fruit-Trees, producing A-
bundance of Cotton, Indigo, Sugar, Pimento,
Ipecacuana, and other Drugs of great Value.

The

The Plains are full of Horſes, Mules, black Cattle, and Herds of Sheep ; the Mountains contain vaſt Treaſures of Gold and Silver ; of which, however, the Fathers ſeem to have no Deſire, ſince, for ought the World knows, not one of theſe Mines hath ever been open'd or wrought.

Originally ſome forty or fifty Families of *Indians* having ſhewn a Propenſity to be in-ſtructed in the Chriſtian Religion, ſome Je-ſuits went amongſt them, accompliſhed that deſirable Work, and the Peace and Happi-neſs in which theſe People lived after their Converſion, had ſuch an Effect upon their Neighbours, that by degrees the Miſſion ſpread, till it attained its preſent Extent, which com-prehends at leaſt three hundred thouſand Fa-milies, who are in all Things ſubject to the Fathers, and who revere them as much as it is poſſible to reverence Mortals.

Theſe *Indians* are divided into forty-two Pariſhes, all on the Banks of the River *Para-guay*, and none above ten Leagues Diſtance from another. In each Pariſh there is a Je-ſuit, who is ſupreme in all Cauſes, as well Civil as Eccleſiaſtick, and from whoſe De-ciſion there lies no Appeal. By him their Caciques, or chief Officers, are nominated, as alſo are the inferior ones ; and even their military Commanders receive their Orders from him. Nothing can be better contrived than the Regulations under which they live ;

every

every Family hath its Proportion of Land and Labour, of Plenty and of Reft. Induſtry is common to all, yet Wealth is attained by none; the Product of their Harveſt is carried into the Magazines of the Society, whence the Fathers diſpenſe whatever to them appears neceſſary, to every Family according to its Degree. The Surplus, which muſt be very conſiderable, the moſt judicious *Spaniards* at *Buenos Ayres* conceive it little ſhort of four Millions of Pieces of Eight *per Annum*, is ſent either to *Cordova*, or *Santa Fé*, there being at each Place a Procurator-General, who takes Care of what belongs to the Society, and, as Occaſion offers, tranſports their Wealth into *Europe*.

It is impoſſible to imagine any thing in the *Indies* more regular or more magnificent than their Pariſh-Churches. They are capacious, well built, and moſt magnificently furniſhed; Gilding and Paintings ſtrike the Eye on every Side, and all the ſacred Utenſils are Gold and Silver; nay, in many of them they are adorned with Emeralds and other precious Stones. Divine Service is celebrated with the moſt ſolemn Splendor. On one Side of the high Altar are Tribunes for the Civil Magiſtrates, on the other Side are like Conveniencies for military Officers: as to the Father himſelf, his Buſineſs is to officiate, which he does twice a Day with the utmoſt Gravity. Their Muſick, both Vocal and In-

ſtrumental,

ſtrumental, is far from being contemptible; the People having naturally a Genius for that Science, which the Fathers have taken care to cultivate.

The Dwelling, or rather Palace of this ſpiritual Prince, is like the Church, a thing extremely grand for the Country in which we find it. It conſiſts of various Apartments, ſuited to the various Functions performed by its Maſter. In the Morning, after having performed his private Devotions, he gives Audience to ſuch as have any publick Buſineſs with him About Noon he hears Confeſſions, in which he is very exact, that being the principal Pillar on which his Sovereignty reſts. In the Afternoon he walks abroad, gives Directions, inſpects the publick and private Affairs of his Pariſh; in the Evening he catechiſes, explains the Principles of the Chriſtian Religion, and diſcourſes on moral Subjects to ſuch as attend him, by Rotation. In ſome Part of his Conduct he is extremely modeſt and praiſe-worthy, in others not a little lofty and aſſuming. To the firſt I refer his ſimple manner of Living, faring coarſely, ſleeping moderately, and uſing few or no Diverſions, if we except ſuch Recreations as he allows to his People, and eſpecially to the Youth. I am led to accuſe him of the latter by obſerving the mighty Diſtance at which he keeps his People, cauſing even their Magiſtrates to be corrected before him with Stripes,

and

and allowing the beſt Man in the Pariſh to kiſs his Sleeve, as the very higheſt Honour he is ever to hope for. I might add, deſtroying all Notions of Property ; for, except the Father himſelf, there is no body poſſeſſes any thing which he can call his own, nor dares he ſo much as to kill a Duck or a Chicken who has bred them in his Yard.

There is an annual Meeting of all the Fathers, who then confer on the Methods neceſſary to be taken for promoting the common Concerns of the Miſſion, for making new Laws, or aboliſhing old ones, as the Neceſſity of Affairs may require. This is the ſupreme Council, over which, for ought that appears, neither his Catholick Majeſty nor the Pope himſelf has any Power. The firſt they have perſuaded, that all Intercourſe between the *Indians* and the *Spaniards* is dangerous to the Salvation of the former, and on this Pretence have obtained a Prohibition to the latter. As for the Holy Father, he is either ſo thoroughly ſatisfied with the Conduct of the Jeſuits, or is elſe ſo little acquainted with it, that he never interferes therewith, but leaves all Things to be guided by the Order. To this Council, or Congregation, the Caciques are accountable, and from them they receive ſuch Orders as concern the Miſſion in general; whereas, in Matters relating to their particular Pariſhes, they are intirely directed by the preſiding Prieſt. One great
Point

Point under Confideration at each of thefe Affemblies, is preventing Strangers from having any Intelligence of the State of the Miffion ; another, the reftraining the *Indians* from learning the *Spanifh* Tongue, or applying themfelves to any Studies, fave fuch as may render them ferviceable to the Society ; amongft which they reckon Architecture, Painting, and Mufick; all which they are taught in every Parifh.

The Military Eftablifhment is very confiderable; each Parifh hath a confiderable Body of Horfe and Foot, exercifed duly, as the *Swifs* are, every *Sunday* Evening. Thefe Troops are divided into Regiments, confifting each of fix Companies, and every Company of fifty Men. The Regiments of Cavalry confift of the fame Number of Troops, that is, of fix; but every Troop contains but forty Men. Thefe Regiments are regularly officer'd, and the whole Eftablifhment is faid to confift of about fixty thoufand Men, under the Command of feveral general Officers; but whenever any Body of thefe Forces takes the Field, one of the Holy Fathers always commands in chief; for it is a Maxim which they never depart from, not to permit their *Indians* either in Peace or in War, to acknowledge any Authority but their own. This *Indian* Army is furprizingly well difciplin'd, and know not only how to handle their Mufket and Bayonet, like *European* Troops; but

also

alfo how to ufe their Slings, out of which
they throw Stones or Bullets of between four
and five Pound Weight with prodigious Force
and wonderful Dexterity.   Thefe Forces, the
Fathers pretend, are kept up to fecure their
Subjects againft the *Portugueze*, who were
formerly wont to make Inroads upon them ;
but there is another Ufe the Fathers make of
their Troops, which feems to be at leaft as
much their Concern, and that is, fcowering
the Country, to prevent either *Spaniards* or
Strangers from coming privately into the
Quarters of the Miffion.

  If, in fpite of all thefe Precautions, a Stranger infinuates himfelf into their Territories,
the Father, into whofe Parifh he happens to
come, fends for him immediately, takes him
into his own Houfe, affigns him a handfome
Apartment, ufes him with all imaginable
Refpect, but affords him no Sort of Liberty.
If, at his Requeft, the Father permits him to
fee the Town, it is altogether in his Company ;
and the *Indians*, having previous Notice, fhut
up their Gates and their Windows, and keep
as clofe as if they were afraid the Sight of a
Stranger would give them the Plague.   As
foon as an Occafion offers for his embarking
at *Buenos Ayres*, he is fent thither under the
Guard of a Detachment of *Indians*, not one
of whom can fpeak a Syllable of any *European* Language : fo that it is fimply impoffible he fhould carry over with him any more
than

than a fuperficial Account of the State of the
Miffion, fuch as this is; nor is every Tra-
veller able to carry over fo much, fince his
Lights muft depend upon the Humour
of the Father, in whofe Territory, or rather under whofe Cuftody he lives; fome
being much more auftere than others. The
Jefuit, with whom I fojourned, was a Native of *Toledo*, a Man feemingly of a frank
Difpofition in all Things of which he accounted it lawful to fpeak freely; yet, in all
Matters relating to the Miffion, he was filent
as the Grave, and, except himfelf, I faw no
Perfon during my Stay in the Country, with
whom I could exchange fo much as a fingle
Word. The *Indians*, though of themfelves
gentle and courteous, yet, in confequence of
the Father's Inftructions, are fhy of fo much
as looking on an *European*, tho' they know
not a Syllable that he fays.

It is certain that in thefe Countries there
are many, and thofe very rich Mines both of
Gold and Silver, that there are befides abundance of valuable Commodities, efpecially
the Herb of *Paraguay*: fo that if this was
as much under the King of *Spain*'s Dominion as the reft of his Provinces in *America*,
it would yield him a very fair Revenue. As
it is, he draws very little, if any thing, from
it; nor are Things like to be in a better Condition. The Fathers ought, indeed, to pay
him a Piece of Eight for every Head under
their

their Jurifdiction ; which Capitation-Tax,
though fmall in itfelf, would however produce a very large Sum.   But they have found
two Ways to elude this ; firft, by making a
very confiderable Prefent to the Governor of
Buenos Ayres, they hinder him from vifiting
the Miffion as he ought to do, once in five
Years, which affords them an Opportunity of
fixing the Tax at a Third of what it ought
to be ; and even this they take Care not to
pay ; for, being obliged fometimes to furnifh
Detachments for the King's Service, during
which Time they receive Pay, they prevail on
the Governors to certify thefe Detachments
to be thrice as numerous as they are, and fo
balance the Account.   Alas ! what can be
expected in a Country where the King can
neither rely on the Honour of his Officers,
nor on the Faith of his Priefts !

F   I   N   I   S.

Books printed for J. STAGG in *Weftminfter Hall*, and DANIEL BROWNE at the *Black Swan* without *Temple-Bar.*

1. MEMOIRS of the DUKE DE RIPPERDA, firft Embaffador from the States General to his moft Catholick Majefty, then Duke and Grandee of *Spain* ; afterwards Bafhaw and Prime Minifter to *Muly Abdallah*, Emperor of *Fez* and *Morocco*, *&c.* Containing a Succinct Account of the moft remarkable Events which happened between 1715 and 1736. Interfpers'd throughout with feveral curious Particulars relating to the Cardinals del *Giudice*, and *Alberoni*, the Princefs of *Urfins*, Prince *Cellamere*, the Marquis *Beretti Landi*, M. de *Santa Cruz*, and other Perfons of Diftinction in the *Spanifh Court.* As alfo a diftinct and impartial Detail of the Differences between the Courts of *London* and *Madrid.* With many Memorials and other valuable Papers. And an Alphabetical Index. The 2d Edition with the Addition of an Appendix.

2. The WORKS of *John Sheffield* Earl of *Mulgrave*, Marquis of *Normanby*, and DUKE OF BUCKINGHAM; containing all that ever was publifhed of his Grace's either in Profe or Verfe, with his Laft Will, Character, *&c.* The 3d Edition corrected. In 2 Volumes.

3. The MEMOIRS of CHARLES LEWIS BARON DE POLINITZ. Being the Obfervations he made in his late Travels from *Pruffia* through *Poland*, *Germany*, *Italy*, *France*, *Spain*, *Flanders*, *Holland*, *England*, *&c.* Difcovering not only the Prefent State of the moft noted Cities and Towns, but the Characters of the feveral Princes and Princeffes, and of their moft noted Generals, Minifters, and Favourites both late and prefent. Interfpers'd with divers curious and entertaining Narratives as well regarding Affairs of State as thofe of Love and Gallantry. In 4 Volumes. The 2d Edition.

4. MEMORIA TECHNICA ; or a new METHOD of ARTIFICIAL MEMORY : applied to and exemplified in Chronology, Hiftory, Geography, Aftronomy ; alfo *Jewifh*, *Grecian* and *Roman* Coins, Weights and Meafures, *&c.* with Tables proper to the refpective Sciences, and

Books printed for J. STAGG *and* D. BROWNE.

and memorial Lines adapted to each Table by RICH. GREY, D. D. Rector of *Hinton* in *Northamptonſhire*. The 3d Edition corrected and improved.

5. A SYSTEM of ENGLISH ECCLESIASTICAL LAW, extracted from the *Codex Juris Eccleſiaſtici Anglicani* of the Right Reverend the Lord Biſhop of *London*. By RICHARD GREY, D. D. Rector of *Hinton* in *Northamptonſhire*; the 3d Edition.

6. LETTERS writ BY A TURKISH SPY, who lived five and forty Years undiſcovered at *Paris :* giving an impartial Account to the Divan at *Conſtantinople* of the moſt remarkable Tranſactions of *Europe*, and diſcovering ſeveral Intrigues and Secrets of the Chriſtian Courts, (eſpecially of that of *France*) continued from the Year 1645 to the Year 1682. Written originally in *Arabick*, tranſlated into *Italian*, and from thence into *Engliſh*; the 10th Edition, in 8 Volumes.

7. The JEWISH SPY; or a Tranſlation of LETTRES JUIVES : being a Philoſophical, Hiſtorical, and Critical Correſpondence by Letters, which lately paſſed between certain *Jews* in *European* and *Aſiatick Turkey*, with others of that Denomination travelling through *Spain*, *France*, *Italy*, *Swiſſerland*, *Germany*, the *Netherlands*, *Great Britain*, &c. Which treat not only of Ancient and Modern Philoſophy, Hiſtory, and other Parts of Learning, but of the Religion, Sects, and Ceremonies in the ſeveral Countries, together with the Manners and Cuſtoms of the Courts and Cities, which they travelled through ; interſpers'd with many curious and diverting Incidents of Love and Gallantry, firſt tranſlated from the Original Letters into *French*, by the MARQUIS D'ARGENS, and now into *Engliſh*, with copious Alphabetical Indexes, in 5 Volumes.

8. The HISTORY of FRANCE, from the Time the *French* Monarchy was eſtabliſhed in *Gaul* to the Death of *Lewis* XIV. Written originally in *French* by FATHER DANIEL, and now tranſlated into *Engliſh* The 2d Edition ; to which is added, an Eſſay towards comparing *Pere Daniel's* Hiſtory of *France*, with Rules laid down by the Ancients for writing Hiſtory, ſhewing its Excellency above any other. Alſo the Heads of all the Kings of *France*, engraved by Mr. *Vandergucht*, with a compleat alphabetical Index. In 5 Volumes.